a queer history of adolescence

a queer history of adolescence

DEVELOPMENTAL PASTS, RELATIONAL FUTURES

gabrielle owen

The University of Georgia Press

Athens

Most University of Georgia Press titles are
available from popular e-book vendors.

Printed digitally

Library of Congress Cataloging-in-Publication Data
Names: Owen, Gabrielle, 1981– author.
Title: A queer history of adolescence :
developmental pasts, relational futures / Gabrielle Owen.
Description: Athens : The University of Georgia Press, 2020. |
Includes bibliographical references and index.
Identifiers: LCCN 2020025386 | ISBN 9780820357454 (hardcover) |
ISBN 9780820357461 (paperback) | ISBN 9780820357478 (ebook)
Subjects: LCSH: Adolescence. | Teenagers. |
Adolescent psychology. | Maturation (Psychology)
Classification: LCC BF724.2 .O94 2020 | DDC 155.5—dc23
LC record available at https://lccn.loc.gov/2020025386

for max and ollie

contents

preface

It seems grotesque to speak of a society without teenagers.
—Albert K. Cohen, foreword to Musgrove, *Youth and the Social Order*

This book develops a critical, historical, and theoretical framework that brings together questions of queer theory and categories of age, tracking shifts in social conceptions of adolescence from the nineteenth and twentieth centuries to reconceive notions of identity and relationality in the present. I draw from a varied archive, including British and U.S. newspapers, educational treatises, medical papers and pamphlets, popular media, and adolescent and children's literature circulating on both sides of the Atlantic, revealing the ways adolescence operates as a kind of hermeneutic of the self, one closely tied to ideologies of sexuality, science, and the nation. My work here encompasses a wide range of materials and historical moments to explore the ideological dimensions of adolescence as a category and how these ideological dimensions circulate and reappear in specific, located contexts. The category of adolescence emerges out of and reproduces a particular logic, a way of making sense of the world and ourselves that I trace back to nineteenth-century deployments of social evolution and the emergence of developmentalism as a dominant epistemological framework. This temporalizing logic makes the idea of adolescence possible, mobilizing biological growth as a metaphor used to naturalize and maintain existing social hierarchies. I argue that the logic of adolescence is one we must do without if we are to think beyond reproductive futurism and conceptualize queer and ethical possibilities beyond the biopolitical imperatives of adulthood, normative gender, heterosexuality, and the nuclear family.

One of the difficulties with putting pressure on the category of adolescence is its interpretive flexibility, its resistance to revision, its stickiness to the ideas it upholds. In 2004 Philip Graham published *The End of Adolescence* with the Medical Publications series of Oxford University Press, arguing that we do away with the category of adolescence. He uses interviews and his clinical experience as a child and adolescent psychiatrist as evidence for the competence and diversity of young people.[1] He believes that "the idea that the teen years are a separate phase of life, clearly different from the years that come before and after is seriously flawed." He documents "the ways in which adult society fails to take into account the competence of young people and refuses to allow them to use their skills," which "infantilizes and disempowers young people, often with disastrous consequences."[2] Psychology researcher and professor Robert Epstein makes a similar argument in his 2007 book, *The Case against Adolescence: Recognizing the Adult in Every Teen*. A second edition was released in 2010 with a new, more marketable "self-help" title that on first glance appears to affirm common stereotypes about adolescence: *Teen 2.0: Saving Our Children and Families from the Torment of Adolescence*. This book plays into common myths about the "torment of adolescence" to make its argument that teens deserve to be treated with the same respect as adults: "the serious problems faced by America's teens—high rates of depression, drug abuse, drinking, pregnancy, gambling, sexually transmitted diseases and conflict with parents—problems that reverberate harshly through our families and our society—are largely unnecessary." Epstein shows how these "problems" of adolescence are caused by the infantilization of competent teenagers.[3] Both Graham and Epstein argue for specific legal and social changes to improve the status of teenagers. Whether these arguments to do away with the concept of adolescence will shape the future of research in medicine and psychology, however, remains to be seen.

Graham and Epstein are also not the first to make attempts to pressure the concept of adolescence. In 1996 the independent researcher Mike Males wrote a book called *The Scapegoat Generation: America's War on Adolescents*, using the state of California as a case study to argue that both children and adolescents have been abandoned by government policy, law, education, and even the family. Males points out how adolescents are continually made the center of a crisis in these systems, positioned as the root of a shifting set of social problems. By constructing adolescents as the source of these social problems, government officials do not have to take responsibility for their role in the extreme poverty, economic stress, and disenfranchisement of children and families.[4] In his second book, *Framing Youth: 10 Myths about the Next Generation*, Males debunks popular myths about adolescents— including those about violence, drugs, suicide, and teen pregnancy —using meticulous data from the state of California to show how these myths are in fact lies perpetuated by the media and government agencies alike. So far, these works by Graham, Epstein, and Males have failed to shift social conceptions of adolescence—not by lack of effort or expertise but because of the centrality of adolescence in the maintenance of other social realities. Adolescence plays a key role in naturalizing systems of social hierarchy, creating normalizing structures for identity and selfhood, and providing a scapegoat to distance social ills.

We can find arguments similar to these researchers even as early as 1965, in Frank Musgrove's *Youth and the Social Order*. Musgrove writes about the diminished status of youth in the 1960s, which "has profound consequences for the kind and quality of relationship which exists between generations." Using interdisciplinary research methods from history, sociology, and anthropology, Musgrove addresses the "problem of youth"—the assumption that young people have rebelled against the values and authority of earlier generations—and finds instead that "what emerged with the greatest clarity was the rejection of the young by adults." Musgrove argues that youth movements driven by "impetus towards social experimentation and change" do not occur when young people are granted too much social power but rather precisely "when they are denied it."[5] Citing studies in biology, Musgrove believes that sexual and physical maturity is being reached at earlier and earlier ages at the same time that social and institutional mechanisms have been working to keep the young even longer in a state of economic and legal dependence.[6] This dependence is lobbied for as a means of protecting young people, and yet, Musgrove states, "Protective measures are a two-edged device: while they may signify concern for the welfare of the young, they also define them as a separate, non-adult population, inhabiting a less than adult world." The consequences of this prolonged state of dependency are similar to those described by Epstein and Graham. For example, Musgrove finds that those elite youth chosen for university study in Britain, which further delays their entrance into the adult world, reported feeling more alienated and depressed than their modern school (the British equivalent to high school) peers who identified themselves more closely with the adult world.[7] These researchers strongly suggest that the infantilization of teenagers is having a profoundly negative impact on even those young people who are conforming to societal expectations and succeeding in school.

The resistance of the category of adolescence to revision can be seen in the foreword to Musgrove's *Youth and the Social Order* by Albert K. Cohen. Surprisingly, Cohen undermines Musgrove's argument, beginning the foreword with a curious declaration: "When I was a teenager, in the early depression years, there were no teenagers!" On the one hand, Cohen may be right if what he is remarking on is the difference between social conceptions of adolescence in the 1960s compared to the 1930s. The word "teenager" did not even come into popular usage until the 1940s. And yet, Cohen's insistence that there were no teenagers when *he* was teenaged demonstrates a distinct form of disavowal, an insistence that the contempt toward young people in the 1960s never belonged to him. Cohen accurately summarizes Musgrove's arguments, stating how the book calls into question a "conception of young people as a species apart" and how Musgrove finds problematic the idea that "young people need a protracted period of preparation *for* life but must not participate directly *in* it together with adults, not even under their benevolent tutelage and authority." But the phrasing of this summary exposes Cohen's conflicted perspective, at once acknowledging the problem of preventing young people from participating *in* life "together with adults" while defensively over-emphasizing the "benevolent tutelage and authority" of adults like himself. At one point Cohen announces, "Dr. Musgrove's conclusions could be wrong," but he says that they should be considered anyhow because of the good intentions with which they were made. Cohen, a college professor potentially complicit in prolonging the dependency of adolescence through higher education, dejectedly remarks that "Dr. Musgrove has some . . . rather bleak thoughts on the matter." At each point Cohen summarizes the arguments made by Musgrove while seeming to undermine them, inadvertently reinforcing some of the very assumptions about youth that Musgrove's research refutes. The foreword ends by shifting the blame back onto young people themselves for perhaps too naively "believing the rhetoric of the commencement address and the brochure from the college's public relations office" and so, he implies, becoming the agents of their own disempowerment.[8] For someone who grew up in a time when there weren't any teenagers, Cohen seems unable to let go of his belief in them.

Articulating the stakes of deconstructing adolescence, my introduction situates my work at a key theoretical intersection between queer theory and the fields of children's literature and childhood studies, among tensions between the discursive and the material, gender and the body, the category child and the people called children. I show how poststructuralist critique in both fields emphasizes language and discursive meanings to complicate, revise, and restore our view of the actual people called children. As a theory that accounts for the relation between the discursive and the material, I focus on the performativity of categories of age—the ways that childhood, adolescence, and adulthood structure how we experience ourselves, others, and the world around us. I use the phrase "categories of age" as a way of signaling that the categories "child," "adolescent," and "adult" are discursive and performative, historically contingent processes and practices that produce subjectivity. As such, I argue adolescence has a logic, a way of thinking that emerges over the course of the nineteenth century and that survives in various forms to this day. It is this logic that makes the idea of adolescence possible and that naturalizes our historically specific ways of conceptualizing time, development, social hierarchy, and the self. This book goes beyond critique to work through the question of what we might do to more ethically understand categories of age and relate to the people named by them.

G. Stanley Hall is often called the father or the inventor of adolescence, a claim that locates the origin of adolescence at the turn of the twentieth century. Drawing from British and U.S. nineteenth-century newspaper archives, chapter 1, "G. Stanley Hall and the Logic of Developmentalism," complicates this history by tracking the circulation of the term "adolescence" in the hundred years before Hall's 1904 two-volume work *Adolescence* to show a pattern of positive descriptors accompanying adolescence, such as the "vigor of adolescence" and "healthy adolescence," in the first half of the nineteenth century. I mark a significant change in usage in 1870, where positive descriptors are replaced by negative and condescending descriptors like the "absurdities and crudities of adolescence," a change that I link to an epistemological shift over the course of the nineteenth century called "historicism" or "developmentalism." Developmentalism describes an interiorized conception of time, history, and the self as a process of development leading to the present. Categories of age were not the source for this epistemological shift but rather were reinterpreted as distinct stages and types of people within developmentalism. Developmentalism is a temporal logic, one that orders the growth of the child, the growth of individuals, and the growth of entire nations or societies along a developmental timeline toward an ideal outcome. Conversely, non-European people or nations can be imagined as regressive, stuck in an earlier developmental time. I show how categories of age served as a way to naturalize existing social hierarchies within these new ways of understanding the social world and how existing social prejudices made their way back onto adolescence by 1870. The logic of adolescence is developmentalism, the way of thinking that makes the category possible in its modern form at the turn of the century. I end with an interrogation of the normative futurity projected by developmentalism in order to contend with violent uses of futurity while making space for the alternative logics of queer futurity, remapping more ethical relations to children, development, and time itself.

Chapter 2, "Temporality, Selfhood, and the Politics of Difference," turns to the early twentieth century, contextualizing the "discovery" of adolescence as a narrative belonging to the emerging institutions of medicine, psychology, and education at the turn of the century as they negotiated for new forms of authority and expertise. Childhood and adolescence serve separate functions in this process. Whereas childhood often represents potentiality and futurity—the fantasy of a stable, knowable truth that science can discover and direct toward the future—adolescence, on the other hand, stands in for the unknown, the limits of social control, and the aspects of being and experience that these institutional discourses exclude as pathological. Though childhood and adolescence appear to be universal stages of human development, the specifically modern form of adolescence that emerges in the late nineteenth century is a fundamentally racial category from the start, operating within the logic of developmentalism to naturalize existing social hierarchies on the level of both individuals and groups. Through the logic of developmentalism, categories of age function as temporal categories in which anyone, but particularly marginalized people or groups, can be relocated in developmental time as regressive, immature, or underdeveloped while masculinity, whiteness, and wealth operate as the normative characteristics of adulthood. Drawing on archival examples from nineteenth-century racial science, the history of endocrinology, and early twentieth-century medical and public health documents from the Wellcome Library in London, this chapter shows how categories of age work together to manage anxieties about race, class, gender, and sexuality. These performative functions continue to this day, in which adolescence serves as a site of disavowal and desire, a disciplinary mechanism of selfhood used to maintain existing social norms and social hierarchies. The idea of adolescence imposes a narrative, progressive, developmental structure onto human experience and conceptions of identity. While I do not think it is possible to do away with narrative or to find an essential truth beyond it, unraveling these threads allows us to question what the narrative constructs as real, natural, and inevitable.

My aim is to put pressure on these developmental narratives through the history of adolescence in order to imagine alternate ways of conceptualizing the stages of human life, ways that grapple with but do not resolve the ever-shifting ground of identity and selfhood. Chapter 3, "Perverse Reading and the Adolescent Reader," draws from social discourse surrounding adolescent reading and from fictional scenes of reading to unravel the cultural logic of adolescence as it has been deployed throughout the twentieth century. Hall's work is deeply anxious about the corrupting and stunting influence of reading, an anxiety that permeates discussions of adolescent reading and young adult literature in publishing, library science, and educational discourse today. Like the classifications of adolescence found at the turn of the century, the "adolescent reader" is defined with a set of qualities so flexible and amorphous they are synonymous with the perpetual unknown. As a counterpoint to institutional delineations of the adolescent reader, I look to fictional scenes of adolescent reading from late nineteenth-century novels, twentieth-century classics, and contemporary young adult fiction to illuminate queerer possibilities for being and knowing. Novels are complex forms that interact with cultural meanings in any number of ways, pushing against or complicating commonly accepted knowledge and ways of thinking. The act of reading, likewise, might be carried out in any number of ways, with or against meanings invited by the text. The tensions surrounding adolescent reading and interpretation echo tensions between social norms and queer possibilities, and I engage these tensions to explore the issues of identity and agency central to childhood and adolescence. I approach fictional representations as compact, interpretively supple negotiations of being in the world, showing how these diverse representations of self and world play with notions of age, identity, and norms. Drawing on queer and psychoanalytic schemas, I theorize adolescence as a hermeneutic of the self that shapes the ways we experience ourselves and others.

Chapter 4, "Toward an Ethics of Relationality," synthesizes the work of my previous chapters to think through the question of what we might do to more ethically care for and relate to the people called children or adolescents. Drawing on Karen Barad and feminist science studies, I propose a theory of ethical entanglement for conceptualizing agency, subjectivity, and autonomy within relationality. Working through relational circumstances such as compulsive obedience, overachievement, parent-child projections of trauma, the infantilization of adolescents, and suicidality, this chapter illustrates the consequences of developmentalism in the present, which invites the *use* of children to meet parental needs as well as the unethical control of children's actions and self-concepts under the guise of protection. I examine two books for young people, Kate Bornstein's *Hello, Cruel World: 101 Alternatives to Suicide for Teens, Freaks and Other Outlaws* and Cory Silverberg and Fiona Smyth's *Sex Is a Funny Word*, to demonstrate and elaborate the dynamics of a more ethical relationality, the limits of our control over others, and the urgent need for queerer possibilities to live and stay alive under the suffocating productivity and isolation normalized by late capitalism.

I conclude by reflecting on the present moment as one quite different from the nineteenth-century episteme that made the category of adolescence possible. The epilogue, "Queer Theory in the Age of Alternative Facts," considers the role of queer theory and the work of critique in the context of post-truth, neoliberalism, and what Rebekah Sheldon calls "somatic capitalism," a form of biopolitical exploitation that no longer relies on conceptions of the unified subject or a coherent sense of interior selfhood but profits from the utilization of separable, vital capacities.[9] In many ways the academic reevaluation of critique has been prompted by witnessing the explicit harm of neoliberal capitalism playing out before our eyes. Social norms are no longer operating through myths about the greater good but rather through new logics of commodification, privatization, and profit. My project emerges out of this context, participating in the ethical turn in childhood studies and the field of children's literature, part of a larger shift in the humanities toward the constructive, world-building work that comes after deconstruction. I argue that queer theory's antinormative methods have a key role to play, allowing us to imagine ourselves and the world otherwise.

My stakes in interrogating constructions of childhood and adolescence are not only discursive but relational, concerned with unfolding a new logic for speaking about and relating to people called children and adolescents. This is at once a deeply personal undertaking, touching on the ways we see ourselves and the ways we care for others, and an abstraction that aims to unravel the institutional logics that have shaped these relations without our consent or control. This project brings to light a nonlinear history that reframes present assumptions about adolescence and opens up the category as a powerful site for work in queer theory, childhood studies, and children's literature.

acknowledgments

When I try to think about how I got here, I am overwhelmed with gratitude. This book would not have been possible without the support of the Department of English at the University of Nebraska–Lincoln, especially my department chair, Marco Abel, who was tireless in his advocacy of me and my research before I was on the tenure track. I am thankful for the many colleagues who discussed parts of this work with me and encouraged me along the way, including Matt Cohen, Maureen Honey, Amelia Montes, Ken Price, Timothy Schaffert, and Roland Végső. Many thanks also to those colleagues who worked with me to expand our children's literature curriculum, including Amanda Gailey, Mike Page, Pascha Stevenson, Laura White, and our undergraduate chair, Guy Reynolds. Thank you to all my friends old and new in Lincoln who let me complain, talked theory, and made me feel less alone while writing—James Brunton, Emily Kazyak, Lauren Gatti, Allison Rusler, Robert Lipscomb, Anne Johnson, Celie Knudsen, Kamryn Sannicks, Rachael Shah, Pete Capuano, Katie Anania, and Mel Plaut.

My heart is still full of love for the University of Pittsburgh, where this project began. I am forever grateful to my committee members Jean Carr, Steve Carr, Nancy Glazener, Marah Gubar, and Kathleen Blee for their guidance, sharp questions, and investment in my work. Jean was exactly the chair I needed, open to the expansive scope of this project and willing to accept me exactly as I was. I will never forget Steve's sound advice to go back to an early draft and to state my argument in its most ambitious terms. With his characteristic brand of humor and honesty, he said, "Would you rather be shot as a sheep or a goat?" These words have shaped the spirit of my work ever since, giving me permission to appear in my writing as myself from the beginning. Thanks to the faculty and friends at Pitt who were with me along the way, including Dave Bartholomae, Julie Beaulieu, Troy Boone, Jess Enoch, Beth Matway, Todd Reeser, Mariolina Salvatori, Jim Seitz, Pamela VanHaitsma, Annette Vee, Courtney Weikle-Mills, and Emily Wender. A special thanks to Jim Kincaid, who read work in progress and offered many words of support during the time he spent at the University of Pittsburgh in the fall of 2009. I am forever grateful to Bill Scott, who had the great insight to encourage me to apply to Pitt in the first place, when I was still a master's student at New Mexico State. Likewise, the support and mentorship of Brian Rourke and Liz Schirmer at NMSU was vital in my survival as a graduate student and as a human, when I was really alone and had no idea what I was doing. And Barbara Ryan, who was my professor at University of Missouri–Kansas City, may be the origin of it all, radically disrupting social norms and traditional literary study in an undergraduate survey course where I encountered Foucault for the first time. Thank you, for everything.

I am immensely grateful to friends and colleagues who have talked with me over the years about this work at conferences and over email, especially Jules Gill-Peterson, Angel Daniel Matos, Jacob Breslow, and Kate Slater. A special thanks to Sarah Chinn and Rebekah Sheldon for providing reader reviews of this book for the University of Georgia Press—this feedback was instrumental in bringing the book into its current form. Thanks also to my editors at UGA, including Elizabeth Crowley, who first encouraged me to develop this project into book form, as well as Patrick Allen and Nate Holly, who saw it through its beginning stages to the very end.

The generous support of an Arts and Sciences Research Travel Grant from the University of Pittsburgh allowed me to spend a number of weeks at the Wellcome Library in London and at the American Antiquarian Society in Worcester, where I was able to immerse myself in sets of materials that continue to complicate and enrich my thinking about adolescence to this day. And grateful acknowledgment to the publication venues in which I had the opportunity to work through earlier versions of the arguments that appear in this book as well as all the anonymous readers and line editors that gave their time to my writing and ideas. A small section of my introduction was published as "Adolescence" in the inaugural Keywords issue of *Transgender Studies Quarterly* 1, nos. 1–2 (2014): 22–24, and it appears here with the permission of Duke University Press. An abbreviated version of chapter 1 was previously published as "'The Absurdities and Crudities of Adolescence': Nineteenth-Century Logics of Development and the Politics of Difference," in *Nineteenth Century Studies* 31 (2019). Special thanks to Sarah Wadsworth for her clarifying edits on this piece. An abbreviated version of chapter 3 was published under the title "Toward a Theory of Adolescence: Queer Disruptions in Representations of Adolescent Reading," in *Jeunesse: Young People, Texts, Cultures* 7, no. 1 (2015): 110–34.

Writing this book has clarified for me more than ever that the change I want to see in the world can happen only in the practices of my lived life, not just as words on the page. I could not have anticipated how profoundly my small children would challenge me, not only to think about childhood beyond the level of academic critique, but to continually do the healing work needed for me to meet them where they are and love better than my parents could. Ruth Schwartz and my therapists over the years, Joellen Popma, Rose Zingrone, and Anne Gilligan, were guides in this process that pushed this project to another level. Thanks also to my dear friend Danielle Meister for all that we have learned together and to my brother, Chad Owen, and sister-in-law, Tara Beeston, for being my family. And to Stacey Waite, for whom there are no words—everything good in my life is because of you. Thank you for believing in me when I did not believe in myself. Thank you for loving me when I could not love myself. Thank you for the countless hours listening and problem solving when I thought I could not write any more. Thank you for reading every word as I wrote it and then reading it again. Thank you for the endless hours of solo parenting you did so that I could write. This book exists because of you.

a queer history of adolescence

introduction

QUEER THEORY AND CATEGORIES OF AGE

Possibility is not a luxury; it is as crucial as bread.
—Judith Butler, *Undoing Gender*

Seemingly, this society wants its children to know nothing; wants its queer children to conform or (and this is not a figure of speech) die; and wants not to know that it is getting what it wants.
—Eve Kosofsky Sedgwick, *Tendencies*

Each of us is here now because in one way or another we share a commitment to language and to the power of language, and to the reclaiming of that language which has been made to work against us.
—Audre Lorde, *Sister Outsider*

I have always found great personal urgency in the work of queer theory. In a world in which normative gender and heterosexuality are often still preconditions for social recognition as a person, the methods of queer theory are first and foremost methods of survival. At the heart of a Foucauldian discourse analysis is a resistance to regimes of truth that aim to tell us who and what we are. Drawing from psychoanalysis, Judith Butler explains the "critical promise of fantasy" as the ability "to challenge the contingent limits of what will and will not be called reality."[1] Audre Lorde calls it the power of the erotic, the recognition of value and self-worth in feelings that exceed and surpass any existing system of meaning-making.[2] When queer desire is so often represented as invisible or impossible—ghosting the gay child or ending queer stories with scenes of social ridicule or suicide—the urgency of challenging the boundaries of reality is the same urgency as finding pathways to be and to stay alive.[3] Eve Kosofsky Sedgwick begins *Tendencies* with statistics on queer youth suicide and writes, "I look at my adult friends and colleagues doing lesbian and gay work, and I feel

1

that the survival of each one is a miracle." How did they do it? For her, perverse reading is not only an intellectual practice foundational to queer theory but a way to resist the overwhelming message that queer people should not exist: "We needed there to be sites where the meanings didn't line up tidily with each other," and this is the way she could "struggle to wrest from [books and poems] sustaining news of the world, ideas, myself, and (in various senses) my kind."[4] Queer theory is much more than a field of study or area of specialization. My work is self-sustaining. Queer theory allows me to look at the world and say, *they are wrong about me.*

I have also found great personal consolation in the controversial, oft-quoted claim in the field of children's literature by Jacqueline Rose: "There is no child behind the category 'children's fiction,' other than the one which the category itself sets in place, the one which it needs to believe is there for its own purposes." This claim, too, tells me that they have been wrong—when children's literature constructed norms for me, when adults dismissively treated me as a "child" and later a "teenager," they were wrong about me. Rose's theory speaks to the degree to which adult projections and fantasies shape cultural understandings of what a "child" is and thus shape what types of interactions are possible between adults and children. This type of cultural analysis is a moving target—it changes depending on context, whether historical, situational, or personal. And yet, I find it urgently necessary to be able to expose what is represented as the "truth" about children and childhood and to begin to ask a different set of questions about these encounters and these contexts. Rose provides a necessary social critique in which she reveals the categorical force of "childhood" in creating "an impossibility, . . . the impossible relation between adult and child."[5] This impossible relation is constituted by the very social norms that she seeks to make visible. In other words, she is not making the claim that adults and children cannot relate to one another but rather describing a culture that renders such a relation impossible within the systems of meaning defining childhood itself. If childhood is understood as something entirely separate from adulthood, if the idea of the child describes someone who is naive, unknowing, innocent, who is without agency or desire, then it is this construction that renders the relation between adult and child impossible—impossible because the child is emptied so significantly of anything we might recognize as being ontologically meaningful. And so we are left with the question: What might a more ethical conception of childhood look like? That is, how might we rethink categories of age so that a more ethical relationality among children, adolescents, and adults is possible?

Both queer theory and Rose rely heavily on the methods of post-structuralist critique to make these arguments. The methods and postures of critique have come under great scrutiny in recent years, notably in Sedgwick's sharp descriptions of paranoid reading, in Rita Felski's *The Limits of Critique* from literary studies, and in theoretical interventions in the field of children's literature by Marah Gubar and others.[6] Using Paul Ricoeur's phrase "hermeneutics of suspicion" to diagnose what is ailing contemporary academic discourse, these scholars suggest that we move on from critique and expand the parameters of our work.[7] As Sedgwick puts it, "Paranoia knows some things well and others poorly."[8] Or, as Felski puts it, "Critique is not always the best tool for the job."[9] Gubar worries that the profound influence of Rose's claims in children's literature studies has had the contradictory effect of further silencing and eclipsing children themselves because scholarship has tended to focus solely on the oppressive functions of discourse. Additionally, she suggests that the methods of critique have prevented children's literature scholars from engaging in productive dialogue with the wider field of childhood studies: "If we want developmental psychologists to pay more attention to what the rest of us are saying, for instance, then we probably should not describe their discipline as 'hegemonic.'"[10] While I agree, I am not so eager to say that the work of critique has exhausted its usefulness in the study of categories of age or that critique itself is what has prevented more constructive, innovative work. Many queer theory books from the past two decades have been accompanied by a disclaimer responding to Sedgwick's charge of paranoia, which of course can have the effect of only seeming more paranoid. I do not think that this was Sedgwick's intention. The problem Sedgwick addresses is the emptiness of critique for the sake of critique—a concern shared by scholars like Felski and Gubar—and the failure of critique itself to take us where we need to go. Once we disassemble our constructions, what do we do then? How do we live? What world do we make?

Felski clarifies that she has "no desire to reverse the clock" and return to older or more traditional modes of thought.[11] Rather, her goal is to find alternate ways of articulating the value of literary study and the work of the humanities more broadly. I think this is key for any method or project: Why are we doing what we are doing? It is true that the methods and moves of critique are not themselves equivalent to the aims of social transformation. (And, for that matter, one could potentially use the postures of critique and poststructuralist methods to uphold the status quo.) Likewise, as Sedgwick points out, to engage in modes of intellectual thought other than critique does not necessarily "entail a denial of the reality or gravity of enmity or oppression." I want to join Gubar and others in expanding the work of children's literature and childhood studies, and this book is possible in part because of these shifts in the field. I am cautious, however, about claims to move beyond critique. I am cautious about returns to tradition, to claims of absolute truth, to speaking for children and their needs in essentializing ways. What is the difference between the romantic idealization of childhood and the trend to celebrate child agency in some recent children's literature scholarship? Just as we have reevaluated the efficacy and aims of critique, we must also ask of alternate methods: "What does knowledge *do*—the pursuit of it, the having and exposing of it, the receiving again of knowledge of what one already knows? *How*, in short, is knowledge performative, and how best does one move among its causes and effects?"[12] When it comes to analyses deeply connected to questions of social justice, I find the insights of poststructuralist critique to be the essential ground from which to rethink and rebuild, particularly when it comes to categories of age, an area that has so infrequently been considered in terms of social justice in the first place.

I find the methods of poststructuralist critique that have been foundational to queer theory to be vital and essential tools for both personal survival and for the work of this book. And alongside many queer and feminist projects before me, this book attempts to go further than critique, to work through the question of what do we do.

What in our real lives is at stake in the work of critique and how do we address those stakes head on? For me, these stakes come down to questions of ethics and relationality. And I find categories of age to be at the center of many of the cultural assumptions preventing our most ethical relations to one another.

The Logic of Adolescence

This book pivots around a set of logics and conceptual linkages connected to categories of age, both present and historical. I have chosen to group these links and organize them around what I call the logic of adolescence because, I contend, a particular set of assumptions and beliefs about hierarchy, development, and age emerge at the same time as the category of adolescence appears as a socially significant age group in the nineteenth century. What I am calling the logic of adolescence consists of observable historical phenomena, identifiable ways of thinking and acting on the world found in my archives, while it also informs a set of practices continuing to this day. The logic of adolescence is connected to many other logics, and perhaps I could have named it something else, but I have chosen adolescence as the frame, or what Karen Barad might call the *apparatus*, through which to interact with my archive because I believe it can show us something important about the habits of mind shaping age relations, social hierarchy, and the politics of identity today.[13]

The idea of adolescence is a relatively recent social category, emerging in the late nineteenth century alongside medicolegal notions of homosexuality and the concept of inversion, which conflates gay or lesbian desire with trans phenomena. While the word "adolescence" dates back to the fifteenth century in English and can be found to designate a stage of human life through the seventeenth and eighteenth centuries, adolescence begins to function later in medical discourse and early psychology as a type of person, one that can be shaped and directed away from perceived social ills, such as homosexuality and prostitution, and toward social aims such as marriage and reproduction. By the turn of the century, G. Stanley Hall's *Adolescence* claimed that adolescence was the key to the advancement of civilization, the developmental moment of state intervention that would propel humankind into the next stage of evolutionary history.

We might understand the idea of adolescence as a mechanism of Michel Foucault's biopower, a technology of self put into the service of the nation-state. One of the ways biopower regulates and disciplines queer and trans phenomena is by locating it in the presumably pliable stage of adolescence, where state intervention appears to be developmentally natural and necessary. In the mid-nineteenth century, both childhood and adolescence became intense sites of disciplinary anxiety and control.[14] Parents, doctors, and teachers were instructed to watch for the warning signs of degeneracy, disease, mental illness, and criminal tendencies. Emerging institutions of medicine, psychology, and education deployed childhood and adolescence to construct institutional knowledge and to establish authority and expertise. For example, it is adolescence that allows Sigmund Freud to claim "complete certainty" about the cause of homosexuality in a young woman in the 1920s, and Richard von Krafft-Ebing similarly uses childhood and adolescent experiences to explain various sexualities and trans phenomena in his 1894 book *Psychopathia sexualis*.[15] In these contexts adolescence serves a narrative function. It becomes the moment of subjective fluctuation before the presumed stability of adulthood.[16] And, as such, it constructs the narrative inevitability of a normative adulthood.

Adolescence constructs and reifies adulthood as the stage of life when selfhood is final, established, known. And so the idea of adolescence contains transition, movement, and change in which the perceived turbulence of puberty is loaded with meanings about the discovery of self. Adolescence is constructed as the moment that gendered *becoming* occurs. Adolescence sustains assumptions about what is normal, natural, right, and good, instructing us as to which of our feelings belong to the past and which to our future, which of them we should disavow and which we should own. Adolescence directs us toward the ways in which we are supposed to develop and also secures the ways in which we are not to go. However, this developmental narrative is one we impose on experience, locating moments of transition, change, and rebellion in adolescence and locating moments of arrival, stability, and conformity in adulthood. Queer sexualities and transgender phenomena suggest a much more varied and complex range of possibilities for bodily experience and gendered subjectivity, drawing our attention to the contingency of any subjective arrival, whether it be normative, queer, or trans-identified. Adolescence functions simultaneously as a site of discovery and disavowal, sustaining assumptions about what childhood was and what adulthood should be, manufacturing narrative coherence for moments of arrival and creating distance for moments of contradiction, contingency, or change.

The question of adolescence inevitably becomes a question about the present, a question about the meanings we use to make sense of ourselves and others. I am interested in exploring these ways of making meaning, how they are constituted, and in what ways it might be possible to think differently. One way to consider the question of adolescence, then, is as a hermeneutic of the self.[17] How does adolescence work as a frame for interpreting our memories, thoughts, and feelings?[18] As a hermeneutic, it has a great degree of flexibility, albeit within its conceptual and definitional limits. This hermeneutic of self is also closely tied to other ways of interpreting and producing the self, closely tied to sexuality, to science, to the nation and its notions of citizenship. Within the logic of adolescence there is a sequence in which we are to order our experiences and to feel that we know what they mean.[19] This hermeneutic unavoidably extends to our interpretations of others as well. That is to say, we live in a world with an ever-shifting group of people called adolescents, without their consent, and any of us might be tempted to say that we know them because we have been through adolescence ourselves. Often what is known as adolescence is taken for granted, and as such it functions both empty of meanings and full of meanings at the same time.

The meaning of adolescence appears at first to be shared meaning, to be something everyone has or will have experienced, to be something any of us might speak about. But I want to question that we can or should claim to know adolescence in this way. People twelve to eighteen years old are called adolescents, talked about as adolescents, and grouped as such for research studies, marketing strategies, and school curricula. We find adolescence deployed for complex and even contradictory goals in fields like education, psychology, library science, and public policy. Adolescence can be used as a rationale for schooling, for censorship, for religion, for approaches to parenting, and for the production of young adult literature. More than any one set of rationales, adolescence is remarkable for its adaptability to a wide range of arguments about how things should be. The notions of adolescence we encounter are not stable, not fixed in time, not objectively defined or even definable. The idea of adolescence moves, and yet, in this movement adolescence has a logic, a logic that shapes the ways we see ourselves and the world.

I use the phrase "logic of adolescence" to describe the conceptual ways of being and knowing that make the idea of adolescence possible today. The logic of adolescence does not lay claim to the origin of these ways of thinking but rather constitutes a distillation of various, historically locatable logics brought together by the emergence of adolescence as a key concept in the early twentieth century. In many ways this project is about uncovering that logic, tracking it through texts and through time, and articulating the work it does today. I could put this agenda more broadly: What are the meanings we attach to categories of being, like age, race, gender, or sexuality, and how is that shared meaning sustained and shifting over time? Where and when do these shared meanings break down, radically split, or dissolve? I want to make the claim, then, that to study the history of adolescence is to practice a kind of historical ontology, or study of being.[20] We might say it was not always possible *to be* an adolescent, since this term and the social meanings we attach to it emerged only as recently as the nineteenth century, though this claim is more complicated than it may at first appear. A claim like this about the history of adolescence speaks to a much larger question about the relationship between the names of things and things themselves, a question that forms one of the central lines of inquiry in the chapters that follow.

Child Trouble

This is also a book about childhood and the people we call children. People called adolescents are sometimes included in the logics surrounding children and childhood because they are legally defined as dependents and because they exist relationally if not *as* children then as *someone's* children. I also see categories of age—including child, adolescent, and adult—as constitutive of one another, interdependent categories that produce the "truth" or "reality" of the others. Many important works on childhood have appeared in recent years, but the tendency has been to acknowledge the capaciousness of childhood rather than to consider categories of age in relation to one another, as part of the same regulatory systems.[21] By focusing on adolescence, and more broadly on the logic of adolescence as a way of knowing the self and the world, I hope to complement and extend important work happening in the fields of children's literature and childhood studies.

But what does it mean to talk about categories of age like "child"? This question is usually framed as a problem in existing scholarship, an ever-present tension between the category child and the actual people called children. We find this tension in other places too. In gender studies, it is the question of how to account for the social construct of sex/gender and also the materiality of the body. In science studies it is the question of how to account for the social production of scientific knowledge and the material world itself. These questions stem from the difficulty of reconciling some of the insights of poststructuralism with the lived reality of being in the world. And the persistence of these tensions indicates that we still do not have good methods to account for the discursive and the material at the same time or an adequate theory for understanding the relation between them. I engage with this problem directly; however, I confess, the longer I have spent working on this problem and reading outside my discipline, the less I have come to see it as one. What if it is not actually a problem at all but a misrecognition of different types of work?

In children's literature the profound influence of Rose's *The Case of Peter Pan, or The Impossibility of Children's Fiction* has resulted in the perception that it is "risky business" to talk about actual children in literary criticism, and different critical approaches are sorted into opposing camps—those who follow Rose and those who do not. Gubar argues that, since *The Case of Peter Pan*, children's literature scholars have inadvertently rendered children as passive, alien Others despite their critiques aiming to expose these ways of thinking. "Rose and company," she explains, avoid speaking about actual children, but in doing so they reinscribe "the radical alterity or otherness of children, representing them as a separate species, categorically different from adults."[22] Gubar believes that Rose "makes statements which presuppose the *success*" of efforts to "entrance, colonize, and reify young readers," even though Rose makes clear that she will not make claims about the experiences of actual children.[23] Robin Bern-stein seems to agree, stating that her work "challenges the position, espoused by Jacqueline Rose and James Kincaid," that children are passive recipients of culture.[24] Bernstein locates this error in Kincaid's claim that "a child is not, in itself, anything," and she characterizes his descriptions of the child as a "wonderfully hollow category" and a "ruthless distribution of eviction notices" as arguments about the lived experience of Victorian childhood rather than the functions of the category child.[25] While Kincaid argues that the modern category of child (and of woman too) carries with it instructions to evacuate—to empty and deny the self—this does not mean that he believes wom-en and children simply moved out. Bernstein is interpreting Kincaid as presuming the success of these cultural instructions, much in the same way that Gubar reads Rose.

At another point in *Child-Loving*, Kincaid writes, "One wonders why, facing this sort of thing, children would not be quick to denounce innocence altogether and take their chances with depravity? Indeed, many children tried (and try) hard to escape the burden of innocence. But it is not easy. Innocence is not, as we said, detected but granted, not nurtured but enforced; it comes at the child as a denial of a whole host of capacities, an emptying out." Though Kincaid argues that innocence is *enforced*, that it "comes at the child," these statements do not refer the responses of actual children as Gubar and Bernstein suggest. Children, on the contrary, are described as inventively taking "their chances with depravity."[26] What I think is happening in these interpretations of Rose and Kincaid is a slippage between descriptions of the "child" and descriptions of actual children, one that equates the functions of the category child—emptiness and erasure—with the beings and doings of actual children. One reason for such interpre-tations is that the relation between the discursive category child and the lived experiences of children is not well understood. While Rose and Kincaid at moments imply some kind of relation between the two, as Kincaid does with his "eviction notices"—notices that could be received by those who are called children—or as Rose does with her reference to "the child who is outside the book, the one who does not come so easily within its grasp," this relation between the discursive and the material remains undertheorized in their works.[27]

The persistent assumption that children function as passive recipients of culture cannot be traced back to Rose or to poststructuralist approaches like Kincaid's. This passivity is built into the very idea of a child that we can trace back to both Enlightenment and Romantic thinking, and it takes hold as a culturally dominant idea by the late nineteenth century. While Gubar and Bernstein both point to an important problem in children's literature and childhood studies scholarship—in which children are inadvertently rendered vulnerable, inactive, or passive—these are ironically the very same problems that Rose and Kincaid aim to describe and historicize. The fact that child passivity haunts critical scholarship on childhood is not so much a failing of the scholarship itself as it is a function of the language available to do our work. Karen Sánchez-Eppler notes, "the very potency of the discourses that surround childhood may ultimately prove blinding, masking children's experience" and "perpetuat[ing] historical and cultural inattention to children."[28] The more incisive and accurate the cultural analysis, the more difficult it is to see the people called children who are obscured by social ideas about childhood. Every time I use the term "child," I evoke the idea of passivity inherent in the meaning of "child" itself, even if my intention is to deconstruct the link between the two. I think such deconstructive analysis is essential if we hope to see beyond the "child" to grapple with the bodies, lives, and experiences of the people called children. But, like the gender of Butler's *Gender Trouble*, the "child" resists analysis, reasserts itself as its own origin, emerges as undeniably real at every turn. It is for this reason that we must begin with child trouble, both by identifying the trouble with the category and by making trouble for it.

Like Rose, Kincaid is widely cited for his argument that the child is an empty category that functions in relation to adult projections of desire: "The child is functional, a malleable part of our discourse rather than a fixed stage; 'the child' is a product of ways of perceiving, not something that is *there*."[29] I would follow that what *is* there is a person, one perceived to be a child and thus with particular social and cultural effects. This functional aspect of the category child is what Lee Edelman polemically describes in *No Future: Queer Theory and the Death Drive*, in which the child becomes "the fantasmatic beneficiary of every political intervention."[30] Both Kincaid and Edelman point to a contradiction inherent in discursive constructions of the child: as an idea, the child functions independently of and sometimes in direct opposition to the realities of any living, breathing people called children. Noting this distinction between the idea of the child and actual children, however, creates some methodological awkwardness for scholars.

Analyses are full of disclaimers. Kincaid explains, "I hope it is clear, then, that the terms 'pedophile' and 'child,' point, for me, not to things but to roles, functions necessary to our psychic and cultural life."[31] It is not clear at all, though, unless we recognize Kincaid's focus on the performativity of knowledge—that is, on the *roles* and *functions* of what we think we know rather than what actually is.[32] Edelman, likewise, explains that his claims are "not to be confused with the lived experience of any historical children."[33] And Rose writes that "it will be no part of this book's contention that what is for the good of the child could somehow be better defined, that we could, if we shifted the terms of the discussion, determine what it is that the child really wants."[34] Statements like these are necessary only because language is usually assumed to represent real things.[35] If we want to analyze how language and knowledge work—what I consider the primary work and expertise of scholars in the humanities—then such disclaimers become necessary to disorient our usual ways of thinking. Statements like these, however, do not mean that no one can speak of anything real or material or that we shouldn't ever try. Rose, for example, resists the misunderstanding that *she* is trying to determine what is good for children, and she challenges the presumption of "speaking to *all* children" and references to "any generalised concept of the child" by others. She must do this in order to describe the functions of these claims to really *know* children: the ways the child and childhood are used to "hold off a panic, a threat to our assumption that language is something which can simply be organised and cohered, and that sexuality, while it cannot be removed, will eventually take the forms in which we prefer to recognise and acknowledge each other."[36]

Rose's focus on discursive practices risks leaving out the matter of bodies and lives. This is mainly a problem of emphasis. And, as many scholars are recognizing, the need to overemphasize that language *does* things is not as urgent or necessary as it was twenty years ago, since this is becoming a more widely accepted view.[37] The sociologist Alan Prout writes that childhood, "like all phenomena, is heterogeneous, complex and emergent, and because this is so, its understanding requires a broad set of intellectual resources, an interdisciplinary approach and an open-minded process of enquiry."[38] What this means is that there is value to be found in different types of work. What I have found in the archives and outside my discipline is that it matters less what a particular text says about actual children than what it *does*. What I am paying attention to is the performativity of knowledge—the effects of a particular set of claims. The disciplinary conventions of one field or another may invite or require generalizations, but, in the context of a particular work, what do these generalizations *do*? A book like *The Drama of the Gifted Child* by the psychologist Alice Miller, for example, radically breaks with the social and institutional practices of simplifying children and denying agency, while at the same time it makes generalizing statements about children. I have found Miller's book to be unique in its characterization of childhood and invaluable in its ethical implications for adult-child relationality (discussed in chapter 4). To dismiss Miller's book offhand would be to misrecognize her efforts to understand the perspectives and emotional lives of children. To dismiss Rose or Kincaid, on the other hand, would be another type of misrecognition, forgetting the importance of their work on the dubious effects of childhood as a social construct. Neither are these two types of work opposed: Miller comes to the same conclusions as poststructuralist approaches do in her exploration of the ways adult projections can powerfully eclipse the actual people called children.

This book aims to do both at once, attending to the discursive functions of categories of age with the aim of understanding their effects on actual bodies and lives. This type of approach has never been far from the work of queer theory in the first place. Even Edelman, whose infamous claim of "fuck Annie" secured his reputation as decidedly antichildren, evokes the "violence" that "actual, flesh-and-blood children" suffer in the name of the figural "Child": "Institutional violence, for example, of a near universal queer-baiting intended to effect the scarification (in a program of social engineering whose outcome might well be labeled 'Scared Straight') of each and every child by way of antigay immunization."[39] An analysis like Edelman's "rejects not the child, but those who make use of the child for their own ends."[40]

Likewise, Sedgwick's essay "How to Bring Your Kids Up Gay" works primarily on the level of poststructuralist critique to expose the heterosexist bias implicit in evocations of childhood by practicing psychologists and psychoanalysts, but she also states that she does so for the gay and protogay children harmed by these institutional practices specifically designed for their erasure. She explains that she is departing from the standard practice of "constructivist arguments" that have "tended to keep hands off the experience of gay and proto-gay kids" so that she can advocate for a "strong, explicitly, *erotically invested* affirmation" of the "felt desire or need that there be gay people in the world."[41] Sedgwick's personal investment, one that underpins much queer theoretical work, takes the form of an appeal made on behalf of children (albeit gay and protogay kids), invoking futurity in a way Edelman eschews. But Sedgwick's vision of futurity is a far cry from the mechanisms of reproductive futurism described in *No Future*. Rather than set them in opposition to each other, I would argue that Edelman and Sedgwick are at work on a similar problem in relation to the social functions of childhood—namely, the ways childhood is conceptualized to extinguish queer ways of being and queer persons themselves (even when those queer persons happen to be children). That said, they propose different possibilities for survival—the affirmation of queer life or the embrace of the death drive. And although Edelman and Sedgwick provide foundational queer theoretical work on the child, neither provides a clear methodology for navigating both the figure of the child and the material beings and doings of actual children.

The Performativity of Categories of Age

Gubar finds an adequate method also missing from the fields of children's literature and childhood studies, despite the interdisciplinarity of work from these fields. Citing a range of scholars from English departments, philosophy, and sociology, she notes the general reluctance to theorize childhood in constructive terms—that is, to say what *is* about children and childhood. And yet, Gubar observes that complex treatments of children and childhood have been written despite the absence of such a theory.[42] She gives the example of Sánchez-Eppler's *Dependent States*, which accounts for children on three levels: as the focus of adult interventions including parenting and education, as an ideological figure deployed for various political and national discourses, and as people who are children—that is, "individuals inhabiting and negotiating these often conflicting roles as best they can." With these three levels in mind, Sánchez-Eppler aims to practice "a method that will analyze and illuminate the ties between the powerful discourses of childhood and the lives—sometimes competent, sometimes vulnerable—of individual children."[43] Gubar sees *Dependent States*, however, as falling short of this goal and instead moving between "two extremes," rendering children on the one hand as passive to "structural and institutional power" and on the other hand as fully independent agents.[44] I think that this representational tension speaks more to the language and concepts available to us to talk about children than to the limits of Sánchez-Eppler's argument, a point she herself articulates: "The tension in these chapters between depicting childhood as a rhetoric for the articulation of social norms, and recognizing children as particular persons affected and often betrayed by those very norms is ultimately discernable as a tension inherent in America's attitude toward childhood." In other words, scholars are bound by the very social conditions that we wish to make visible. In Sánchez-Eppler's case the assumed passivity of childhood and the mythology of full autonomy are most visible as "two extremes" because they uphold each other, both working to obscure her argument that "interdependence or partial independence may be far more accurate terms for understanding civic life."[45]

Gubar's work in *Artful Dodgers* represents the child as an independent agent in her revision of Golden Age histories, arguing that children's authors did not produce images of children as naive and passive, as is commonly accepted, but rather constructed complex child characters shown negotiating their agency in cunning and powerful ways.[46] Gubar's analysis of Golden Age literature brings us back to the question of *why* the passive child is still so often what is seen when we look at children, fictional or actual. Likewise, Bernstein's *Racial Innocence* emphasizes child agency, using children's dolls, diaries, and letters to show how nineteenth-century white children were "co-producers" of racism and not merely passive recipients of a racist culture's messages.[47] Both Gubar and Bernstein make important interventions in the pervasive and enduring construct of the child as passive, though these interventions may overemphasize child agency to do so. The challenge we all face is how to recognize and describe at the same time the complex ways discourse acts on social persons as well as the ways social persons act on discourse. An edited collection like Anna Mae Duane's *The Children's Table: Childhood Studies and the Humanities* represents an array of approaches to the problem of "how to bridge the relationship between the rhetorical child (the cultural construct of "childhood") and the historical child (actual young people making their way in the world)."[48]

Building on this conversation, I aim to articulate a theory for categories of age that bridges the divide between the discursive and the material, between social meanings and the body, between poststructuralist critique and the need to construct knowledge about ourselves and our world. This means working through not one, the other, or even both, but seeking to represent the complex relations between them. These relations are always there, even when they are not acknowledged. An earlier work on childhood that negotiates these divisions with great success, Carolyn Steedman's *Strange Dislocations*, contains a disclaimer in the preface, strangely disavowing the role of discourse in the production of reality: "I do not . . . understand language as a force that shapes or forms people living in the past, or texts and narratives as productive of meaning or human identity."[49] And yet, the book itself offers a sophisticated account of a modern form of subjectivity made possible through radical shifts in nineteenth-century conceptions of the self and the child.[50] Though Steedman's disclaimer might be contextualized as a 1990s remnant of debates about language and culture, even Sedgwick expresses in *Touching Feeling* her dissatisfaction with the seemingly totalizing theories of discourse in two foundational queer texts: volume 1 of Foucault's *History of Sexuality* and Butler's *Gender Trouble*. Though in later writings Foucault extends and complicates his theories from volume 1, Sedgwick explains that the overconfidence of the "repressive hypothesis" cast its mechanisms as so pervasive that they encompassed even the work of critical analysis itself. Seemingly, there was no *outside* to the regulatory functions of discourse. The excitement of the "repressive hypothesis" was the promise of a way out, a way of thinking otherwise. However, Sedgwick finds that volume 1 could not deliver on this promise, and she laments the unfortunate effect of "propagating the repressive hypothesis ever more broadly" through interpretations of Foucault that continue to fixate on prohibition as the most important part of his argument. The binary opposition between repression and liberation that Foucault aimed to dismantle has persisted in the critical analysis that followed, as we see in opposing constructions developed later like the hegemonic and the subversive.[51]

Conceptualizing cultural analysis in terms of oppositions like these—like passivity and agency, the "child" and actual children—close down possibilities for thinking otherwise about the very things we intend to study and critique. Setting up two opposite poles like the hegemonic and the subversive obscures the complex and even paradoxical forms of resistance that can occur in the spaces between acceptance of the status quo and complete refusal of it. Much like Gubar's urging to "chart a middle course" in the study of children and childhood, Sedgwick argues that it is "only the middle ranges of agency that offer space for effectual creativity and change."[52] The disclaimer by Steedman and this critique of Foucault by Sedgwick both stem from some unanswered questions within poststructuralism. What can we do within the constraints of language and culture? What interventions will have meaning?

Sedgwick's dissatisfaction with Butler's *Gender Trouble* likewise suggests some strategies for answering these questions. Though Sedgwick expresses great affinity for Butler's early work, she traces a theory of performativity beginning with J. L. Austin to Jacques Derrida and Butler, in which she observes how the move "from *some* language to *all* language" was seemingly "required by their antiessentialist project." One of the consequences of this move "to *all* language" is that the original playfulness of Austin's examples is lost—what was "originally both provisional and playful, can persist only as reductively essentializing" when *all* language is understood to be productive of a normalizing reality. Sedgwick does not reject the antiessentialist project as a whole but rather sees what she is doing in *Touching Feeling* as a "step to the side" and a "relative lightening of the epistemological demand on essential truth." If the antiessentialist project must vigilantly expose "truth" as contextual and contingent, Sedgwick seems to suggest that we can relax this requirement—one of the requirements of critique—perhaps even strategically leaving room for a truth to be. Here is where I think Sedgwick makes space for different types of work to be evaluated by their functions and effects rather than by their specific methodological loyalties. Declining to interrogate a "truth" does not make the truth any less contingent or any more stable, but it does provide the opportunity to assess what that truth is *doing*, what it might be able to do, and to try to do something ourselves by making an attempt at saying what *is*. Sedgwick also highlights her own departure from "analyzing apparently nonlinguistic phenomena in rigorously linguistic terms," a method characteristic of poststructuralist critique. Though Sedgwick's priorities align with many deconstructive methodologies, she does not privilege language in *Touching Feeling*, clarifying that "the line between words and things or between linguistic and nonlinguistic phenomena is endlessly changing, permeable, and entirely unsusceptible to any definitive articulation. . . . Many kinds of objects and events *mean*, in many heterogeneous ways and contexts, and I see some value in not reifying or mystifying the linguistic kinds of meaning unnecessarily."[53] I think this intervention in poststructuralist critique is key to bridging the division among scholars in the study of childhood and categories of age more generally.

I do not see the need for scholars to agree on a method or to participate equally in the various ways we might approach the study of categories of age. Our project, on the contrary, might be to embrace the interdisciplinarity of our field and to value methods that depart from our own, cultivating the kind of cross-disciplinary collaboration Gubar hopes for in the future of childhood studies. Sedgwick refutes the charge that theories of discourse like performativity ignore or deny the significance of bodies, matter, and lives. Like interpretations of Rose that take her argument to mean that we cannot (or should not) speak of actual children, a similar accusation has plagued interpretations of Butler's theory of gender performativity since *Gender Trouble*. But Sedgwick does not reject performativity on the whole; she nuances and clarifies its usefulness for both discursive and nondiscursive phenomena. Barad similarly clarifies that "performativity, properly construed, is not an invitation to turn everything (including material bodies) into words; on the contrary, performativity is precisely a contestation of the excessive power granted to language to determine what is real."[54] This contestation of language is vital to work in queer theory, and I would argue that performativity is equally crucial to the study of categories of age, in which the discursive weight of the word "child" eclipses again and again our efforts to complicate, revise, and restore our view of the actual people called children. As I show in the pages that follow, the idea of adolescence similarly obscures the group it purports to name.

Performativity describes a relation between matter and meanings: contrary to "the misconception that would equate performativity with a form of linguistic monism that takes language to be the stuff of reality," Barad explains, "performativity is properly understood as a contestation of the unexamined habits of mind that grant language and other forms of representation more power in determining our ontologies than they deserve."[55] Butler describes performativity "as the reiterative and citational practice by which discourse produces the effects that it names."[56] One of the primary analytic modes of this book is to describe the problematic ways in which categories of age produce the effects that they name—the ways the logic of adolescence produces particular subjectivities or senses of self, how these categories shape particular bodily and experiential phenomena as real and true while excluding others, and how the logic of developmentalism naturalizes social hierarchies of race, class, and nation. This analytic mode is not to suggest that categories of age cannot or have never aimed to describe something material and phenomenological about the experience of being a child or adolescent. Rather, it is to say that these concepts far exceed this function. It is to recognize with Barad that

> discursive practices and material phenomena do not stand in a relationship of externality to one another; rather *the material and the discursive are mutually implicated in the dynamics of intra-activity.* The relationship between the material and the discursive is one of

mutual entailment. Neither discursive practices nor material phenomena are ontologically or epistemologically prior. Neither can be explained in terms of the other. Neither is reducible to the other. Neither has privileged status in determining the other. Neither is articulated or articulable in the absence of the other; matter and meaning are mutually articulated.[57]

Both Barad and Butler theorize materiality alongside discourse and its effects, insisting that materiality cannot and should not be determined by the limited representationalist view of language as merely descriptive of matter. Whereas Barad expands performativity to include the agency of matter within her concept of agential realism, Butler primarily describes materiality in terms of its relation to discourse— where materiality describes what we are able to see through existing social meanings, what we can even recognize as material or having matter. Butler does not make the specifics of bodily phenomena or the physical world central to her inquiry, but queer and trans analyses engaging and extending her concept of performativity account for both mechanisms of constraint or erasure and the productive function of bodily phenomena—that which appears within discourse as normative and that which appears to us only as it is excluded—inviting materialist and intersectional approaches that aim to account for the lived phenomena of bodies produced by the performative categories of race, class, gender, sexuality, and age.

The performative functions of categories of age often prevent the recognition that children and adolescents are already people now (rather than not-yet-adults to be shaped and formed), that they are complex beings (rather than metaphors for nature, the future, innocence, or evil), and that they are as various in personality, feelings, and needs as adults. These somewhat obvious statements form the basis for developing an ethical relationality to the people called children and adolescents. This work is and has been engaged by psychologists, teachers, parents, and caregivers. I draw from a variety of sources, wherever I have found ethical knowledge practices that I might build on. It is interesting to note, though, how often these ethical articulations are made possible by their acknowledged opposition to the cultural norms for describing children and adolescents and their needs. I see these two types of work as inextricably linked, both cultural critique and the practical matter of young people's lives. More ethical practices with regard to childhood and adolescence are made possible by identifying the ways that categories of age produce and regulate the bodies and experiences of children and adolescents.

Knowledge is performative, and so we can recognize varying and even opposite *doings* or effects for the same types of claims. Seemingly opposite claims might have similar goals or effects depending on context. It is this awareness that leads Sedgwick, writing in the aftermath of the AIDS crisis, to caution that both social constructivist and biological explanations for gay identity might be put to the use of an "overarching, hygienic Western fantasy of a world without any more homosexuals in it"—social constructivist approaches on the one hand emphasizing "choice" to invalidate the legitimacy of gay identity, and biological explanations on the other hand paving the way for the discovery of a "gay gene" in order to develop protocols to prevent or correct it.[58] Likewise, the idea of "storm and stress" associated with adolescence illustrates the importance of attending to the performativity of knowledge because of its opposite functions in different contexts. Turn-of-the-century theorizations of adolescence following Hall take storm and stress to be a biologically driven part of adolescent development, and this essentializing view has had the effect of producing other dehumanizing conceptions of adolescents as uncontrollable, rebellious, hormonal, or criminal. Disagreeing with Hall, Margaret Mead deployed a constructivist argument in the 1920s, contrasting U.S. American adolescence with the Samoans, to suggest that storm and stress was social and thus preventable.[59]

Contrasting Hall's and Mead's approaches, it might appear that a constructivist point of view is more ethical. However, there is today a countercultural trend among fundamentalist Christians *also* arguing that adolescence is socially constructed, but for the purpose of denying their adolescent children the space for individuation usually associated with storm-and-stress phenomena.[60] Adolescent children are expected to move directly from an obedient childhood into a dutiful adulthood without questioning the authority or beliefs of their parents. With Hall and fundamentalist Christians, one essentialist and one constructivist, we find two unethical uses of adolescence designed to control others, one based in the claim that adolescent stress is natural and the other based in the idea that it is entirely a social construction. Rather than tackle this problem within the well-worn nature-versus-nurture debate, as constructivist and essentialist positions invite us to do, we might ask instead through an ethical frame what such knowledge does and how it might shape the experiences of adolescents in different contexts. Performativity also allows us to recognize the potential for ethical uses even in essentialist claims. For example, the idea of storm and stress could be used to recognize and accept a fuller range of emotional experiences in a young person, or a skeptical view of storm and stress might similarly allow for a fuller recognition of adolescents as people deserving of respect. What matters in this range of examples is what a claim to knowledge is doing, what its effects are, and whether these effects are harmful or helpful in a particular context.

What I aim to do in this book is to describe the broader social and historical functions of categories of age while attending to the complexities of context, the ways that ethical pathways have been and might be forged through our existing concepts despite the misuses I have identified. Such an analysis aims to sort through these performative functions of our knowledge of children and adolescents to discover what ethical uses it might serve while abandoning uses based on dominance, control, and oppression. Bringing the insights of poststructuralism to bear on the lived realities of being in the world make possible this more ethical enactment of knowledge, one that grapples with the performative effects of our knowledge-making about an agential world. Performativity does not mean that language is in control; on the contrary, Butler explains, "the iterability of performativity is a theory of agency, one that cannot disavow power as the condition of its own possibility."[61] This understanding makes an active engagement with the ethics of our relationality all the more urgent and necessary.

Queer Historical Method

This project deploys the performativity of knowledge as a historical method. One of the central tensions between constructivist and essentialist approaches to history has to do with what the archives can be said to tell us. While traditional historical methods might use archives to make claims about the material realties of the past, and constructivist methods might use those same archives to make claims about language and meaning, performativity as a historical method acknowledges the entanglement of matter and meaning. The archives neither give us direct access to reality nor do they merely represent ideology. As Barad reminds us, "The relationship between the material and the discursive is one of mutual entailment." What this means for the study of history is that

> *performative* approaches call into question representationalism's claim that there are representations, on the one hand, and ontologically separate entities awaiting representation, on the other, and focus inquiry on the practices or performances of representing, as well as the productive effects of those practices and the conditions for their efficacy. A performative understanding of scientific practices, for example, takes account of the fact that knowing does not come from standing at a distance and representing but rather from *a direct material engagement with the world.*

Though Barad offers scientific practices as her example, her description is indicative of the potential for historical study as well. My approach to history and to my archives attends to both the situatedness and productive effects of my sources as well as my own interpretations of them. Neither my sources nor myself as a writer are before or after language, neither productive of unmediated knowledge *or* entirely constrained by a regulatory discourse. Barad asserts that *"theorizing, like experimenting, is a material practice."*[62] This insight is as relevant to Hall's theorizations of adolescence at the turn of the century as it is to my own arguments in this book. My principal historical questions indicate this consideration of mutual entailment, investigating the specific ways that adolescence became historically possible, and later essential, to what we understand as real and true about ourselves and the world.

The idea of adolescence raises questions about identity and the self, about what it means to be in the world and to experience ourselves and others in relation to language and meaning. These are questions about the present, about being in the present, though we can consider notions of *being* themselves historically located and contingent, shifting over time and place. The question of adolescence is not simply one of terminology, not simply a matter of linking earlier notions of youth with twentieth-century notions of adolescence; rather, it is a historical inquiry into the ways we conceptualize identity and the self, agency and power, language and reality. In this sense I find that there are both radical contingencies in notions of adolescence in the present and significant conceptual links between past and present notions of youth. If we understand language and meaning as performative, as moving with each iteration and reiteration, then my framing historical question is not whether adolescence existed in earlier centuries but how its logic existed in shifting, fragmented, and interconnected discourses over time. This methodology allows me to speak to the perplexing question of how language constitutes social realities and modes of knowledge.

The availability of widely circulating historical newspapers and periodicals in electronic databases, in conjunction with searchable full-text books online, makes an investigation of this scale possible, allowing me to trace patterns of meaning that both echo and depart from the big thinkers we now associate with adolescence. While Foucault is interested primarily in tracking the big thinkers of each age in *The Order of Things*, I am interested primarily in the broader dispersal of modes of thought, how and in what form certain ways of thinking circulate in public discourse. Through wide reading of these archives, I have found a significant number of shifting, multipurposed conceptualizations of youth, not only those articulated by experts but also those that circulated in more popular forms. My primary focus in the archives is on tracing and articulating broad patterns of thought connected to categories of age, the logic underpinning such knowledge production, and the beliefs and assumptions that make the category of adolescence possible in its particular forms from the nineteenth century to the present. There is value to very specific, contextualized historical analysis, but such analysis tells us more about a particular context than about how shared cultural meanings appear and persist through time. To argue that a set of logics surrounding adolescence emerges and shifts over time, I use a broad and varied archive, demonstrating ideological connections among disparate sources sometimes separated by a hundred years or more. This project takes a somewhat promiscuous and nonlinear approach to time, drawing from the past and the present in each chapter. Likewise, I move between British and

U.S. archival sources throughout the book, following the influence of Hall's ideas as well as his educational and professional background, which spans both sides of the Atlantic. In this regard, what I have found examining sources from both Britain and the United States are meaningful commonalities leading up to conceptions of adolescence today.

For Carla Freccero the "spirit of queer analysis" involves a "willful perversion of notions of temporal propriety and the reproductive order of things." She describes a method of "reading 'against' history," because her method of analysis "at times works counter to the imperative—appearing in many discourses called literary as well as those called historical—to respect the directional flow of temporality, the notion that time is composed of contiguous and interrelated joined segments that are also sequential." Importantly, however, she asserts that "this does not, nevertheless, mean that the work is anti- or ahistorical."[63] The "imperative" to regard time as directional, sequential, and progressive can itself be historicized within the arguments of my book, as it refers to a particular way of viewing the passage of time (and categories of age themselves) that emerges over the course of the nineteenth century. I think it is useful here to think of Barad's keen observation about Einstein's theory of relativity: "Time isn't an abstract idea for Einstein; time is what we measure with a clock."[64] Time exists in its material instantiation as a unit of measure, not as the epistemological ground of all knowledge. What makes Freccero's disregard for historical imperative "queer" is the fact that this developmental view of time is normative and, I would argue, foundational to the continued production and maintenance of normativity itself. As Michael Warner reminds us, the emergence of "normal" as a social value is a recent phenomenon, located in the explosion of measurement, categorization, and documentation of people in the nineteenth century.[65] In "Queering History," Jonathan Goldberg and Madhavi Menon describe a "rigorously historical" study of the past that would simultaneously "refuse what we might term the compulsory heterotemporality of historicism."[66] This is something like the methodology Freccero describes: "These analyses proceed otherwise than according to a presumed logic of cause and effect, anticipation and result; and otherwise than according to a presumed logic of the 'done-ness' of the past, since queer time is haunted by the persistence of affect and ethical imperatives in and across time."[67] It is precisely these "ethical imperatives" that motivate my reading of the archives for what possibilities they open up for thinking otherwise about adolescence, temporality, and selfhood.

My questions proceed from a queer relation to history, one that muddles the separateness of the past and the present and resists the urge to create a historical narrative in which the past forms the justification for the present state of things. The logic of adolescence is a temporal logic, a way of understanding the stages of human life, selfhood, the past and future. This developmental logic of life-as-a-progressive-story, one that overlaps the interiority of selfhood with the biological growth and aging of the body, constitutes the epistemological ground from which the stages of human life and history itself are perceived and known. That is, "history" within this schema refers to a progressive narrative of development toward the present. But the idea of history *as a thing itself* rather than a sequence of discrete events comes out of the profound epistemological shift in the nineteenth century known as "historicism" or "developmentalism." The dominance of historicism has made it difficult to see the past as anything other than a point in time within a historical process that has led to our present. This viewpoint illustrates a logic in which the primary significance of the past is to search for developmental *causes* for the present. My project does, at times, participate in the methodology I am aligning with developmentalism here, in which I speculate about causes and effects. Steedman puts it this way: "My conviction that events marshalled into a chronology can *explain* something is a turn of thought connected to the very development of childhood in its modern sense, and one that I cannot escape, even should I want to."[68]

However, my critique of developmentalism carries over into the organization of this book. Thus, I do not attempt to string together historical events as a cohesive story of what happened in the past. My departures from this method are not to dismiss it altogether but to acknowledge that developmentalism "knows some things well and others poorly," to reuse a phrase from Sedgwick.[69] I want to know: What happens if we look backward with another goal in mind? What can we see if we look at the past outside these narrative and developmental logics? What becomes visible when we disregard national boundaries and the usual periodizations of academic study? What connections emerge through wide reading of a broad archive? This is not a disregard for the past (which is the complaint often lodged against queer theory) but rather a different sort of attention to it.

In this sense my project is one of opening up rather than closing down meanings, moving my inquiry inside its very questions rather than attempting to answer questions while I stand outside them. One way I have approached the problem of discourse is to overlap language, text, and world, a strategy that makes visible the performative and hermeneutic dimensions of any engagement with these contradictory and shifting constructions of self and other. Certainly, the objective of critique is to challenge existing interpretations, to shift or stretch the interpretive possibilities of self, text, and world. Scholars in queer theory emphasize the performativity of gender and sexuality because of an often personal awareness of ways of being that fall outside of language, outside of the existing definitions and categories. Performativity reminds us that lived realities are always more complex, contradictory, and queer than the discursive ways of being we use to make sense of those realities. This book attempts to hold open some of these possibilities, to acknowledge the vast range of being and knowing that exceeds discourse. Sarah Chinn suggests that childhood studies can "maintain its rigorous historicism" while incorporating from queer theory "a less materialist recognition of the unknowability of children." She explains, "We can recognize the historically and culturally specific narratives that construct 'childhood' while also understanding that actual children are and have always been far more mysterious, perverse, incomprehensible, antisocial, productive, and embodied—that is to say *queer*—than our scholarship has given them credit for."[70] Like gender or sexuality, adolescence is not a *thing* in and of itself but constituted through discourse, and, as such, it is unstable and contradictory, shifting through time and space. This is not to disregard the material world, the body, or our experiences of them, but on the contrary to attend to the ways discursivity shapes what it is possible to see and know about such material phenomena in the first place.

Of course, adolescents and children are people. But the privilege of personhood is not granted to all children or adolescents and such privilege is highly dependent on social factors beyond the control of young people themselves, at times contingent on the discretion of a few parents, teachers, doctors, or social workers. The logics of childhood and adolescence powerfully function to justify the denial of personhood to this person who is not yet recognized as a person, to those who may never achieve personhood. Childhood obscures these abuses of childhood. And adolescence so often serves as reason enough to deny a young person the dignity of their own meaning-making. As I have inhabited throughout this project so many evocations of adolescence and childhood, I have paid particular attention to those that seemed driven by projects of control. What were these projects of control, and what did they want? What seemed to motivate their values and assumptions and grounds for justification?

We cannot control other people. I say this, perhaps, at the risk of stating the obvious. And yet, for some the idea of allowing others control of themselves ushers on visions of anarchy and chaos, visions of a world in which all hope of freedom and security are gone forever. Here we find the utopian project of imagining a better world to be only one side of the coin, which on the flip side is merely a dystopian nightmare. The ominous phrase, for example, "the end of the world as we know it" gives away its investments in preserving to the end the known over the unknown, this threat hinging on apocalyptic fear. I am interested in understanding the vexed relationship between the productive, even utopian, project of imagining a better social world and the regulatory impulse to manage those aspects of the social world that we cannot know, anticipate, or control. Figures of youth can be used to hold apocalyptic visions at bay, coming to represent both the cause and the cure for fears of the unknown, both what propels us toward the end of the world and back toward its beginning. It is perhaps the fantasy of control that adolescence promises, the illusion that there are origins we can discover or return to, futures at which we can arrive.

Adolescence is a fiction, but one that cannot be so easily undone. It is always difficult to see the present *as* the present. That is, a critical inquiry that aims to describe the present is perpetually enmeshed in the very culture it seeks to describe. My hope is to pry apart language and begin to wriggle it free from the natural, the normal, and the known of our present. With this objective in mind, I have sought after the perverse interpretive possibilities of both past and present. I have sought after the submerged and explicit ways that we *need* adolescence, what functions it serves, and whether we are best served by it. I do not know if we can ever do away with adolescence, whether the disciplines of medicine and psychology will move away from it in the twenty-first century, whether changes will occur in public policies on the age of consent, voting rights, driving, drinking, and compulsory schooling. For now my hope is to dislodge adolescence from its present knowability and, with it, the logic that sustains it.

chapter 1

G. STANLEY HALL AND
THE LOGIC OF DEVELOPMENTALISM

What is philosophy today—philosophical activity, I mean—if it is not the critical work that thought brings to bear on itself? In what does it consist, if not in the endeavor to know how and to what extent it might be possible to think differently, instead of legitimating what is already known?
—Michel Foucault, *The Use of Pleasure*

We can find some measure of liberation, I believe, by examining the directions we receive for reading the past and then disobeying them as brazenly as we can, flaunting them, turning them back on themselves.
—James Kincaid, *Child-Loving*

U.S. psychologist and educator G. Stanley Hall (1846–1924) is often referred to as the father of adolescence, and it is common practice in academic scholarship across the humanities and social sciences to mention Hall and the start of the twentieth century as a key moment in medical, psychological, legal, and educational discourse about adolescence. This moment has even been called the invention of adolescence, and Hall's massive two-volume *Adolescence: Its Psychology and Its Relations to Physiology, Anthropology, Sociology, Sex, Crime, Religion and Education* is largely taken for granted as the point of origin for a stage of human life previously unrecognized or unacknowledged.[1] My research, however, reveals more than 700 references to adolescence in U.S. newspaper databases dated before 1900, one of the earliest dated 1769, and nearly 1,400 references in British newspaper databases.[2] What did the word "adolescence" mean, then, over the course of the nineteenth century? Using Hall as an anchor point, this chapter, drawing primarily on U.S. and British newspaper archives, tracks the word "adolescence" up through the nineteenth century to uncover the assumptions and beliefs about adolescence that shaped the use of this word in the past and that continue to inform our present. Social histories are not wrong to emphasize the importance of Hall's work in the history of adolescence, but a wide survey of nineteenth-century newspapers reveals trajectories of fragmented, multipurposed conceptualizations of adolescence—trajectories that precede Hall and continue after him. The abundance of references to adolescence prior to 1900 raises the question of what specifically Hall's work distilled and condensed and what specifically was new.

While distinctions can be made between the content of U.S. and British newspaper archives, the word "adolescence" reveals strikingly similar patterns of usage on both sides of the Atlantic.[3] Newspapers provide a record of common usage—the way a word carries meaning through time—demonstrating both the tenuousness and stickiness of meaning-making.[4] In other words, I track the word not for some essential meaning but for its usage in specific textual contexts. What does a particular use of "adolescence" indicate about the work that word does, the knowledge it conveys? This method acknowledges, above all, the performativity of knowledge. While I do not claim that adolescence is central to nineteenth-century thought, I demonstrate how a focus on adolescence allows us to see a nexus of larger shifts in the organization of the social world. In this chapter I describe a set of logics and conceptual linkages connected to categories of age, both present and historical.

One of the most frequent uses of the word "adolescence" in the first part of the nineteenth century was as a metaphor for nation and for various civic institutions, such as a city hall. In the United States, this metaphor had very positive connotations, heavily weighted with the triumphant narrative of the newly independent nation. When I searched British newspapers, I expected to see the opposite pattern of usage, assuming the British would refer to the United States as "adolescent" in a derogatory way. Surprisingly, however, the pattern was the same. Adolescence was frequently invoked as a metaphor to justify the self-governance of former colonies with references to the "rights of adolescence" and qualities such as the "strength of adolescence" and "vigorous adolescence."[5] In the first half of the nineteenth century, I was also surprised to find in both U.S. and British newspapers a striking pattern of positive descriptors accompanying the word "adolescence," including the "treasures of adolescence," "joys of adolescence," "vigor of adolescence," "healthy adolescence," and "bloom of adolescence."[6] These examples provide a stark contrast to the negative and often condescending associations of adolescence that would become common in the twentieth century. A significant shift occurs around 1870, when we see the first negative generalizations accompanying the category of adolescence. Likewise, over the course of the nineteenth century, the use of adolescence as a metaphor for nation changed, invoked instead to justify the prolonged dependence of states and territories rather than their independence.

In this chapter I show how a larger epistemological shift over the course of the nineteenth century—the logic of developmentalism— makes the category of adolescence possible. Today the notion of development is synonymous with our conceptions of growth and learning. Valerie Walkerdine argues that developmental psychology produces the very object it claims to know: the "developing child." She observes how the discourses of developmentalism "forget the constructed nature of consciousness," a mechanism that "covers over exploitation and oppression, just as wealth, poverty, race and gender inequalities are understood within developmentalism as producing a lack, a backwardness."[7] Claudia Castañeda likewise argues that developmentalism is central to the construction of racial hierarchies, in which "the Now of the primitive was not only placed in the time of childhood, but also in the child-body: the child was seen as a bodily theater where human history could be observed to unfold in the compressed timespan of individual development."[8] Like Walkerdine and Castañeda, I use the term "developmentalism" to underscore the difference between development as a value-neutral description of change over time and the goal-oriented narrativizing epistemology that emerges over the course of the nineteenth century, what Maurice Mandelbaum describes as "historicism" and Michel Foucault as "historicity."[9] Remarkably, categories of age were not the model for developmentalism. On the contrary, as Carolyn Steedman reminds us, "'Childhood' was a category of dependence, a term that defined certain relationships of powerlessness, submission, and bodily inferiority or weakness, before it became descriptive of chronological age. The late nineteenth century fixed childhood, not just as a category of experience, but also a time span."[10] References to categories of age in nineteenth-century newspaper databases likewise suggest that developmentalism, as an epistemology, reconfigures notions of childhood and, later in the century, makes possible the concept of adolescence we recognize today.

What I am attempting to define is the "*a priori*" of adolescence, the unacknowledged and unarticulated beliefs that become the occasion for knowing "its conditions of possibility."[11] Developmentalism emerges out of a temporal logic that imagines the growth of the child's body, people as individuals, and entire nations or social groups as ordered along a pathway in time toward an ideal or normative outcome. Through a new conception of time, the stages of human life took on new significance as political metaphors that were used to maintain the inferiority of other categories of difference. At the same time the ontological categories of age, race, class, gender, and sexuality emerged as classifiable types of people placed within the temporality of developmentalism to justify existing social hierarchies. These categories function in different ways, but they can be understood as strands of the same hierarchical mechanisms that emerged over the course of the nineteenth century. Developmentalism is the dominant logic through which categories of age are understood today. Indeed, our very definitions of parenting and educating seem to hinge on these ways of thinking, though not without consequence. My purpose is to understand what patterns of thought inform these logics and perpetuate them so that we might imagine more ethical possibilities for knowing and relating to one another.

Nineteenth-Century Newspapers

The word "adolescence" was not widely used in English prior to the mid-nineteenth century, and the earliest references in newspaper databases suggest the word's capaciousness at this time.[12] The first reference in the archive of U.S. newspapers appears in a 1769 parody titled "The Use and Abuse of Time" with the phrase "Adolescence of Youth" employed to mock the wordiness and redundancy of philosophical writing.[13] A similar use of the word appears in an 1811 article by a "Philologer" titled "Pompous Reflections No. 1," which contains mock reflections on the "cogitation of man," such as this formulation: "From his ablactation to his adolescence, with respect to ethics, he is nearly adiaphorous."[14] A joke appearing throughout the middle of the nineteenth century continues this pattern, though it addresses a person called by the name "Adolescens," which distinguishes it from earlier uses. The humor of the joke, though, still hinges on the perceived verbosity of those who use the word: "A dabbler in literature and the fine arts, who prided himself upon his knowledge and proper use of the English language, came upon a youngster sitting upon the bank of a mill pond, angling for shiners, and thus addressed him:—'Adolescens, art thou not endeavoring to entice the finny tribe to engulph into their denticulated mouths a barbed hook, upon whose point is affixed a dainty allurement?' 'No,' said the boy, *'I'm fishin!'*"[15] The joke's introduction, with the dismissive word "dabbler" and the phrase "prided himself," indicates that the joke is on the adult speaker and his pretentious language rather than the boy, with whom the audience is invited to identify. Likewise, the reference to the "proper use of the English language" may be ironic, expressing resistance to the normalizing attempts of grammar books circulating at this time. The joke sometimes appears without the introduction, beginning simply with the dialogue, suggesting that the introduction was not necessary for readers to get the joke. But an 1870 version changes the introduction to read somewhat more sarcastically: "A gentleman, whose learning does not appear to have sat very lightly upon him, addressed a boy whom he found fishing, in the following simple and unaffected manner."[16] This change may reflect only a version of the joke recalled from being told in person rather than from being read in print. But it is interesting that this intensification of the joke's sarcasm corresponds with the first negative descriptors accompanying the word "adolescence" around 1870. It may have been necessary by this point to craft an introduction that guarded against its interpretation as a joke on the boy.

In the first half of the nineteenth century, a pattern of positive descriptors accompanies the word "adolescence." An early example, reprinted from a London paper, appears in New York's *Commercial Advertiser* in 1798. This article, reportedly written by a French officer of engineers regarding the art of sculpture, describes the work of the Italian sculptor Antonio Canova (1757–1822): "This delicious abandonment—this picture of youthful pleasure—these treasures of adolescence, have a grace, beauty and delicacy, which no description can reach."[17] Similarly, an 1806 advertisement for an aromatic confidently claims to "have inspired the feeblest decrepitude with the vigor of adolescence."[18] And a political story in the *Monitor* from 1808 describes how two characters "seized our guns with all the gaiety and vigor of a healthy adolescence."[19] Another account from the *Middlesex Gazette* in 1826 describes a character who "seemed in the very prime of adolescence, having just arrived at that period when the slender and less powerful graces of youth are strengthening into and blending with the firm and muscular symmetry of full manhood."[20] Another 1827 article in the *Norwich Courier* talks about the "enchantments of youth" and the power of memory to "restore to the autumn of age the adolescence of youth."[21] In the phrase the "adolescence of youth," the word "adolescence" is used positively to describe the health, vigor, and strength of feeling belonging to youth.

Vigor and health were primarily associated with male adolescence, with maleness operating as the default and assumed point of reference in most usages. When adolescence referred to a woman or girl, the descriptions change. In 1828, for example, the *Washington Whig* described "the innocent face of the blooming girl, just shooting up from the first period of childhood, in to the more sedate age of adolescence."[22] The "sedate" age of adolescence contrasts starkly with contemporaneous references to strength and vigor. Similarly, an 1848 short story in the *Boston Daily Atlas* states, "so sad a year had taken from Joanna the almost infantile character of adolescence, which had given her so much naivete and charm."[23] The "infantile character of adolescence" here sounds more like childhood than adolescence. As this example suggests, the characteristics attributed to girls are not strongly negative, but such usages are condescending, evidence of the hierarchical subordination of femininity to masculinity.

John Springhall notes that while the biological changes of puberty were recognized in earlier centuries, the cultural significance attached to puberty was not the same as it is today: "Prior to the middle of the nineteenth century, contemporaries associated puberty with rising power and energy rather than the onset of an awkward and vulnerable stage of life which would later become known as adolescence."[24] And Joseph Kett observes that it was not until the turn of the twentieth century that "young people, particularly teenage boys, ceased to be viewed as troublesome, rash, and heedless, the qualities traditionally associated with youth; instead, they increasingly were viewed as vulnerable, passive, and awkward, qualities that previously had been associated only with girls."[25] Kett's observation suggests that the changes surrounding perceptions of adolescence at the turn of the century were strongly linked to other social hierarchies, in this case gender: specifically, the feminized qualities of passivity and vulnerability used to naturalize the hierarchical relation between men and women were used later in the century to demote adolescence as a whole. It is worth noting that it is not evident what ages correspond to adolescence in these examples about girls or whether any specific age range is even intended. In nineteenth-century articles concerned with health or educational prescriptions, childhood and adolescence are often mentioned together in a single phrase, such as "infancy and adolescence," or as part of a list that includes terms such as "manhood" and "old age."[26] These uses emphasize interconnectedness and the inevitability of aging—the march of life—over discrete categories of existence with essential, defining characteristics.

For example, a short piece called "The Periods of Human Life" that appeared in at least eight U.S. newspapers and periodicals in 1825 lists fifteen stages of life divided into spans of seven years each (see fig. 1.1).[27] Adolescence is only the second stage listed, following childhood. In this rendering adolescence spans from ages eight to fourteen and is the "age of hopes, improvidence, curiosity, impatience." Puberty, extending from ages fifteen to twenty-one, follows adolescence and consists of "triumphs, desires, self-love, independence, and vanity." The majority of life stages are ascribed to adulthood, an arrangement that significantly deemphasizes what the twentieth century would later consider the "developmental years." The fifteen stages suggest the inescapable passage of time rather than a developmental process; they neither imply a hierarchical organization nor position adulthood as an arrival point. Considering the fact that the average life expectancy was fewer than forty years in the first half of the nineteenth century, most people would not have lived to experience the majority of these stages.

"The Periods of Human Life" first circulated in papers without interpretive commentary, but in 1840 a medical doctor named E. G. Wheeler reproduced it in the *Boston Medical and Surgical Journal*

Childhood.—From 1 to 7 years of age. The period of accidents, griefs, wants, sensibilities.

Adolescence.—From 8 to 14. The age of hopes, improvidence, curiosity, impatience.

Puberty.—From 15 to 21. The age of triumphs and desires, self-love, independence, vanity.

Youth.—From 22 to 28. The age of pleasure, love, sensuality, inconstancy, enthusiasm.

Manhood.—From 29 to 35. The age of enjoyments, ambition, and the play of all the passions.

Middle Age.—From 36 to 42. The age of consistency, desire of fortune, of glory, and honour.

Mature Age.—From 43 to 49. The age of possession, the reign of wisdom, reason, love of property.

Decline of Life.—From 50 to 56. The age of reflection, love of tranquillity, foresight, and prudence.

Commencement of Old Age.—From 57 to 63. The age of regrets, cares, inquietudes, ill-temper, desire of ruling.

Old Age.—From 64 to 70. The age of infirmities, exigency, love of authority and submission.

Decrepitude.—From 71 to 77. The age of avarice, jealousy, and envy.

Caducity.—From 78 to 84. The age of distrust, vain-boasting, unfeelingness, suspicion.

Age of Favour.—From 85 to 91. The age of insensibility, love of flattery, of attention and indulgence.

Age of Wonder.—From 92 to 98. The age of indifference, and love of praise.

Phenomenon.—From 99 to 105. The age of hope, and—the last sigh !

Figure 1.1. "Physiology: The Periods of Human Life," in *Classic Cullings and Fugitive Gatherings* (London: Arnold, 1831), 246.

alongside his own commentary. Wheeler discusses a number of alternative organizations for human life, including six stages outlined by the "ancients" and five from the physiologist Dr. Robley Dunglison (1798–1869) with additional subcategories for infancy. About the fifteen periods of human life, which he admits is a "curious division of the age of man," he remarks, "there may be some inaccuracies in regard to the names of the different periods in the above quotation, particularly as regards adolescence and puberty, but the passions, qualities of the mind, &c., as therein attached to the several stages of life, are principally, if not altogether, correct, as I have no doubt every observing mind will at once admit."[28] Despite his claim of "inaccuracies," Wheeler offers no correction and instead appeals to his readers' commonsense observations to discern the "truth" of the list. The appearance of this list in a medical journal, along with its wide circulation on both sides of the Atlantic in the early nineteenth century, supports my contention that categories of age themselves were not the model or origin point for developmentalism. None of the organizations for human life discussed by Wheeler indicate a process of development but rather reflect an earlier episteme (in Foucault's terms) of representationalism—that is, "language as the spontaneous *tabula*" for representing things.[29] Three separate organizational schemes for depicting the human life course are offered side by side and on equal footing as alternative representations of the same thing. Life is not a story or a process, according to this view, but a sequence of stages that can be represented in language with varying degrees of accuracy.

How were the stages of life understood, if not as a story of development? Prior to representationalism, Foucault explains, "The history of a living being was that being itself, within the whole semantic network that connected it to the world."[30] Importantly, the shifts between epistemes is not clean but rather involves a "middle region" that is "continuous and gradual or discontinuous and piecemeal."[31] On this note "The Periods of Human Life" suggests these earlier epistemes in its division by seven years, based on numerology and resembling a division by the ancient Greek Solon or one corresponding to the plants (of which there are seven) that can be found in many medieval texts. We also see stages of seven years reproduced (among other organizations) in the early twentieth century along with the attempt to match them to biological phenomena and developmental theory, showing how conceptualizations from different periods can be refunctioned.[32] Philippe Ariès describes popular organizations for the stages of life prior to the eighteenth century and their difference from today: "It was the inevitable, cyclical, sometimes amusing and sometimes sad continuity of the ages of life; a continuity inscribed in the general and abstract order of things rather than in real experience." Life had clearly defined stages "corresponding to certain modes of activity, physical types, social functions and styles of dress" rather than biology, and these stages "had the same fixity as the cycle of Nature or the organization of society."[33] The order of this organization did not come from an internal process of development but from forces perceived to be outside the human body such as God, Nature, or Divine Law. Under this pre-nineteenth-century episteme, the stages of life were not a story of development but rather evidence of the fixed and cyclical inevitability of birth and death alongside the perceived stability of hierarchical order in the social and natural world.

As early as 1825, we can find calls for the study of adolescence, though the method of this study is quite different from the agenda outlined by Hall almost a century later. The *Newburyport Herald* declares, also appealing to commonsense, that "we are all disposed to regard the age of adolescence with affection, for its beauty as well as its feebleness invites our sympathy and attachment." It is for this reason, the *Herald* continues, that "we should do more, we should consider it with grave attention, study it, and in learning and improving from its simplicity, bend our best energies to its direction and encouragement."[34] These assumptions about adolescence seem to align more closely with an idea of childhood "feebleness," and the argument expressed seems to encourage a perceptiveness in caregivers that would adapt according to what is seen rather than the application of a predetermined method based on an authorized knowledge or "truth" about these stages of life. The appeal to affection, sympathy, and attachment also assumes a very positive feeling about adolescence that is quite different from the fears of degeneration expressed a century later.

In the 1830s, 1840s, and 1850s, adolescence was still accompanied by highly positive descriptors. In 1831, for example, a rave review of the child actor Master Burke declared how "the soul of adolescence kindles in his eyes, and breathes in all his acts," making it "delightful to regard so singular a combination of youth, genius and renown."[35] And, in 1834, a lecture reprinted in the *Richmond Enquirer* refers to the "luxuriance of adolescence."[36] In 1840 "adolescence" is used as a complimentary term for an adult, who, despite his age, wrote an article "exhibiting all the elasticity of adolescence."[37] A moral tale reprinted from the *Ladies Companion* in both the *Salem Gazette* and the *Pennsylvania Inquirer* in 1841 declares, "My children are now grown to adolescence—wealth and honor and goodness are theirs."[38] In 1847, too, an article on the opening of an exhibition in New York reported that all ages were actively interested, including "vigorous manhood, happy adolescence, and squalling babyhood."[39] In another example from 1851, the word "adolescence" is used to compliment Col. Washington Daniel Miller (1814–66), secretary of state in Texas, whose "countenance, still indicative of adolescence, and flushed with robust health, bespeaks in language plainer than words."[40] Similarly, in 1853, a short story in the *Boston Daily Atlas* describes "the young and flexible strength of adolescence."[41]

Alongside these positive uses, adolescence was commonly invoked as a metaphor for national independence with strongly positive connotations as well. For example, a Fourth of July commemorative speech, printed in Boston's *Daily Advertiser* in 1809, casts the United States in terms of the stages of human life: "Yes, my friends, we are now the nation. As such we have arrived at that epoch when instead of looking back to with wonder upon our infancy, we may look forward with solicitude to a state of adolescence, with confidence to a state of manhood. Tho' as a nation we are yet in the morning of life, we have already attained an elevation which enables us to discern our course to its meridian splendor."[42] Adolescence has a very positive association here—it is a moment of looking forward first with care and then with confidence to a state of manhood. An article in the *Washington Federalist* in the same year uses the words "infancy" and "adolescence" to make an argument for why the United States should not get involved in the war in Europe: "Will this country, as yet, comparatively speaking, in a state of infancy, certainly not advanced beyond a state of adolescence, be able to meet the shock of such a war?"[43] In contrast to the preceding example, here the reference to adolescence indicates the need for protection and caution, though it is worth noting that this is accomplished through the indeterminancy of the boundary between infancy and adolescence. In another example, an 1813 address printed in *Poulson's American Daily Advertiser* uses "infancy" and "adolescence" to assert the power of the United States: "Other countries by gradual accretions of strength, by slow and painful step, had risen, through an arduous and toilsome course, to the same degree of maturity, to which we ascended with the rapidity of a single impulse: The period of their infancy and adolescence had been long precarious and exposed; America was like the infant Hercules, and in her cradle strangled the serpent anarchy."[44] Infancy and adolescence describe the metaphorical growth of the nation. Notably, in this comparison, the United States' adolescence is *not* precarious but heroic and strong.

The invocation of adolescence as a metaphor for the growth of national sentiment was quite adaptable, as we see in an article from 1815 supporting the mental advantages of reading newspapers: "And to what are we to attribute the implantation and adolescence of patriotism in our fellow-citizens, but to a knowledge of the heroic deeds of our fathers in establishing our Republic."[45] In this case it is not exactly the nation, but U.S. patriotism that is in its adolescence, and, as such, this patriotism is described as well established and enthusiastically felt. An 1820 article in the *Daily National Intelligencer* celebrates the opening of the city hall in the District of Columbia using adolescence as a metaphor characterizing the population of the city: "We, of this city, are now passing from an infancy in which we were surrounded by difficulties, to an adolescence which is full of promise."[46] The positive connotations of this metaphorical adolescence echo the positive characteristics we see in references to adolescence as a stage of life in the early nineteenth century—a stage that evokes vitality, health, and strength.

Adolescence, used as a metaphor for nation, often functioned as a narrative device used to justify or predict particular outcomes, and it is this ideological force that we see harnessed by Hall nearly a century later. Take, for instance, an 1816 campaign piece for the upcoming presidential election. The *Daily National Intelligencer* declared, "What citizen, then, has greatly merited the suffrage of his country by a series of public services and patriotic sacrifices from the age of adolescence to the maturity of years of wisdom? Who is he who at the age of sixteen took up arms to assert his country's independence?"[47] The answer was James Monroe, and the narrative evoked here, the story of adolescence that would justify the choice for the future president, was reprinted in at least four U.S. newspapers in February 1816, including the *Baltimore Patriot*, the *Essex Register*, and the *Vermont Republican*. Usually, when we see adolescence used as evidence of one's future greatness, it works through back-formation, like in a biography of Napoleon, for example, where the literal or metaphorical adolescence justifies the achievements of the present or recent past.[48] This example is notable because adolescence is being used to construct a future result, a story that hasn't happened yet, a narrative arc that begins with patriotic adolescence and ends with the election of James Monroe, one that suggests to voters what they should do to make the story complete. Indeed, this campaign piece spends most of its time instructing readers how to think about voting, what questions to ask, what requirements they should have for the next president. The narrative here works to make the desired future outcome, the election of James Monroe, feel inevitable and the rightness of it indisputable. Narrative tends to construct its own inevitability, but these narratives around adolescence are not natural or inevitable; rather, the concept of adolescence begins to function here as a narrative of developmentalism, a story of self and nation, one that has intersected over time with shifting ideological investments.

As a metaphor for nation, adolescence continued to be referenced in positive expressions of national independence in both U.S. and British newspapers throughout the nineteenth century. That pattern changed in the middle of the nineteenth century, however, when it became available as a term of condescension to justify the continued dependence of states or territories. For example, an article from 1845 in the *New York Herald* about territory disputes in the recently annexed state of Texas makes an unflattering comparison with the state of Florida, which "became saucy" and "in the very first days of its adolescence, gets too big for its breeches."[49] Unlike earlier examples, Florida's metaphorical adolescence does not suggest its right to independence but rather its failure to show proper deference. Another example from 1856 in the *Wisconsin Patriot* argues for Congress to provide some form of law and order for new territories "at least during their adolescence." The article states, "It seems to us a matter of indispensible [*sic*] necessity, that when Congress organizes a Territory, it should extend the blessings of a limited code of laws and somebody to enforce them—otherwise all would be anarchy and confusion—the people would be without law and order at least during their adolescence, or the period of intervening between their being a territorial Government, and the time they could enact and enforce their own laws."[50] Here adolescence functions as a metaphor to indicate the need for prolonged dependence rather than a territory's ability to self-govern.

chapter one

This example, preceding the strongly negative characterizations of adolescence that would crop up in 1869 and 1870, appears the same year as two outlying examples from the same paper in which we see the word "adolescence" accompanied by somewhat idiosyncratic descriptors: the phrases "gangrene adolescence" and "effeminate adolescence" are used to criticize the state government in Wisconsin in separate articles in 1856.[51] These early examples provide a clarifying contrast for the negative generalizations that appear later because the category of adolescence does not carry the weight of the insult. In other words, the descriptors "gangrene" and "effeminate" are not generalizations about adolescence itself; rather, these adjectives do the work of the critique (in this case, of the Wisconsin assembly and the Wisconsin legislature, respectively). These phrases do not imply that adolescence is characteristically gangrene or effeminate; rather, they suggest that these are the signs of a weak and inferior political body that will, metaphorically speaking, grow up inherently perverse and diseased, in contrast to the robust masculinity implied by contemporaneous references to "healthy adolescence" and "vigorous adolescence." However, the logic of developmentalism enables these contrasting constructions, in which adolescence begins to designate a location on a developmental pathway heading toward an ideal, normative outcome or away from it.

In newspapers from the middle of the nineteenth century, evocations of adolescence as a national metaphor demonstrated significant temporal variability, sometimes representing U.S. independence in the present, other times representing the past or a future that was just ahead. In 1842 an article in the *Madisonian* places the United States just past adolescence: "When this system was resorted to before, we were in our adolescence: we have now grown up into the bone and sinew of manhood."[52] But, only a few years later in 1845, an article in the *New York Herald* positioned the United States as on the verge of a triumphant adolescence: "All these combined together form the annual increase in the wealth of the United States, and indicate to the world at large, that in everything that constitutes power, wealth, civilization, abundance, and national prosperity, the United States are almost in a state of adolescence."[53] Later, in 1845, the *New York Herald* depicted the entire world as in its adolescence: "Society is constantly in a state of transition—of progress. That which many are accustomed to call the old age of the world, was but its infancy, and it is yet in the days of its adolescence."[54] All these examples utilize adolescence as a metaphor linked to the triumphant story of U.S. independence, but there is another layer of meaning indicating the progress of human civilization as a whole. The idea of revolution by human efforts blends with the idea of an evolutionary progress that is inevitable. This layer of inevitable but unpredictable development, expressed in the idea that "society is constantly in a state of transition," is one that we see emphasized in Hall's *Adolescence* more than half a century later.

A significant shift in nineteenth-century newspapers occurs around 1870, when we begin to see some of the first negative, dismissive, and condescending references to adolescence. In 1870 we find one of the most unambiguously negative examples, printed in *Pomeroy's Democrat*: "We certainly would have never intentionally accused John Q. A. of the absurdities and crudities of adolescence. It is strange how often the young prove inadequate to represent the sound sense of their progenitors."[55] Here the words "absurdities" and "crudities" provide a stark contrast to the positive pattern of descriptors we saw earlier. This example is significant because "absurdities" and "crudities" function as negative generalizations about adolescence itself, and I didn't find any analogous negative generalizations before this date. The word "progenitors" resonates with the language of evolutionary theory, connoting biological ancestry, not just parenting. Moreover, this quip evokes the concept of generational deterioration—the idea of children devolving into something weaker or lesser than their parents—not as a fear but as a fact. In the 1870s, in British as well as U.S. papers, the word "adolescence" began to appear with a number of negative and condescending descriptors like "feeble-minded adolescence" and "gushing adolescence."[56] Throughout the 1860s the *London Times* contains phrases like "fresh and vigorous adolescence," "the strength of adolescence," and "healthy and vigorous adolescence," with the first negative descriptors appearing in 1869 with the "temptations of adolescence" and, even more striking, the "perpetual state of rabid adolescence."[57] Like the example from *Pomeroy's Democrat*, these kinds of negative generalizations about the category of adolescence do not exist in the newspaper archive before this date. The positive descriptors accompanying adolescence in the first part of the nineteenth century continue past 1870 (particularly "vigorous adolescence"), but there are no earlier examples of negative generalizations comparable to the instances found in 1869 and 1870, when adolescence becomes available as a term of insult. This shift also occurs more than thirty years before the publication of Hall's *Adolescence*, calling into question the ways he is positioned in social histories as the source of the negative associations we see in the twentieth century.[58] This shift also raises the question: What happened circa 1870?

Foucault names 1870 as the year "the homosexual was now a species," meaning that particular sexual acts, which previously anyone might have participated in, began to be understood as indicative of a classifiable type of person. He writes, "The nineteenth-century homosexual became a personage, a past, a case history, and a childhood." At the same time something similar happens with the category of adolescence, which is used less to describe a stage of life and—by the time we get to Hall—more to describe a generalizable *type* of person belonging to this stage, a particular species of human. There were all kinds of categories invented for people in the nineteenth century that were being subjected to new forms of institutional management and control. Some of these categories appear at first to be more obviously contingent on historical context—like Foucault's tracing of the "homosexual" or Ian Hacking's case study of the emergence of multiple personality disorder in 1875.[59] But the history of adolescence raises questions about how these new ways of classifying people impacted the social functions of seemingly more "universal" or "durable" categories like gender, age, race, or class.

Analyzing multiple categories of difference at once reveals that these forms of classification functioned primarily as new ways of maintaining existing social hierarchies. Siobhan Somerville suggests "that it was not merely a historical coincidence that the classification of bodies as either 'homosexual' or 'heterosexual' emerged at the same time that the United States was aggressively constructing and policing the boundary between 'black' and 'white' bodies" in the period following the U.S. Civil War in 1865. Somerville's analysis of late nineteenth- and early twentieth-century discourses shows the mutual constitution of sexuality and race through practices that "demanded a specific kind of logic" to give "coherence to new concepts" for classifying human beings.[60] My research suggests that categories of age played a pivotal role in the "specific kind of logic" described by Somerville and that these new classifications of race, sexuality, and age relied on one another for definition. Recent scholarly work also takes up the centrality of childhood and adolescence to one or more intersections of identity, illuminating the interdependency of categories of difference in the late nineteenth and early twentieth centuries.[61] Building on this work, I want to emphasize the mutual constitution of categories of difference in the nineteenth century, including categories of age, and the necessity of understanding them as part of the same reorganizations of power whose logics inform conceptions of human difference to this day. Through the logic of developmentalism, childhood and adolescence began to function as temporal categories in which any marginalized person or group could be relocated along a developmental timeline as regressive, immature, or underdeveloped. In the next section I show how categories of age served as a way to naturalize existing social hierarchies within the logic of developmentalism and that, as a result, prejudicial descriptors were mapped back onto evocations of adolescence by 1870.

Rethinking G. Stanley Hall

In *Adolescence* Hall set adolescence at the forefront of evolutionary progress, claiming that this stage of human life was foundational to the progress of civilization as a whole. He made this argument through a series of developmental narratives that structured history, civilization, and human growth in correlating, linear lines of progression. These narratives offered a rationale for the surveillance and control of young people, including the measurement of their height and weight and limbs, the study of their minds and feelings, and the direction of their education and interests toward Hall's particular vision of progress. These narratives continue to construct the illusion of control over an unpredictable future through the watchful and guided upbringing of youth. For Hall adolescence was essential to this future, at once a developmental stage of human life and a literal embodiment of the evolution of all humankind. Hall felt that the United States as a nation was in a unique developmental predicament as well, one that echoed the precarious conditions of adolescence as he imagined them. In this sense Hall deployed the stage of adolescence as a metaphor for nation, reinvigorating a metaphor that was at this point over a century old. But Hall made that metaphor literal by equating the development of individual adolescents with the development of the nation as a whole.

Hall's interpretation of all life, civilization, and growth within a developmental narrative can be understood as part of a much larger epistemological shift that occurred over the course of the nineteenth century. Mandelbaum, who describes this shift as "historicism," defines it as "the tendency to view all of reality, and all of man's achievements, in terms of the category of development." He writes, "Historicism is the belief that an adequate understanding of the nature of any phenomenon, and an adequate assessment of its value, are to be gained through considering it in terms of the place which it occupied, and the role it played, within a process of development." Importantly, this idea is about reinterpreting changes and events as implicitly leading to one another within a narrative of progress. So "historicism," in this sense, suggests that change occurs in a specific direction, that what comes later is caused by earlier stages, and that the end result is better than the beginning.[62] In *The Order of Things*, Foucault describes this epistemological shift as "historicity," a new way of thinking that "penetrates into the heart of things" and "imposes upon them the forms of order implied by the continuity of time." Before the nineteenth century, Foucault remarks, "life itself did not exist," only "living beings," a distinction that illustrates a new understanding of "life itself" as a story rather than a reference to one's present embodiedness in the world.[63] And time, which was previously understood as a linear chronology of events with no significance apart from those events, became abstracted into a concept of Time as a progression within which events might be interpreted.[64] This way of thinking has had particular consequences in the present, "effectively shaping the contours of a meaningful life."[65] Elizabeth Freeman describes the ways "properly temporalized bodies" are linked "to narratives of movement and change"—that is, "teleological schemes or events or strategies for living such as marriage, accumulation of health and wealth for the future, reproduction, childrearing, and death and its attendant rituals."[66] Within this new conception of time, the idea of "life itself" indicates a conceptual frame of development or progression within which each individual "life" takes place, a narrative within which all of its parts might be understood.

Mandelbaum's "historicism" and Foucault's "historicity" both refer to an interiorized conception of development that significantly impacted how categories of age were understood in the nineteenth century. Nancy Lesko notes that "adolescence and the modern temporal order were creations of the same historical period."[67] Steedman describes how "child-figures, and more generally the idea of childhood," began to "express the depths of historicity in individuals," a particular "kind of configuring of the past" that "emerged at the same time as did the modern idea of history and modern conventions of historical practice."[68] The logic of developmentalism requires this convergence of categories of age, interiorized selfhood, and narrativized history that we see in Hall's idea of adolescence. External processes having to do with the nation, nature, or biology were connected to internal processes of subjectivity though a "new mode of relation between history and life," what Foucault describes as "this dual position of life that placed it at the same time outside history, in its biological environment, and inside human historicity, penetrated by the latter's techniques of knowledge and power."[69] This is a process that incorporates external events into a cause-and-effect relation, but also one obligated to locate the significance of such events within oneself, within a notion of "self" constructed as progressive and narrative.

Freeman describes it this way: "In the eyes of the state, this sequence of socioeconomically 'productive' moments is what it means to have a life at all. And in zones not fully reducible to the state—in, say, psychiatry, medicine, and law—having a life entails the ability to narrate it not only in these state-sanctioned terms but also in a novelistic framework: as event-centered, goal-oriented, intentional, and culminating in epiphanies or major transformations."[70] Charles Taylor writes that the "objectification of time," or the "new time sense," altered "our notion of the subject: the disengaged, particular self, whose identity is constituted in memory"—that is, someone who "can only find an identity in self-narration." He argues, "life has to be lived as story."[71] By the beginning of the twentieth century, the concept of adolescence starts to function as a key narrativizing device in this process, one that makes possible the conceptualizations of self that we understand today as the "search for identity," a process in which one's psychic life is organized into a before and after the arrival point of adulthood.[72] The category of adolescence plays a key role in naturalizing these temporal logics as biological rather than ideological.

Mandelbaum writes that there were two sources for historicism, or what he calls the "developmental view": one is late eighteenth-century Romanticism and "its tendency to view historical development on the analogy of the growth of living things" and the other is a nineteenth-century carryover of Enlightenment thinking that sought a "science of society which would be based on the discovery of laws of social development."[73] These two sources were only foreshadowing historicism, he claims, whereas it was Charles Darwin's theory of the origin of the species and the widespread acceptance of evolution that led to the dominance of historicism as a nineteenth-century epistemology. However, Steedman remarks that "we fail to recognise that much thinking about change and development was not connected to biological thought at all, but was associated with physiology." She explains, "It was a form of evolution conceived of in terms of growth. It took as its analogy, or explanatory figure, the pattern of individual development (of a plant, an insect, an embryo, a human being). The growth model allowed those who used it to comprehend evolution as purposeful, orderly and goal directed and, perhaps, as divinely planned or ordained."[74] Thus, it is more accurate to say that the social uses of evolutionary schemas were responsible for these problematic applications of the logics of developmentalism in that they sought to reinscribe older hierarchical conceptions of human life and of existing social order within a new epistemological framework.

We can see these dynamics at play in Hall's belief that the human race was in a single stage of its evolution and that this stage was a "late, partial, and perhaps essentially abnormal and remedial outcrop of the great underlying life of man-soul." He explains, "Man is not a permanent type but an organism in a very active stage of evolution toward a more permanent form." The descriptors "abnormal" and "remedial" in this passage do not describe adolescents but the entire human race, which has veered off course and has yet to fully evolve into a "more permanent form" equivalent with adulthood. Hall thought that humankind, as a whole, was in its evolutionary adolescence: "While his bodily form is comparatively stable, his soul is in a transition stage, and all that we call progress is more and more rapid. Old moorings are constantly broken; adaptive plasticity to new environments—somatic, economic, industrial, social, moral and religious—was never so great."[75] In one great metaphorical leap, Hall claims the development of adolescents is the key to guiding the advancement of the entire human race to the next evolutionary stage. He did not make this link by analogy only: adolescence became for him a literal embodiment of the state of civilization, both as evidence of its current distress and as singular opportunities for intervention by parents and educators. For Hall evolution was not only a biological process but also a spiritual, social, and psychological one. His extensive study of adolescence was to discover ways to accelerate and maximize human potential in all these areas over subsequent generations. The problem with Hall's thinking is not only false equivalence but also the objectification of the adolescent, who is no longer an individual person in this figuration but the raw material with which to shape the fate of all humankind.[76]

Stating that "the child and the race are each keys to the other," Hall makes human biological development synonymous with the advancement of civilization through the theory of recapitulation, in which the embryos of more "advanced" species are said to represent the adult stages of more "primitive" species, commonly understood as "ontogeny recapitulates phylogeny." In this way Hall's conception of adolescence relies on a hierarchical logic of racism and social class. The theory of recapitulation, developed most extensively by Ernst Haeckel in his "Biogenetic Law" of 1866, was used throughout the nineteenth century to rank humans according to racial characteristics, with the white European male ranked above all others.[77] Hall equates "the animal, the savage, and the child-soul," illustrating the view of racial superiority inherent in his conceptions of categories of age. This developmental logic allows him to argue that "savages, in most respects, are children, or, because of sexual maturity, more properly, adolescents of adult size."[78] Conceptualized as a temporal position, adolescence is not *over* when the body reaches physical maturity but persists as the embodiment of regressive, deviant, or pathological forms of developmental arrival in adulthood.

Stephen Jay Gould explains that the error in Haeckel's theory of recapitulation had to do with his conception of time as progress. There are observable similarities between ontogeny (the biological development of an individual organism) and phylogeny (the evolutionary history of a species). However, Gould points out, the relationship between the two is not one of recapitulation, which posits developmental change "all in one direction—a universal acceleration of development, pushing ancestral adult forms into the juvenile stages of descendants." Haeckel conceptualizes time as a march toward progress, in which adult stages are universally superior to juvenile stages and in which evolution occurs forward toward improvement (though fears of degeneration are never far behind). Haeckel's theory requires an "*active mechanism* that pushes previously adult features into progressively earlier stages of descendant ontogenies—that is, it requires a change of developmental timing." Much more plausible, Gould argues, is a theory put forward by Karl Ernst von Baer, which uses the "conservative nature of heredity" to explain the similarities between ontogeny and phylogeny. So, for example, while Haeckel believes that the gill slits of human embryos were an expression of the same trait present in adult fish, von Baer believes that gill slits "represent a stage common to the early ontogeny of all vertebrates (embryonic fish also have gill slits after all)."[79] Evolution has occurred, and organisms *do* develop, but the development of an organism is scientifically observable and measurable only as value-neutral change over a life span. Haeckel's error stems from conceptualizing this value-neutral change as developmental progress, in a sense imposing a teleology of progress onto a neutral process. This error remains in our notions of development today. Indeed, the word "development" now signals a value-laden notion of progress in which the end result is imagined to be better than the past or even the present.[80]

The theory of recapitulation had been largely discredited in biology even by the time of Hall's writing, a fact that he acknowledges while simultaneously making a claim for its social relevance: "Along with the sense of immense importance of further coordinating childhood and youth with the development of the race, has grown the conviction that only here can we hope to find true norms against the tendencies to precocity in home, school, church, and civilization generally, and also to establish criteria by which to both diagnose and measure arrest and retardation in the individual and the race."[81] Notions of the individual and the race, as Hall deploys them, are ideologically interdependent, conceptualized in relation to each other. For Hall childhood and adolescence are thus literal representations of the evolution of humankind, with the child being the most like the animal or the "savage," whereas he understands the adolescent to have both strong carnal urges and the ability to reason. Hall's use of recapitulation theory favored a long adolescence and the delay of adulthood, presumably while one "advanced" through the adult stages of inferior races, and as a result his theory privileged those who had the luxury of delaying the need to make a living: the wealthy, the educated, and the upper classes. In this view humankind is imagined to be on a pathway through time in which it moves either forward toward the advancement of civilization or backward toward animality. Like Haeckel's "Biogenetic Law," movement through time becomes a value-laden process of achievement and success. What these conceptual layers of bodies, lives, nations, and stories share is a narrativized view of time as progress. Hall incorporates all these layers at once within his idea of adolescence, which he uses to move between biological and social phenomena, indicating causal relationships among them.

Hall was deeply influenced by the theory of evolution and "dreamed of becoming the 'Darwin of the Mind.'"[82] But his understanding of evolution more closely followed that of Herbert Spencer than that of Darwin.[83] Spencer, who coined the phrase "survival of the fittest," wrote essays on evolution—what he called the "Development Hypothesis"—before the publication of *Origin of the Species* in 1859, incorporating social applications from the start.[84] As in Haeckel's theory, the error in Spencer's theory of evolution stems from his conceptualization of time as progress. True Darwinian evolution does not have a purpose, and we cannot know the causes of natural selection since they may be long gone before any changes have even shown up in the next generation. Darwin's theory also emphasized variation, whereas previous theories had emphasized continuities among species. He writes, "During the modification of the descendants of any one species, and during the incessant struggle of all species to increase in numbers, the more diversified these descendants become, the better will be their chance of succeeding in the battle of life." The system of nature, according to Darwin, is contingency, change, and variation. These adaptations are at odds with the evolutionary narrative justifying education that we see outlined by Hall. Indeed, Darwin implies that natural selection confounds the objectives of the older generation: "Natural selection may modify and adapt the larva of an insect to a score of contingencies wholly different from those which concern the mature insect."[85] Castañeda puts it this way: "A developmental system of evolution lays out a specific and more predictable trajectory of change over time, while Darwinian evolution . . . is 'creative' precisely because its trajectory cannot be predicted."[86] To use Darwin's theories to justify existing social hierarchies, this value-neutral, unpredictable, and multidirectional notion of change over time had to be replaced by a fantasy of purposeful, progressive time.[87]

This notion of time as progress played a central role in the construction of a racialized, primitive Other. Johannes Fabian argues that social evolutionists like Spencer could not "accept the stark meaninglessness of mere physical duration," in which the history of humankind "occupied a negligible span on the scale of natural evolution." They instead believed "that Time 'accomplished' or brought about things in the course of evolution." To maintain their belief in Western superiority—that their present and future were the result of what capital-T "Time" accomplished—they adopted a spatial concept of time: as Fabian explains, a spatial concept of time "promoted a scheme in which not only past cultures, but all living societies were irrevocably placed on a temporal slope, a stream of Time—some upstream, others downstream." Fabian identifies concepts such as civilization, evolution, and development as "temporal devices" used to uphold this hierarchical order.[88] Building on Fabian's claims, Castañeda argues that the figure of the child was similarly used as a device of temporal distancing, "a critically important tool for constructing racial hierarchies, primarily in the United States and Britain."[89]

Developmentalism imagines that change occurs in one direction toward an eventual goal, producing a hierarchy in which earlier stages are inferior to later stages. The developmental arrival point, however, is defined as inherently normative, evoking characteristics such as whiteness, masculinity, and wealth. People or nations who do not (or cannot) arrive at the imagined end point of developmentalism are understood as failing to develop, stuck in an earlier stage or actively devolving into a lesser form. Thus, Walkerdine explains how "the very idea of development is not natural or universal, but extremely specific, and in its specificity, occludes other marginalized stories, subsumed as they are within the bigger story. The big story is a European patriarchal story, a story from the centre which describes the periphery in terms of the abnormal, difference as deficiency."[90] Freeman notes how even today "bourgeois-liberal entities from nations to individuals are defined within a narrow chronopolitics of development at once racialized, gendered, and sexualized." She gives the example of Western "modernity," which has "represented its own forward movement against a slower premodernity figured as brown-skinned, feminine, and erotically perverse."[91]

The role of developmentalism in the production and maintenance of racial hierarchies calls into question the ethics of deploying developmental notions of childhood and adolescence at all. Walkerdine shows how the practices of developmental psychology construct childhood as white, wealthy, and masculine in ways that bias researchers and construct girls, non-European, and nonwhite children as deficient.[92] Queer life has also been historically represented as a state of arrested development, an idea popularized by Richard von Krafft-Ebing in the late nineteenth century and later by Sigmund Freud in the early twentieth.[93] The logic of developmentalism thus emerges in the nineteenth century as a way to reinscribe and maintain social hierarchies of race, gender, class, and sexuality within new ways of thinking about the natural world.

Social hierarchy was not new to the nineteenth century, but the ways that hierarchy was justified and understood needed to adapt. If ideas about evolution in the nineteenth century challenged notions of an unchanging divine order (species independently created by God within a stable hierarchy), this challenge was resolved by superimposing a secular notion of time as progress onto scientific knowledge of the natural world. As metaphors for inferiority, the concepts of childhood, and later adolescence, were deployed in the nineteenth century to naturalize existing prejudice and hierarchy, in which colonial subjects were figured as "childlike" and the homosexual was positioned as "stuck" in an adolescent stage. What we see in 1870, when positive descriptors associated with adolescence turn to starkly negative ones, is the result of existing hierarchical thinking in which the intensity of prejudice, focused on race and ethnicity, crops up in evocations of age. It is important to recognize that these negative connotations are not associated with historical ideas of childhood—with the forms of condescension or paternalism we might expect to see directed at children—but instead signal a distinct kind of distancing and disavowal that echoes contemporaneous ideas about racial inferiority. This racialized conception of age is what we see in Hall at the turn of the century. Categories of age provided flexible metaphors to justify the "rightness" of social hierarchy throughout the nineteenth century: what happens around 1870 is that these categories began to absorb the prejudice of those social hierarchies to become versatile terms of denigration. This is one of the performative functions of categories of age coming out of the nineteenth century.

The Ethics of Futurity

At the very moment that negative descriptors of adolescence appeared in British and U.S. newspapers, an 1868 article titled "The Awkward Age" resisted these emerging generalizations. The article argues that awkwardness is not a biological feature of adolescence but instead a function of social hierarchy; the author insists that adolescents are awkward "because they do not know whether they are to be treated as children or adults." Awkwardness is presumed to be a shared social experience but not an essential characteristic of adolescence: "No wonder that your son comes into the room with a confused expression of uncomfortable pain on every feature when he does not know whether he will be recognized as a gentleman, or overlooked as a little boy. . . . No wonder that your tall daughter turns red, stammers, and says foolish things on being courteously spoken to by strangers at dinner, when she is afraid that she may be sharply contradicted or interrupted, and remembers the day before yesterday she was told that children should be seen and not heard." The problem of awkwardness is thus described as a problem having to do with the power relations between adults and children. The solution proposed is therefore to disrupt this hierarchical relation: "Suppose we make a rule that children are always to be treated, in point of courtesy, as if they were adults?"[94] In a sense this article is making the same argument I am by proposing a more ethical relationality based in a critique of the categories themselves. The article participates in an emerging discourse about adolescence—one later synthesized by Hall at the turn of the century—but it does so to undermine the logic of hierarchy contributing to the social and bodily experiences of awkwardness in adolescents. It is grappling with the performative effects of categories of age to challenge an existing discourse about adolescence.

What I am describing in this chapter are functions of the categories themselves, which are not totalizing. The performative function of adolescence to uphold social hierarchies is enacted through specific discursive practices that I am locating in the mid-nineteenth century and that continue to this day. The effects of these practices impact people differently across varying positions of identity and social privilege, and this specific mechanism—whether we call it historicism or developmentalism—is used to maintain the inferiority of other categories of difference. This raises an important question: Are some processes properly developmental, whereas others are not? Or, put another way, is the issue here a misapplication of the concept of developmentalism onto nations and races to justify projects of domination? Such a question implies that categories of age might properly occupy a developmental sequence, whereas nations and races do not. I argue, however, that developmentalism is a hierarchical logic that has no place in understanding either childhood or nations. We might be tempted to think of the stages of human life as the basis for the developmental logics arising in the nineteenth century. But this broader epistemological shift, which encompassed various and even opposing viewpoints in nineteenth-century thought, did not emerge from categories of age. Rather, I have shown that childhood and later adolescence were reinterpreted, discovered anew, through a narrativizing concept of time as progress. This developmental logic is what makes adolescence possible as a new category in the late nineteenth century.

In one sense the project of Hall's *Adolescence* is motivated by a productive and useful question: What do we want the future to look like? Is the problem that we have different answers to this question, or is the problem the investment in futurity inherent in the question itself? Hall bestows teaching and parenting with monumental importance, but this importance comes at great cost, weighting parenthood with an enormous responsibility to society and displacing the relationship between parents and children for one shaped by institutional priorities. It sets in place a supreme rationalization for surveillance by parents and teachers responsible for the development of young people according to what Hall considers the "true norms" of home, school, church, and state.[95] We might understand Hall's work as an enactment of what Foucault describes as biopower or biopolitics, in which childhood and adolescence function as sites of intensifying institutional regulation, part of a larger social and governmental project to "foster life" beginning in the eighteenth century.[96] In the biopolitical sense "life" means *being alive* and putting that life to use in the service of the nation's good. It doesn't necessarily mean having *a good life* or promote ethical questions about how to do so. Claire Colebrook puts it this way: "Modern bio-power can then take the form of the management of life: far from asking *how* we might live, what we might do, or what counts as a good life, life is now that which will ground political decisions."[97] Biopower is not concerned with whether we feel whole or happy or spiritually enlightened. It is concerned with our functional use value as citizens. Thus, Foucault writes that a "normalizing society is the historical outcome of a technology of power centered on life."[98] As mechanisms of biopower, childhood and adolescence continue to function as technologies deployed as the necessary means for directing the future. As we see in Hall's work, the fate of humankind and even "life itself" appear to be at stake in normalizing projects such as the policing of gender norms, the construction and maintenance of heterosexuality, and the affirmation of the reproductive nuclear family as the organizing principle of society.

Today the figure of the child functions as an adaptable symbol for various and even opposing political projects as part of what Lee Edelman calls "reproductive futurism," in which the child becomes synonymous with the future, "the fantasmatic beneficiary of every political intervention," "the logic within which the political itself must be thought."[99] Edelman explains the adaptability of reproductive futurism, showing how opposing arguments over abortion both rely on constructions of the child as futurity: the so-called pro-life position insists that a fetus is a child who deserves a future, and the so-called pro-choice position advocates for reproductive rights for future "sons and daughters."[100] Robin Bernstein further illuminates this contradictory function of the figural child in her discussion of Keith Bardwell, a justice of the peace in Louisiana who refused to marry an interracial couple in 2009.[101] He reportedly justified his decision by saying he "didn't want to put children in a situation they didn't bring on themselves."[102] The couple in question did not have children, so the children he aimed to protect were hypothetical. "I do it to protect the children," Bardwell said. "The kids are innocent and I worry about their futures." Bernstein observes that these statements assume that "imagined children deserve protection more than living adults deserve constitutional rights."[103] Remarkably, she notes, this investment in imaginary children went unchallenged in the public denouncements that followed, which countered his position with arguments for the potential benefits of interracial marriage for the couple's future children. Both Bardwell and those who opposed him made a case for their position based on the image of an idealized child citizen, what Edelman describes as a "universalized subject" whose "notional freedom" is "more highly valued than the actuality of freedom itself."[104]

The figure of the child in these arguments, like the developmental adolescence found in Hall's work, reflects what Castañeda describes as a common "conceptualization of the child as a potentiality rather than an actuality," our seemingly "self-evident" beliefs that the child is "an adult in the making," "a human in incomplete form," and "not yet that which it alone has the capacity to become."[105] This problematic emphasis on futurity places the potential future of a person called a child above the present needs and desires of that person. Noreen Giffney puts it this way: "Reproductive futurism fixates on the future as fetish so the Child becomes but a means to an end; a prosthetic conduit through which access to the future can be achieved."[106] This logic takes an extreme form in Bernstein's example, in which the "needs of imagined children trumped even those of embodied children." Bernstein explains, "Bardwell understood interracial children to 'suffer' and said that therefore he 'won't help put them through it.' Bardwell opposed interracial marriage, then, so as to protect imagined children from becoming flesh, to protect them from life itself."[107] In this example, we clearly see the child evoked as potentiality over the recognition of any actual living, embodied children. This is the ethical problem inherent in futurity. Remarkably, Bardwell's argument *for* children is so far removed from the actual needs of children that it attempts to prevent them from even being born. The figural child of reproductive futurism is not a child at all, but the projection of a normalizing culture.

Social histories of adolescence focus on the material changes in the late nineteenth century under which a population of young people became newly recognizable as a specific group. New legislation excluded young people from the workforce, and educational reforms extended the age required for compulsory schooling in both Britain and the United States. These changes significantly changed the legal agency and status of the people called adolescents in the late nineteenth century. The material changes that resulted are sometimes understood as the reason for the increased visibility of young people, which in turn led to their availability as objects of study in emerging twentieth-century discourses, and I do not disagree.[108] And yet, it is ironic that the very social changes leading to the increased visibility of a segment of the population correspond with the emergence of new ways of thinking about them that directly contribute to their continued erasure. The conditions of this new recognition—the proliferation of institutional discourses harnessing childhood and adolescence as potentiality at the turn of the twentieth century—render adolescents unintelligible as actual people just as they are. At a moment when we might say adolescents were first discovered or seen, the actuality of young people was being eclipsed by narratives of evolutionary progress and a symbolic investment in futurity.

Seeing a young person for their potentiality necessitates a refusal of their actuality—who they are in the present—and, consequently, a denial of their agential possibilities. The logic of reproductive futurism decides *for* children whom or what they should be. Developmental models, both biological and educational, suggest that the changes inherent in growth justify this erasure, since the present of childhood and adolescence is fleeting. The raw material or matter of the child body "as potentiality, is on its way to actualization, and that actuality is determined in advance as what matter *ought* to be."[109] But the idea that adulthood is somehow more stable or continuous, that adulthood is the arrival point of this process of change, is itself a fantasy. Within this logic educational or parental expectations for the future are given permission to eclipse the present as anything other than the opportunity—the obligation—to shape that future in the right direction. It is precisely this "determining in advance" that poses an ethical problem. This model does not distinguish between ethical and unethical mentor relationships, between the parent who just wants happiness for their child's future and the one who has already decided *for* that child how they will achieve such happiness. All forms of investment in the future are understood as "teaching" or "parenting" or "development" itself. Like notions of time or history as a progressive story, the life of the child becomes a narrative for the adult to find meaning, to accomplish something.

How might the logic of developmentalism be resisted? In the past decade, queer theorists have devoted critical attention to the idea of "queer time" as a location of political agency: as Jack Halberstam describes it, "the perverse turn away from the narrative coherence of adolescence—early adulthood—marriage—reproduction—child rearing—retirement—death, the embrace of a late childhood in place of early adulthood or immaturity in place of responsibility."[110] Halberstam's model is about resisting a developmental logic for how different parts of life are to be valued, embracing instead the full range of human existence at any age. Similarly, Kathryn Bond Stockton explores the profound need for cultural representations of "growing sideways" for queer children who avoid or delay the normative, developmental arrival point of heterosexuality.[111] Likewise, Edelman's *No Future* can be understood within this frame, rejecting futurity altogether in favor of the queer jouissance of the death drive. José Esteban Muñoz elaborates yet another alternative, retheorizing futurity *as* queerness, as a "site of infinite and immutable potentiality." Unlike the common conceptualization of the child as potentiality (which is a form of objectification), Muñoz describes a practice of queer temporality in which potentiality is always located in the present, in the right now.[112] This practice requires a queer understanding of potentiality as infinite and immutable—that is, an understanding that potentiality *never* arrives at a normative future, never takes shape as an institutional vision, but manifests in radical aesthetic deployments only *as* potentiality. We might say that the child is conceptualized as potentiality in part to manage and control the radical promise of potentiality that Muñoz articulates. The figure of the child is used to construct a comforting narrative where *only* the figural child embodies potentiality, thus containing all the promise and all the risk in a presumably manageable and controllable form. Muñoz's retheorization gestures toward the possibility of a more ethical engagement with futurity than what we see in Hall. When it comes to categories of age, we might ask how our investment in growth and futurity can be located in the present, in the doing, in the being and becoming of each present moment. We might ask how futurity can function as unlimited possibility, even when those possibilities might include failure, harm, or death. Can the notion of fostering "life itself" ever be conceived of as open-ended rather than as a social obligation to health, growth, development, and productivity?

In *Touching Feeling*, Eve Kosofsky Sedgwick describes the queer temporality of her friendships with three other people, one fifteen years her senior, two fifteen years younger, all academics with much in common with one another. She writes, "In a 'normal' generational narrative, our identifications with each other would be aligned with an expectation that in another fifteen years, I'd be situated comparably to where my sixty-year-old friend is, while my thirty-year-old friends would be situated comparably to where I am."[113] The "generational narrative" she describes is one of developmentalism, in which years correspond to universalized arrival points. The ways that developmentalism instructs us to relate and identify with one another invites a deeply problematic relationality. Age differences, in this logic, imply a normative life sequence that these identifications function to regulate and reproduce. It is not the idea of childhood or adolescence but the compulsory dimensions of adulthood that are reproduced, such as the obligation to be a productive member of the labor force, the pressure to be and stay married, or the social expectation that one should have children. These experiences of being in the world are problematically naturalized by age, as if there were some quality or shared consciousness in being forty-five years old that is shared by all. The developmental logic of generational difference invites projection rather than compassionate understanding. *Someday, you will be where I am.* Predictive and directional. Or the dismissive, *I have been where you are.*

Of course, Sedgwick's friendships fail to occupy this generational logic because she, at only forty-five, is living with advanced breast cancer while her sixty-year-old friend is healthy. Of their two thirty-year-old friends, one is living with advanced cancer and another with HIV. In this queer temporality that fails to participate in the normative sequencing of aging, Sedgwick considers other ways of characterizing their connections with one another. "On this scene," she writes, "an older person doesn't love a younger person as someone who will someday be where she is now, or vice versa." Though her analysis suggests that their friendships depart from the norm only because three of the four are facing shortened lifespans, I want to suggest that her alternative characterization describes a more ethical relationality for age difference than what a developmental model invites: "It is one another immediately, one another as the present fullness of a becoming whose arc may extend no further, whom we each must learn best to apprehend, fulfill, and bear company."[114] This relationality, which Sedgwick describes in coping with the imminence of death, might be used to more ethically account for the rapid biological changes unique to childhood and adolescence or for the inevitable shifts in identity and selfhood anyone might experience over a lifetime. Biological changes are often used to dismiss adolescent experiences and perspectives, as if young people could not possibly know themselves in the midst of such instability or unfinishedness. But what if these changes served instead to remind us of our ethical obligation to see and accept young people in the immediacy of who they are, in each moment, without projecting or anticipating a developmental arc? This ethical relation asks to be contingently learned and known again and again: how best to be with one another in the present moment of becoming, whatever that might look like.

chapter 2

TEMPORALITY, SELFHOOD, AND THE POLITICS OF DIFFERENCE

The adolescent is a very queer creature.
—Dr. Margaret Lowenfeld, "Youth and Health"

The adolescent, like the child, is a mythical figure of the imaginary that enables us to distance ourselves from some of our failings, splittings of the ego, disavowals, or mere desires, which it reifies into the figure of someone who has not yet grown up.
—Julia Kristeva, *New Maladies of the Soul*

Here is a philosopher who fancied that the world was "known" when he had reduced it to the "idea." Was it not because the "idea" was so familiar to him and he was so well used to it—because he hardly was afraid of the "idea" any more?
—Friedrich Nietzsche, *The Gay Science*

The figure of the adolescent evoked at the turn of the twentieth century was openly constructed with an ever-shifting set of characteristics by new institutions negotiating for their own authority and expertise. Through the work of G. Stanley Hall and others, the emerging institutions of medicine, psychology, and education set the figures of the child and the adolescent at the center of their investigations. The function of these figures in institutional discourses was not merely to exercise control over the young, as one might expect, but to compel adults—parents and teachers—to defer to institutional knowledge over their own. Ironically, however, twentieth-century articulations of adolescence were less often accompanied by scientific certainty than they were fraught with the specter of the unknown. For example, Dr. Margaret Lowenfeld (1890–1973), a pioneer in the fields of pediatric medicine and psychology, began her lecture on "Youth and Health" delivered to the British Red Cross Society in 1934 with a bold declaration: "The adolescent is a very queer creature. All of us who are in intimate contact with the adolescent feel at times completely baffled."[1] Like many twentieth-century constructions of adolescence, Lowenfeld's primary definition rests on the strangeness and unknowability of the person called adolescent. The word "creature" echoes the distancing language used for insects and animals. She counts herself among those "in intimate contact with the adolescent" in contrast to others who do *not* know the adolescent in this way, drawing a clear line between those who are authorized to speak about adolescence and those who are not. Despite evoking the "adolescent" as a type of person, a "creature" she is in intimate contact with, an object of study that she can describe in generalized terms, Lowenfeld represents adolescence as synonymous with unknowability and with encounters that leave her "at times completely baffled." This type of statement is common throughout the twentieth century—associated later with the unstable selfhood of the adolescent "identity crisis"—serving a key set of cultural functions to maintain normativity.[2]

Adolescence functions as a location for disavowal, a way to distance phenomena that troubles or baffles Lowenfeld, but it also functions as location for desire. The unknowability of adolescence makes Lowenfeld's lecture all the more urgent and important, functioning to secure her professional role and its authority. The "discovery" of adolescence at the turn of the century as an "unknown" conveniently leaves much undiscovered, setting up the category in a productive relation to the endless pursuit of progress and scientific knowledge. One of the things these institutional discourses have in common is their purposeful evocations of the adolescent as a subject belonging to science and medicine. These purposeful evocations are so common, so insistent, that it is apparent how fragile these constructions were.

The idea that adolescence was discovered at the turn of the twentieth century may itself be a narrative constructed at the turn of the century. For example, the *Journal of Adolescence* confidently reported in 1900 that it was Indiana that "was the first state to formally recognize the study of Adolescence," rather than naming Hall and his colleagues at Clark University in Massachusetts.[3] Competing claims of discovery indicate a shared investment in discovery itself, a legitimizing pattern used in emerging fields of study like education and psychology in the first part of the twentieth century. Take, for example, the celebratory language of an early review of Hall's *Adolescence*, titled "Dr. Hall's 'Adolescence' Considered One of the Most Important in Years." In addition to its abundant praise, the review concludes with a statement that also positions adolescence as a representation of the unknown: "It is astonishing how little we know ourselves. The whole truth about life is coming slowly, but it is certain that we have much yet to learn."[4] Adolescence is cast as a pathway for knowing the self, both as individual selves and collectively as humans, a locus of examination that will provide access to "the whole truth about life." This characterization depicts its own moment—the turn of the twentieth century—as the moment when, at last, the whole truth is within reach. This statement expresses Hall's own boastfulness on the significance of his research, but it also captures a disciplinary context of scientific "discovery" from which his work emerges. As should be apparent by now, the claim that adolescence is new does little to denaturalize it or disrupt its logic. Acknowledging the historical specificity of adolescence alone cannot dislodge it from projects of dominance, since the harkening of adolescence as a "modern" concept, and thus as a confirmation of Western superiority, is part of the work it does.[5] So what is it that we mean when we attribute modern conceptions of adolescence to the turn of the century? What is it that we recognize in Hall, and how do the conditions of this recognition obscure both the past and our present?

As early as the 1920s, we can find claims resembling those in recent social histories, locating the origin of adolescence at the turn of the century. Take, for example, the *Transactions and Proceedings of the National Association of State Universities*, which boasted in 1928 that "another development of the last twenty years . . . is the discovery of adolescence."[6] Claims about scientific discovery were not confined to academic contexts. An 1897 advertisement for Bradfield's tonic appearing in the *Macon Telegraph* proclaims, "The period succeeding youth is now more desirable than adolescence. The strangest thing is that it has not been discovered before with all the examples that exist in history."[7] These examples, above all, demonstrate the appeal of the narrative of discovery itself—a narrative of progress in which the present is our inevitable arrival point. The category of adolescence is made possible by this narrative, which is at its heart a story about the development of civilization, a process of evolutionary growth in which adolescence is an example, a metaphor, and a confirmation of one's investments and projections for the future. It is highly adaptable, used for various and contradictory purposes, and yet it works according to a specific logic, a way of mapping time, selfhood, and social hierarchy along a developmental continuum. Valerie Walkerdine observes that this is how developmental psychology operates to this day, confirming itself through "a grand, totalizing story, *the* story of children's development, a scientific story testable, within limits, in relation to the methodological guarantees given about the treatment of scientific data, science's claim to truth."[8] Claims about the discovery of adolescence throughout the twentieth century participate in this narrative mode of knowledge in which the history of adolescence itself is cast as a developmental story, part of an inevitable process of arrival at scientific truth and institutional accomplishment.

One of the consequences of understanding adolescence and "life itself" as a developmental story was that it required the displacement of situated, contextual, experiential knowledge with the stabilized, presumably objective "truth" of science produced by institutions. We can see this dynamic illustrated by Hall as he defensively asserts the objective "truth" of scientific knowledge in the preface to *Adolescence*. He laments the "dishonorable captivity to epistemology" in existing scholarly methods and the "present lust for theories of the nature of knowledge," which he claims "have become a veritable and multiform psychosis."[9] He dismisses the types of self-reflexive, contingent knowledge that account for one's experience and perspective in order to claim the "truth" for himself and his assertions about adolescence. His choice to call epistemological concerns a "psychosis" is a very telling strategy, one that uses the emerging institutional discourse of psychology to regulate whose speaking will be recognized as legitimate and whose will not. If we understand epistemology—"theories for the nature of knowledge"—to grapple with the limits of what is knowable, the instability of knowledge itself, and the shifting relational contexts within which knowledge is produced, then we can see here how Hall disavows these concerns to assert the authority of science and lay claim to his own expertise.[10] After disavowing epistemological concerns, Hall insists that "we must turn to the larger and far more laborious method of observation, description, and induction."[11]

Expressing his faith in scientific objectivity, Hall wants to use these methods to study the "folk-soul, learn of criminals and defectives, animals, and in some sense go back to Aristotle in rebasing psychology on biology" because, he claims, "we know the soul best when we can best write its history in the world." As discussed in chapter 1, Hall's desire to study the "folk-soul," criminals, defectives, and animals stems from his belief that they represent "earlier," inferior forms from our evolutionary past. As Johannes Fabian reminds us, "there is no knowledge of the Other which is not also a temporal, historical, political act."[12] Hall's history of the "soul" is a form of historicism, which interprets all phenomena within a temporal process of development. He declares, "There are no finalities save formulae of development," which he believes provide a map for directing the "soul" toward "indefinite further development."[13] Hall's methods do not aim to objectively observe what *is* now but rather to interpret all observable phenomena as belonging to the past or to the future of a developmental process, one moving toward or away from a normative ideal that he narrowly defines as white, male, and middle class. Categories of age play a key role in supporting these directional, hierarchical logics of development today.

Adolescence is imagined to exist in a hierarchical relation to adulthood, and this relation reifies and obscures the power dynamics of other social relations, those between doctors and patients, institutions and individuals, as well as hierarchies of race, class, gender, and sexuality. The array of late nineteenth- and early twentieth-century discourses I examine in this chapter contain overlapping categorizations of the criminal, homosexual, ethnic, savage, prostitute, deviant, primitive, queer, and delinquent as ways of dehumanizing marginalized populations within a developmental model as biologically deficient. Categories of age function as a temporal sleight of hand, relocating existing social hierarchies within the seemingly "natural" developmental trajectory of childhood and adolescence. Thus, the specifically "modern" category of adolescence that emerges in early twentieth-century discourses is a normalizing technology of power that both maintains and obscures these forms of dominance. This chapter layers categories of age, race, class, gender, and sexuality because of the historical and present entanglement of these identity positions within the logic of developmentalism. Judith Butler writes, "Though there are clearly good historical reasons for keeping 'race' and 'sexuality' and 'sexual difference' as separate analytic spheres, there are also quite pressing and significant historical reasons for asking how and where we might read not only their convergence, but the sites at which the one cannot be constituted save through the other."[14] The presumed universality of categories of age illuminates the mutuality and coproduction of multiple categories of difference. Within the logic of developmentalism, adolescence appears not as a point of difference but as the ground from which difference itself is constituted.

The Politics of Difference

The category child appears as if it is universal, crossing all social divisions, the category itself seemingly innocent of social division. But this is only one of the more insidious functions of childhood as a Western concept. Jacqueline Rose points to how the fantasy of childhood "serves as a term of universal social reference which conceals all the historical divisions and difficulties of which children, no less than ourselves, form a part."[15] James Kincaid explains it this way: "By formulating the image of the alluring child as bleached, bourgeois, and androgynous, these stories mystify material reality and render nearly invisible—certainly irrelevant—questions we might raise about race, class, and even gender."[16] The category child, then, does not work in the same ways for all children, and its presumed universality obscures the ways that it functions to produce and maintain social hierarchies. The figure of the child—the child of reproductive futurism, the innocent child, the child who needs protection—this figural child is white. Robin Bernstein historicizes the link between childhood, innocence, and whiteness, noting the shift in the nineteenth century toward childhood "not as innocent, but as innocence itself; not as a symbol of innocence, but its embodiment." She makes clear that "this innocence was raced white."[17] By the turn of the twentieth century, middle- and upper-class white children were "priceless," no longer regarded as a potential source of family labor or income but sentimental objects now assigned increasing monetary value in adoption fees and insurance policies.[18]

And yet, it might be surprising to discover that child-protection laws that were passed around the turn of the century in the United States were put into motion by making the argument that children were like animals. Presumptions of innocence did not confer respect to children but rather linked children and animals, as we see in the naming of organizations such as the Board of Child and Animal Protection in Wyoming and Colorado, what eventually became the Humane Society. An article from 1904 in the *Philadelphia Inquirer* makes an argument for the Wyoming and Colorado models to be put into law at the national level: "A measure will be introduced into Congress, asking for the establishment of a National Board of Child and Animal Protection, with a secretary and offices in Washington. It was shown that there are a number of states without legislation of any sort for the protection of either children or animals. The horrible conditions connected with cattle shipped from the West suggested the project for a national law and bureau."[19] The "horrible conditions" prompting action here refers to an incident in which a herd of cattle worth $500,000 froze to death on a ranch in Texas the previous winter.[20] This logic linking the monetary loss of cattle with the need to protect children is a fascinating historical phenomenon, occurring at the moment when white children were identified as being the most precious and the most in need of protection. It seems clear that adoring, idolizing, or protecting the innocence of children is not the same as recognizing the personhood of children.

Kathryn Bond Stockton overlaps her theorizations of "the child queered by innocence" and "the child queered by color" under the same heading in her introduction to *The Queer Child*, a choice evocative of the ways these seemingly opposing constructions have something in common. The child queered by innocence is idealized, made distant and strange from an adult point of view, which can work also to make children distant and strange to themselves. But the child queered by color is not seen as innocent and thus is queered by exclusion from the category child. This construction is similarly mapped onto children whose families struggle to make financial ends meet: Stockton writes, "Experience is still hard to square with innocence, making depictions of streetwise children, who are often neither white nor middle-class, hard to square with 'children.'"[21] Many scholars have recognized the degree to which black and brown children are imagined in ways that exclude them from the conditions of dependency, protection, and innocence imagined to belong to the category child, but these observations do not always account for the "insidiousness of infantilization."[22] The assumption that innocence reflects a universal view of children obscures the complex reality of *all* children's lives, but in particular the lives of protogay, queer, and trans children, poor children, and children of color.

Like childhood, the category of adolescence presupposes universality even while it does the work of differentiating and naturalizing racial hierarchies. In this sense adolescence, as it emerged in the late nineteenth century, is a fundamentally racial category. Adolescence works within a developmental logic alongside childhood to embody *not* innocence and potentiality but more often regression and deviance. This tension between innocence and deviance in categories of age occurs because, as Jacob Breslow writes, childhood and adolescence "are not straightforwardly ontological; they are also, to varying degrees, temporal positions. They name subjects who are defined by a relation to futurity, growth, delay, and a temporal 'estrangement' from an adulthood that they are simultaneously defined in opposition to yet destined to become." Breslow describes how categories of age work as temporal mechanisms, accounting for the contradictory ways that childhood and adolescence function to uphold existing social and hierarchical structures while themselves appearing to be transitory stages of life shared by all people.[23] Toby Rollo, for example, argues that it is the alignment of blackness with childhood, rather than the exclusion from childhood, that is responsible for racist depictions in which black people are represented as biologically grown but without "mature intelligence and self-control," which continues to perpetuate notions of criminality and deviance recurrent in antiblackness.[24] Breslow accounts for this contradiction through temporality. Through present and historical examples, he suggests that "childhood and adolescence, as ambivalent categories with blurred boundaries, *do and do not* stick to black children and young people," while black adults remain temporally suspended in a subject position he calls "adolescent citizenship," in which rights and recognition are cast as premature, belated, or inappropriate because they are "out of temporal sync with a fantasy of the nation's present" as postracial.[25]

These contradictions are woven throughout the early twentieth-century medical and psychological discourses discussed in this section, where categories of age can work to justify the behaviors of those who occupy normative categories of identity while they simultaneously work to establish the inferiority of others. Thus, the temporality of developmentalism enables the contradictory construction of black children *outside* the conditions of innocence and protection thought to belong to childhood while simultaneously constructing black adults as childlike, immature, or adolescent. These hierarchical functions of categories of age can work to establish the inferiority of *any* nonnormative or marginalized group.

Hall imagined adolescence as a racial category that replicated the evolutionary development of humankind, one in which the proper environment, guidance, and control were necessary to reach the "higher and more completely human traits" he correlated with the norms of masculinity, whiteness, and wealth. This definition at once constructs adolescence as the developmental period for "higher and more completely human" traits at the same time as it implies the absence of those traits. Who achieves the status of the human and who does not is a matter of time: the longer the adolescence, the more time there is to develop the "higher traits" Hall imagines, but the shorter the adolescence, the more likely a person (or group of people) will reach adulthood without achieving the status of the human. Hall declares that "youth needs repose, leisure, art, legends, romance, idealization, and in a word, humanism, if it is to enter the kingdom of man well equipped for man's highest work in the world."[26] For Hall the "higher and more completely human traits" represent a biological process, an expression of genetic potential possible only through a long adolescence. Masculinity, whiteness, and wealth operate as if they are synonymous with the "higher traits" and the arrival at adulthood itself, constructing minoritized populations including the poor, women, people of color, and those who are queer, trans, neurodiverse, and/or disabled as regressive and subordinate, as *not* quite achieving the "more completely human traits," according to this universalized conception of human development.

For those who occupy these norms, this developmental schema ensures their conformity for the achievement of adult status, whereas others are simply excluded. Claudia Castañeda puts it this way:

> The "normal" child was not assured of being normal until the developing body had traversed childhood and become the normative adult. To be a true adult was to have passed out of development—out of the realm of the pathological (savage, female, racialized, hyper- and hypo-sexual, etc.)—and into the realm of the "normal": to be a "civilized" man in present time. The female, the racialized, the insane, the disabled, and the poor were left behind, in childhood, while adulthood was strictly enforced as a "natural" developmental achievement reserved for the deserving few.

These constructions stem from the logic of developmentalism in nineteenth-century theories of social evolution. Castañeda explains how nineteenth-century racial science posited that white and black children had the same levels of intelligence and capability only to reassert adolescence as the moment of racial differentiation when development presumably stagnated in nonwhite bodies.[27] She quotes the nineteenth-century British phrenologist Robert Dunn, who wrote in 1864: "The Negro child is not, as regards the intellectual capacities, behind the white child." However, Dunn goes on to say that the brain of the "Negro child" cannot grow after a certain point: "No sooner do they reach the fatal period of puberty than, with the closure of the sutures and the projection of the jaws, the same process takes place as in the ape. The intellectual functions remain stationary, and the individual, as well as the race is incapable of further progress."[28] Childhood represents potentiality and receptivity to institutional intervention, the fantasy of directing all human potential into the evolutionary future, but adolescence, with the arrival of adultlike physical characteristics, represents the *failures* of this directive action, the closing of potentiality.

Within Dunn's racist logic, white children continue to advance past puberty, but black children cannot. Biological determinism supersedes any responsibility for the social conditions black adolescents and adults might endure because of racism, extreme poverty, or lack of educational opportunity. Similarly, Hall understands most non-white, non-European people as "adolescent races."[29] This use of the word "adolescent" does not designate an age category but a temporal position of development fixed in nonwhite adult bodies: "for they are the world's children and adolescents," Hall writes.[30] Whether Hall imagines adolescence as the acquirement of the "higher and more completely human traits" or as the stasis of regressive traits in "savage" populations, these opposing constructions are mutually enabled by the temporalizing functions of developmentalism in which subjects are ordered along a developmental timeline, heading toward or away from a predetermined arrival point.

Jules Gill-Peterson's concept of "racial plasticity" in *Histories of the Transgender Child* illuminates these temporal functions in the history of endocrinology. Gill-Peterson argues that the early twentieth-century concept of biological plasticity worked to "bind sex to race" by interpreting the "sexed form of the internal and external body" as an identifiable characteristic of one's racial (understood as genetic) heritage.[31] The words "plastic" and "plasticity" appear more than sixty times in Hall's two volumes to describe adolescence, representing a fantasy of both biological and psychological impressionability available to parents and educators to shape the future. Early twentieth-century endocrinologists likewise deployed this fantasy of control, suppressing the notion that biological plasticity might have an agency of its own by locating it in the growing body of the child. Childhood figured a docile, manageable potentiality available for manipulation by scientists and doctors despite the fact that children's bodies grew and changed in surprising and unexpected ways under their care. However, childhood plasticity was synonymous with whiteness, symbolizing the biological potential of white children to achieve a normative, idealized human form in contrast to children of color, whose bodies were imagined as atavistic and resistant to institutional intervention. These are two opposite, but conceptually linked, ways of interpreting biological development as a linear, value-laden process either toward or away from an ideal form.

Like the idea of the child as pure potentiality (the raw material of an idealized future directed by science), racial plasticity expresses an institutional and profoundly eugenic fantasy about the ability of scientists and doctors to shape the direction and form of human evolution. But only some children were perceived as embodying such genetic potential. This symbolic investment in normativity had real conse-quences in the practice of endocrinology, in which doctors "regarded black children as suitable experimental subjects because of presumed access and disposability, whereas white children were framed as exhib-iting the potential for a normative cure or at least improved normali-ty." Likewise, white trans children and adolescents in the 1960s were often offered "curative" medical support while trans black children were frequently misdiagnosed as either homosexual or schizophrenic and then institutionalized or imprisoned. These differences describe two very different degrees and types of harm carried out as eugenic fantasy: black children and children of color were confined and their possibilities for life extinguished, whereas "plasticity as an abstract whiteness" was projected on white children, justifying "altering the body without consent and in nontherapeutic ways in the name of a universalizing humanity." These effects demonstrate the vast degree to which reproductive futurism disenfranchises *all* children, since it is invested in an abstract futurity rather than the present or future lives of actual people, child or adult. The consequences of racial plasticity stretch into the present, where trans women of color appear almost ex-clusively in news reports about their murders, representing "ongoing forms of social death that reduce their personhood to the barest zero degree," while trans children appearing in the media today are exclu-sively white, standing in for a normative futurity achieved through medical technology.[32]

In the history of trans medicine, adolescence emerges as the limit point for plasticity's normative potentiality by the 1970s, when "plasticity was understood to undergo an important change in form during adolescence, becoming less receptive to cultivation by med-ical science and more unruly in puberty before it began to recede altogether." This is what allowed Lawrence Newman, a psychiatrist at UCLA in the 1960s, to imagine that he could prevent or cure trans-sexualism in childhood, but not after puberty.[33] The plasticity of the adolescent body, then, was recognized as having an agency of its own, one that the doctor might intervene in but not, ultimately, control. If the biological plasticity of the child allowed doctors to imagine they could redirect or control developmental outcomes, the stage of ado-lescence took on the action more like a runaway train, a time of rapid

chapter two

growth whose course could no longer be stopped. According to these temporal logics of developmentalism, scientists could interpret any nonnormative or marginalized group as exhibiting excessive, deviant, or pathological growth that was unresponsive to institutional control or changes in environment. The temporal order of developmentalism structures adulthood as the achievement of normativity, and thus *any* variation from this narrow teleology constructs adolescence as inferior or developmentally regressive.

Doris Odlum, for example, echoes Hall in her 1931 pamphlet called *The Psychology of Adolescence*, where she remarks on how "the actual age at which adolescence occurs shows a very marked individual, racial and climatic variation."[34] She confidently explains that climate, a coded reference to racial difference, determines these developmental variations:

> Those races with a highly developed civilization "adolesce," if one may use the term, later than those which are more primitive. The peoples inhabiting the Arctic regions have a slower development than those which inhabit the more temperate zones, and these, in turn, are slower than the subtropical and tropical peoples. The more Western nations develop later than the Eastern, and the Nordic stock more slowly than the Latin. Thus the people of the British Isles have a comparatively late and long adolescence, and this is an important factor in modifying the relations between the developing child and its environment.[35]

Like Hall, Odlum correlates a prolonged adolescence with a "highly developed civilization" and the people of the British Isles, whereas Eastern, Latin, subtropical, and tropical peoples develop more quickly and thus represent more primitive civilizations.[36] Odlum blurs the distinction between biological processes and the social and cultural mechanisms that structure the transition from childhood to adulthood. The social structures of "civilization" and wealth provide access to what Odlum and others perceive as normative development and thus the category of human itself. Odlum states that "adolescence marks the first real appearance of the social sense" in which "the developing human being begins to . . . appreciate its rights and duties in relation to the community." But these "rights and duties" are functions of normativity, describing the conforming behavior of "good" citizens. And so, markedly, "with the mental defective, even with a relatively high intellectual capacity, the sense of social responsibility is more than correspondingly deficient."[37] Within developmentalism Odlum overlaps figures of the primitive and the mental defective as both perpetually halted without "social sense" in the temporality of adolescence.

We see a similar logic in claims that homosexuality is caused by "arrested development," a theory popularized by Sigmund Freud, but circulating earlier in medical and sexological discourses.[38] For example, a 1955 report by a committee for the British Medical Association treats concerns about prostitution and homosexuality together as coexisting deficiencies.[39] This is because, the report claims, "the normal development of the sexual drive passes through auto-erotic and homosexual phases in childhood and adolescence before it reaches the normal heterosexual maturity," thus homosexuality and male prostitution represent "some immaturity of development which may be due to a variety of causes."[40] In 1947 we see the idea of "arrested development" constructed as specifically adolescent in a paper by Dr. Albertine Winner, read at a meeting of the Section of Psychiatry at the Royal Society of Medicine: "In dealing with large numbers of Lesbians one of the most striking things is the recurrent traits of immaturity, mainly emotional, but showing themselves in many unexpected ways, that one meets in women of high intellectual or artistic development. This certainly bears out the view that the homosexual relation is an immature one, an arrest of normal sexual development at an adolescent stage."[41] Winner sees no contradiction in her assessment of the developmental discrepancy between intellect and emotion, reading high-achieving lesbian women as "immature." This contradiction is enabled by the logic of developmentalism in which heterosexuality is synonymous with adulthood. Thus, the emotional "immaturity" Winner identifies is merely the lesbian's unmarried status and her attachment to women rather than men. The problem, which Winner struggles to describe *as* a problem, is adolescent in nature and thus beyond the corrective reach of the institution. The lesbian, if we circle back to Odlum's terminology, might have a "high intellectual capacity" but lacks a "sense of social responsibility" to marry and reproduce.

Adolescence functions to explain and hold queer phenomena

within adolescence so that such phenomena pose no challenge to the norm of heterosexuality. Within a developmental logic, queer phenomena are excluded from the spectrum of adult human experience because they signify arrested development. Though Freud continued to use the phrase "arrested development" throughout his career, he attempted to recast it in later years as mere human variation, as he does in a 1935 letter to a mother about her homosexual son: "Homosexuality is assuredly no advantage but it is nothing to be ashamed of, no vice, no degradation, it cannot be classified as an illness; we consider it to be a variation of the sexual function produced by a certain arrest of sexual development."[42] Despite Freud's impulse to reserve judgment, the problem with this developmental logic remains: all change, growth, or variation is temporally located in childhood or adolescence (regardless of the age of the person) in order to avoid acknowledging variation and change in human phenomena at all ages.

Eugene S. Talbot's 1898 *Degeneracy: Its Causes, Signs, and Results* covers *all* kinds of "degeneracy," which he believes to be inheritable and detectable through physical abnormalities in childhood. Thus, Talbot writes, "This work has been written with a special intention of reaching educators and parents." Educators and parents, Talbot hopes, should be especially watchful of children for the physical traits he describes so that they can be identified as degenerate before doing harm to themselves or society. Childhood functions as a period in which institutional control, and perhaps intervention, can take place, the period in which degeneracy is identifiable and manageable. These educators and parents are called on to be guards of the institution, its gatekeepers, its whistleblowers. Talbot includes homosexuality, trans phenomena, or mere gender nonconformity in his book under the terms "masculinism" and "feminism," physical conditions that, for him, indicate a range of degenerate conditions.[43] Talbot was inspired by the work of Italian criminologist Cesare Lombroso, who rejects the idea that crime is a part of human nature and suggests that some people are born criminals, what he understands as a biological reappearance of the traits and behaviors from an earlier evolutionary stage, one replicated in childhood development.[44] Lombroso writes, "Just as the fetus shows deformities that in the adult would be considered monstrosities, so, too, does the child lack moral sense. When adults possess the following impetuous passions of children, psychiatrists call them moral madmen, and we call them born criminals." Lombroso's equating of the child and the criminal stems from recapitulation, as seen in Hall, suggesting at once that criminals are childlike and children are like criminals. Lombroso adds, "Anomalous and monstrous sexual tendencies, like criminal behavior, begin in childhood."[45] Through its presumably identifiable location in childhood, criminality becomes more manageable, something that can be identified before the crime is committed, something the doctor can control. At the same time generalizing the "criminal" as a type of person requires the figure of the child, deploying developmentalism to distance and exclude the criminal from the category of human.

This developmental logic can be found not only in condemnations of criminality but also in more sympathetic depictions of "sexual delinquency." Dr. Robert Sutherland, in a 1939 address to the National Association of Probation Officers, speaks of the "hormonic intoxication of the adolescent, during which there is a tremendous drive towards some form of sexual experience," as a way to garner sympathy and compassion for those charged with delinquency. Here those charged with delinquency are imagined as human and deserving of sympathy, but their behavior is attributed to the "hormonic intoxication" of adolescence, escaping rational control. Sutherland uses the same dubious evolutionary arguments as Talbot and Lombroso, but he uses them in this instance to recast so-called illegal sexual behaviors as natural: "The work of anthropologists has shown that it is quite a natural thing among primitive people for children to engage experimentally." Citing research from the Kinsey Report, Sutherland claims, "The youngster who has been indicted for sexual delinquency differs from the average youth only in degree and in the fact that he has been found out."[46] Whereas Talbot and Lombroso evoke the temporality of childhood to distance and disavow the "criminal," Sutherland uses it along with the evolutionary time of "primitive people" to explain and excuse the behavior of British young men who are presumably on their way to a normative adulthood.

As a normalizing and regulatory concept, adolescence continues to produce the temporal and developmental logic used to sustain social hierarchies today. When young people occupy normative categories and roles, such as middle-class whiteness, they are often imagined to be on their way to maturity and thus on their way to social recognition of their personhood and right to civic participation. Legal scholar Patricia J. Williams comments on this phenomenon with regard to Columbine shooters Dylan Klebold and Eric Harris, young white men who, even after committing mass murder, left the media and the predominantly white community of Littleton, Colorado, in disbelief: "Still their teachers and classmates continue to protest that they were good kids, good students, solid citizens. Even their probation officers (assigned after Klebold and Harris were caught burgling a car) had released them to their parents while praising them as intelligent young men with lots of promise."[47] The strong association of masculinity, whiteness, and wealth with the potentiality of an ideal adult citizen made it difficult, impossible even, for parents, teachers, and the media to reconcile the reality of Klebold and Harris's crimes with these positive social expectations.

However, we can see adolescence work similarly to exclude others from the benefit of the doubt extended to some white, middle-class teenagers. The temporality of categories of age enables these contradictory constructions, in which movement through time can be just as easily imagined as regression or decline as it can potentiality or promise. For example, we might look to Trayvon Martin, an unarmed black teenager murdered by a neighborhood watch vigilante while walking home from a convenience store. Despite Martin's youth (he had turned seventeen only weeks before) and the fact that he was doing nothing wrong when he was followed and killed by George Zimmerman, media representations following his death focused on his presumed guilt and potential for criminality. While many scholars have remarked on the exclusion of Martin and black boyhood more broadly from conceptions of childhood innocence, it is also notable that media evocations of Martin's adolescence produced a different set of assumptions than the "promise" of white adolescence stirred by the Columbine shooters. Breslow points to how these representations "locate Martin firmly in a deviant adolescence" in order to imply "that it is understandable to not just question Martin's foreshortened life, but also to question the grievability of his death."[48]

In these recent examples, we see the insidious echoes of nineteenth-century racial science, how white adolescence is perceived as a developmental stage on the way to the "higher and more completely human traits" (in the words of Hall), while black adolescence is constructed as developmentally stagnant, with no projected arrival point for personhood or civic participation. Depending on who is looking and what they want to see, the nonconformity, rebellion, or even criminal behavior of white, middle-class teenagers can be perceived as nonthreatening because they already represent the ideals of normalization, whereas the ordinary behaviors of young people of color can be seen as dangerous and criminal, a threat to the social order, because they are always already measured against standards of normalization implicitly defined as white, male, and middle class. These versatile functions of adolescence attest to the urgency of rethinking categories of age as developmental epistemologies complicit in the construction and maintenance of social hierarchies.

Sex Education Pamphlets

Sarah Chinn argues that the specifically "modern" concept of adolescence belonging to the twentieth century is defined by an "assumption of antagonism between adolescents and their parents," what by the 1990s looked like a "combative relationship between the adult power structure and teenagers," which "seemed both comfortable and convenient for all involved: older people could rest assured in their sense of superiority and confidence that this new resistance at worst opened up new market possibilities, and young people could occupy various postures of rebellion and independence through combinations of different commodities." She explains that most social histories attribute the origin of this antagonism to "the 1920s and 1930s, with the flaming youth, the flappers, and the sexual freedom that cinemas and automobiles afforded young people of the middle classes." And yet, she notes, historians have shown that young people from this period were "remarkably passive in relation to their parents (and, in fact, all adults)."[49] Chinn argues that the modern idea of adolescence emerged from anxieties about the behaviors of the teenage children of immigrants who "occasioned an impressive amount of hand wringing among reformers, sociologists, journalists, creative writers, educators, policy makers, and intellectuals of all persuasions." Chinn connects these discourses with assumptions about adolescence today, arguing that "concerns that writers at the end of the nineteenth and in the early twentieth centuries explicitly linked to the young people of immigrant communities—the explosion of commercial sites of leisure (amusement parks, dance halls, theaters, and beer gardens, for example), a loosening of controls on premarital sexuality, rebellion against parents and other authority figures—became the defining characteristics for teen culture more generally as the twentieth century progressed."[50]

Much like the transference of racial prejudice onto categories of age by 1870 (documented in chapter 1), Chinn describes how forms of antagonism directed toward immigrant populations were mapped onto the category of adolescence more broadly during the twentieth century. In this section I show how the new ways childhood and adolescence were being defined in medical and psychological discourse in the early twentieth century contributed to this trend. The ways that immigrant teenagers were being talked about by reformers echo the ways that Hall talks about "primitives" or the "savage," trapped in an immature and uncontrollable adolescence. The logic of adolescence unites these racial evocations with the disparaging ways that teenagers are talked about today. Categories of age are deployed in the late nineteenth and early twentieth centuries as metaphors for heredity, evolution, and the development of civilization. They functioned to maintain the presumed inferiority of categories of difference while appearing to represent universally shared stages of human life, as they continue to do today. Childhood and adolescence have distinct functions in this process, where childhood comes to represent an idealized potential available for direction and adolescence comes to represent the antagonism that Chinn describes, the limit point of social control *and* the embodiment of those traits deemed as needing social control in the first place.

In the inaugural issue of the *Journal of Adolescence* published in 1900, four years before Hall's *Adolescence*, editor L. A. Stout's "Words of Welcome" offered an explicit agenda of control as part of the journal's framing lines of inquiry: "Why do so many young people choose a life for which nature manifestly does not intend for them? What can be done to correct this evil?"[51] It is unclear what evil Stout is referring to in his "Words of Welcome," but the "life for which nature manifestly does not intend" intimates concerns about homosexuality. James E. Russell expressed a similar agenda of control in the *School Review* in 1896, writing, "The important pedagogic consideration is the enormous accession of physical and psychical energy. What shall be done with it? This question the educator must answer."[52] Notably, the question of what shall be done with adolescent energy is *not* one to be posed to adolescents themselves, but one Russell believes the educator must answer.

The title of Louis Starr's 1915 *The Adolescent Period: Its Features and Management* also indicates that management and control are the primary concern when it comes to adolescence, and his book devotes one of six chapters to "The Faults and Criminal Tendencies of Adolescents." Starr's emphasis on management in *The Adolescent Period* is typical of publications on adolescence in Britain and the United States from the late nineteenth century forward, replicating that presumed antagonism described by Chinn and constructing the problem of adolescence as one precisely about control. Likewise, a section called "Discipline, Crime, and Punishment" in T. A. A. Hunter and M. E. M. Herford's 1961 *Adolescence: The Years of Indiscretion*, covers what was still at midcentury being treated as an obligatory topic in any full-length work on adolescence. Both Hall's *Adolescence* and the abridged version called *Youth* devote a large number of pages to adolescent faults and crimes. The frequency with which chapters appear with titles such as "Adolescent Delinquency and Crime" in C. Stanford Read's 1928 *The Struggles of Male Adolescence*, "Some Pathological Cases: The Juvenile Delinquent," and "The Problem of Discipline during Adolescence" in Olive Wheeler's 1929 *Youth: The Psychology of Adolescence and Its Bearing on the Reorganization of Adolescent Education*, for example, suggests that the institutionalized study of adolescence at once emerges out of and reproduces anxieties about deviance and control.

We can see these anxieties about control play out in early twentieth-century sex education campaigns in Britain and the United States. For example, in the 1930s and 1940s, organizations such as the British Social Hygiene Council and the Medical Women's Federation published and circulated dozens of pamphlets with titles such as *The Approach to Womanhood*, *What Parents Should Tell Their Children*, and

WHAT PARENTS SHOULD TELL THEIR CHILDREN.

Published by
BRITISH SOCIAL HYGIENE COUNCIL,
Carteret House, Carteret Street, London, S.W.I.

Figure 2.1. Mary Scharlieb, *What Parents Should Tell Their Children* (London: British Social Hygiene Council, 1933), pamphlet, folder N.2/6, box 106, Medical Women's Federation, Archives and Manuscripts, Wellcome Library, London.

Sex Education of Small Children (see fig. 2.1).[53] The content of these pamphlets is overtly regulatory, aimed at policing the knowledge and behavior of children and adolescents through sex education. In these pamphlets the child is imagined as docile and receptive to guidance, whereas the adolescent embodies the unbridled energies of the sexual body, just beyond the control of parents or teachers. What is surprising, however, is how often this archive of sex education pamphlets seems to be aimed at policing parents, displacing their private knowledge of sex with an institutionally sanctioned, scientific discourse about reproduction. And why? Early twentieth-century medical documents often acknowledge morality as a motivating factor for sex education, and yet these gestures appear perfunctory, only a single layer of a much more widespread, secular project of social regulation with explicitly eugenic aims. In the United States similar campaigns were conducted by organizations such as the American Social Hygiene Association, which produced posters and published educational books. While there are contextual differences between Britain and the United States, the institutional discourses I examine here emerge from a shared context of intellectual and scientific production in which experts on both sides of the Atlantic exchanged and cited similar ideas. They reveal the explicitly eugenic aims of controlling sex, a project of normalization requiring the participation of parents, teachers, and doctors.

In *What Every Mother Should Tell Her Children*, the author emphasizes that it is best to let the child approach the mother about the topic of reproduction, rather than the mother approach the child. But if the child fails to do so before adolescence, "it may be necessary for the mother to ask him point blank if he would not like to hear the beautiful story of birth." This is because "he *must* be taught before he reaches the difficult age of adolescence, when the body is undergoing rapid changes and when the nervous system is sensitive and excitable." Adolescence represents the uncontrollable stage in which hearing the "beautiful story of birth" could have disastrous consequences. The author emphasizes again: "I repeat that it is my opinion, and that of many well-known doctors, that all children must be told the full facts of reproduction before they reach adolescence." The pamphlet explains in technical detail the reproductive organs and the changes in the body during puberty in a singsongy way for the mother to imitate when speaking to her children. It urges mothers to talk to their children before they might hear from anyone else, because "there is always the danger that she may hear frightening things from other sources, and so it is important for you to 'get in first.'"[54] The primary concern is that girls will find out about the pain of childbirth and then fail in their reproductive duty to the nation. Thus, the mother is the only one whose knowledge of sex is authorized by the institution, and the control of this knowledge is considered essential.

The author of this pamphlet, calling herself anonymously a "Workday Mother," then addresses some potential objections from her imagined audience of mothers: "I expect you will say, 'But this is perfectly simple. The difficulty arises when one has to explain the father's part in the scheme of things.' I agree that is not easy. . . . This may seem terribly shocking and embarrassing at first sight, but the point is this: Children who are trained early bring such a pure, unspoilt attitude of mind to the subject, they can see nothing shameful or embarrassing about it, and they will accept what you tell them in the frankest possible way."[55] The difficulty of explaining the "father's part" is sidestepped, emphasizing telling children in the "frankest possible way" without really telling her readers anything very frankly. The child is imagined as innocent of sexuality—"pure, unspoilt"—and receptive: "They will accept what you tell them." All notions of sexual desire are located with the "father's part," denying the sexuality of all children, but especially girls, who are imagined to be passive listeners and (future) passive sexual partners despite their important childbearing and child-rearing roles. It is unclear how an awareness of these technical details—ovaries and fallopian tubes—will effectively impact the child's later successful reproductive practices, let alone her use of pleasure. For all its emphasis on frankness, this pamphlet, like many others of its kind, leaves out any useful information about pleasure or desire. The "sensitive and excitable" nervous system of the adolescent is described as a biological force that must be contained and managed beforehand, when the child is still a child. Aside from the occasional reference to "temptations," and perhaps the "father's part," there is really no acknowledgment that sex might be desirable at all. Desire is irrelevant here, perhaps even a hindrance to the institutional goals of sex itself.

In a 1935 pamphlet called *How You Grow: A Book for Boys* in the Medical Federation Papers, Theodore Tucker and Muriel Pout acknowledge sexual pleasure as a matter of prevention, explaining that "both girls and boys should take care that their clothing does not get tight between the thighs, as it excites nerves connected with the sex glands and starts them off working too quickly." Girls and boys, too, should even be cautious that they do not outgrow their pajamas without noticing, so as to prevent accidental stimulation. And "those of you who roll up into a ball, like hedgehogs" also need to beware that there is enough room in the pajama bottoms. Tucker and Pout caution, if the "sex glands" should get sensitive for any reason, it is important not to touch them because "this would be unwise as if, when something makes your eye smart, you were to start rubbing that, for it will only make it worse." Worse, indeed. Tucker and Pout explain that, luckily, what we have to do is very simple to ensure our good health, but there is one more thing they want us to remember. "That is," they write, "the way we think about these things affects the way the sex glands work." And so they suggest that "as a matter of fact, the less we think about them the better," and now that "you know how they work, and how to keep them healthy, you will not have to bother yourself by wondering about them."[56] They advise plenty of exercise, outdoor activities, and even work to keep the mind clear. And, if we happen to find people who want to talk about sex, it is only because they are very ignorant, and so we need to take great measures to stay away from them.

Doris Odlum repeats the words of caution offered by the "Workday Mother" in her 1931 pamphlet *The Psychology of Adolescence*. In a section on "The Teaching of Sex Knowledge," she explains how it is essential to give the proper information about sexual functions. This information is "not charged with any real emotional significance," since the child "feels very little more personal concern with the matter than he [sic] does with the question of where trees or rabbits come from and how they grow, or how a motor car is made." But, for the adolescent, "the question has become intensely personal, heavily charged with emotion," and that is why the question of sex must be dealt with simply and without shame when children are still children. Odlum regrets that few parents are equipped to do this properly, since they themselves are so full of shame or embarrassment in regard to sex. But if the parents wait until adolescence, it may be too late, since "later on great damage may be done by explanations given by the wrong person or at the wrong time or in the wrong way, and even more damage, perhaps, may be done by withholding necessary explanations."[57]

Childhood is positioned here as the moment when parental and institutional intervention is simple and effective in its goals, but adolescence is the moment when it may already be too late. Odlum puts enormous pressure on the parent to achieve the proper outcome with the teaching of sex education. She writes that "nothing is more fatal than handing an adolescent boy or girl a book dealing with the facts of life, and telling them that they will find everything that they ought to know clearly explained there." This is because no book can "adjust itself to the needs of the person who reads it, and that is quite essential in such a matter as this," since "some of us have all sorts of personal problems and difficulties which make us interpret things in different ways, and a mere statement of facts cannot by any means satisfy all the problems and questions, mostly of a quite personal nature, that trouble the adolescent." The only solution is for sex information to be given in person and adjusted to the needs of the questioner. "If we fail in this," Odlum warns, "we shall be sowing the seeds of fear and distrust, both of life and of self, and in adolescence, at the time when the sex urge is awakening, what should be the most beautiful and wonderful mystery of life is inevitably spoiled from the outset."[58]

Sex education appears here to be placed in the hands of parents—mothers, specifically—when it is really being put in the hands of institutions who aim to regulate what it is the mother says and doesn't say, thinks and doesn't think, about sex. The pamphlet operates under the assumption that mothers will not know what to say to their children, rendering their own experiences with sex and desire irrelevant, since the story they are to tell about sex is the story told by the psychologist, doctor, or expert. Michel Foucault writes that an "entire medico-sexual regime took hold of the family milieu."[59] In this sense instruction is a form of control working backward onto the instructor, quite explicitly a lesson for adults as much as for the children these adults are supposed to teach. In the proliferation of literature on child and adolescent development written before and after Hall's *Adolescence*, parents, teachers, and doctors are made participants in a system of cooperative watchfulness that regulates exactly how a child should develop and at which rate and in what direction. And when that child fails to meet expectations, it is not only the child who is held responsible but even more so the adults who have been charged with that child's progress, who have, in a sense, been charged with the failure to meet these expectations themselves.

In the United States Margaret Sanger, who was an early advocate for birth control, identifies the enormous responsibility placed on mothers and uses it to make a eugenic argument for planned parenthood.[60] In her 1920 book *Woman and the New Race,* Sanger accepts the blame for women as the ones responsible for birthing and producing mental defectives, criminals, prostitutes—all recently developed categories of undesirables named by medical and psychological discourses:

> The creators of over-population are the women, who, while wringing their hands over each fresh horror, submit anew to their task of producing the multitudes who will bring about the *next* tragedy of civilization.
>
> While unknowingly laying the foundations of tyrannies and providing the human tinder for racial conflagrations, woman was also unknowingly creating slums, filling asylums with insane, and institutions with other defectives. She was replenishing the ranks of the prostitutes, furnishing grist for the criminal courts and inmates for prisons. Had she planned deliberately to achieve this tragic total of human waste and misery, she could hardly have done it more effectively.[61]

The book is a polemical argument for women to take this responsibility into their own hands through voluntary motherhood, but this seemingly feminist argument is made through the eugenic project of population control. Her eugenicist arguments appear to operate rhetorically in the text as the *least* controversial part of the book, the most socially acceptable platform for her much more controversial claim that women should have reproductive rights.[62] The eugenic project of "racial hygiene" provides the backdrop for the sex education campaigns of the 1930s and 1940s. In 1938, for example, the medical adviser and secretary for the Central Council for Health Education, Robert Sutherland, gave a report on "Sexual Delinquency" that was equally concerned with preventing "sexual vice" as it was concerned with figuring out how to get married people to have reproductive sex.[63] "Delinquency" in this context includes the failure of married people to produce children. The problem of sex was not simply one of regulating knowledge and controlling the behaviors of young people but of regulating the entire project of reproduction on a national and institutional scale through the family. The family provides the access required for the teacher, doctor, and psychologist to monitor a child's upbringing and education. Reproduction is the first priority here, though not in a strictly moral sense, but rather in regard to producing the nation's ideal citizens under circumstances within institutional reach.

In an undated pamphlet titled *Adolescence,* published by the Mothers' Union, marriage and childbearing are the ultimate goals of educating their members about adolescence. The pamphlet states in its conclusion that "the Mothers' Union stands for the view that the bond should be indissoluble, or rather that marriage is less a bond than a relationship, differing from others only as being the result not of birth, but of choice." It is perhaps surprising that the word "choice" is emphasized here, since the pamphlet goes on to describe marriage as an "obligation" in which "bride and bridegroom completely understand the responsibilities and the conditions of their new relationship to each other." These responsibilities and conditions are to "fully learn the beauty and dignity of sex, and realize it as a solemn trust from God Himself for the happiness of men and women, and continuance of the race in the children."[64] Any spiritual or emotional dimension of marriage is overshadowed by the evolutionary responsibility of married men and women to ensure the "continuance of the race." Likewise, in the 1938 pamphlet called *What Every Mother Should Tell Her Children* circulated by the Medical Women's Federation, the rationale for reproduction is stated directly as an obligation to the nation: "There was never a time when the country was so much in need of fine, healthy citizens, and our children must be armed with the knowledge which will protect them against the dangers and temptations they will meet as they grow older; and which will help them to make a success of marriage and parenthood."[65] The danger against which "children must be armed" consists of any nonnormative sexual behavior, ranging from homosexuality to promiscuity to prostitution. The goal is not just reproduction but reproduction under the carefully controlled circumstances of the white, middle-class British family. The project of managing the production of "fine, healthy citizens" through the sex education of youth is an overt theme in many of these early British pamphlets, which appear to be a response to and a perpetuation of the myth of a "lost generation" of educated, upper-middle-class citizens in World War I.[66] The obligation to produce children carried with it specific assumptions about whiteness and social class within which such production should take place.

Another pamphlet from the 1930s, titled "England's Girls and England's Future," rises to the level of propaganda, overtly stating its intention to "rouse the ambition of the girls of England" with its "ambitious title." However, the direct address for this pamphlet still appears to be for the parent, rather than the girl herself, who is spoken about in the third person. Far from inspirational, the content of the pamphlet quickly turns threatening:

> For if she does not realise her responsibility for that future, and accept whatever the fulfillment of that responsibility entails, she is evading the universal call to service—and service is the payment she is called to make for the great gift of life entrusted to her.
>
> Every girl, then, is bound to realise and accept her responsibility for the future, and if she is to fulfil that responsibility she can only do so by realising that the present, her every-day life and daily actions, are all-important in shaping that future.[67]

We can see here the logic of what Lee Edelman calls "reproductive futurism," in which the freedom and needs of a living, agential English girl must be sacrificed for the future, for children that do not even exist.[68] Thus, if a girl does not realize her "responsibility" to produce children for the nation, she is "evading" her "call to service" and the "payment she is called to make" for having reproductive capacities, the "great gift of life entrusted to her." The class dimensions of this eugenic project are evident in the euphemistic reference to how "her every-day life and daily actions" have something to do with "shaping that future." It is not enough for a girl to live her life as she wishes and then later settle down and produce citizens for the nation. Fears about "vice," promiscuity, homosexuality, and prostitution were coded with class prejudice mapped here onto a girl's genetic potential, as if these behaviors initiated evolutionary decline in the body of a girl. Gill-Peterson writes, "There is no meaningful, nonideological difference between so-called positive and negative eugenics, and the historical binding of race to reproduction remains largely unchallenged, which is to say unmarked and unspoken, in medical science today."[69]

Taken together these sex education pamphlets illustrate the co-constitutive relation between categories of age and categories of difference. While the figure of the child most often represented knowability, control, and the promise of science to direct the future, the adolescent stood in for the unknown, the unmanageable, and the limits of institutional control. One way we might think about the movement of this institutional discourse is through Friedrich Nietzsche's own critique; here the child and the adolescent are the "idea" that allows for classifications of the criminal, the abnormal, the homosexual, and the prostitute to appear "known" to an institutional expertise, an expertise *so well used to it* that they are *hardly afraid of the "idea" anymore.*[70] Adolescence functions in these contexts to contain anxieties about race and class difference, queer and trans phenomena, and the instability of scientific knowledge itself. And when attempts at social control failed (as they inevitably did), the category of adolescence served as the *cause* of those failures, naturalizing resistance into the category itself, a mechanism used to evade the ethical limits for managing the private life and personhood of others.

Identity and Selfhood

In the prologue to Erik Erikson's 1968 *Identity: Youth and Crisis,* he likens the distress experienced by soldiers returning from World War II—who "had through the exigencies of war lost a sense of personal sameness and historical continuity"—with what he understood as the disturbed behavior of adolescents, arguing that symptoms evident of a pathology in veterans were developmentally normal in adolescence: "Since then, we have recognized the same central disturbance in severely conflicted young people whose sense of confusion is due, rather, to a war within themselves, and in confused rebels and destructive delinquents who war with their society." He concludes, "Thus, we have learned to ascribe a normative 'identity crisis' to the age of adolescence and young adulthood."[71] Erikson's conception of identity cannot be reduced to mere social conformity, since he believed that a healthy self-concept resulted from the successful balance between self-determination and social expectations; however, the "confused rebels" and "destructive delinquents" he mentions are nonetheless characterized as failing to accomplish this process of normalization, as if the symptoms of trauma Erikson himself describes in adolescents are not due to traumatic experiences but rather from breakdowns in the developmental process of identity formation. Erikson's concept of identity suggests that adolescence is a time of confusion, instability, and distress while imagining adulthood as the end result of this process, a stable arrival point of independence and self-determination. The nineteenth-century logic of developmentalism, along with its temporal mapping of selfhood as an interiority accessed through memory, makes this mid-twentieth-century notion of identity possible.[72]

The concept of identity emerges in the mid-twentieth century as a conceptually new form for the logic of developmentalism, structuring normative categories as synonymous with the arrival at adulthood while nonnormative or marginalized categories continue to signal arrested development, as they do today. Take, for example, a 2013 article in the *New Yorker* by Margaret Talbot that dismissively frames trans identity as one more form of postmodern self-expression in a world where "plastic surgery, tattoos and piercings have made people more comfortable with body modification."[73] Talbot bemoans the ordinariness of transitioning among adolescents, talking about trans identity as if it is just another teen trend. She writes, "for high-school seniors like Skylar—who live in prosperous suburbs, have doting parents, attend good schools, and get excellent grades while studding their transcripts with extracurricular activities—the hardest part of the college application is often the personal essay." In the context of this wealth and privilege, Talbot all but says Skylar is lucky to be trans so that he has something to set him apart on his college application. She offhandedly acknowledges that some transgender children face challenges, like bullying, but insists that "Skylar's more seamless story is becoming increasingly common." In the liberal town where Skylar grew up, Talbot writes, "nobody seriously challenged his decision to change gender. Some of his peers even expressed a certain envy."

Another mom interviewed by Talbot, given the pseudonym "Danielle," casts doubt on her child's desire to transition by echoing this characterization of trans identity as a trendy, easily available mode of adolescent individuation: "Danielle said that she had met many teen-agers who seemed to regard their bodies as endlessly modifiable, through piercings, or tattoos, or even workout regimens. She wondered if sexual orientation was beginning to seem boring as a form of identity; gay people were getting married, and perhaps seemed too settled."[74] Danielle appears to insinuate that teens who come out as gay or lesbian do so only to set themselves apart from the crowd and that, if they come out as trans, they do so because they are bored with being gay or think that being gay is not "special" enough anymore. Danielle uses common assumptions about adolescence to dismiss trans phenomena as ordinary, widespread experiences of adolescent angst taken too far: "I feel like a lot of these kids, including my daughter, might be going through identity struggles, a lot of them are trying on roles."[75] Talbot briefly acknowledges that "teen-agers who identify as transgender appear to be at higher risk for depression and suicide"; however, her wording implies that these numbers are probably misleading.[76] Danielle remarks, "a lot of these kids are sad for a variety of reasons. Maybe the gender feelings are the underlying cause, maybe not." Conceptions of adolescence as an "identity crisis" construct adolescent self-knowledge as inherently suspect. Adolescent knowing is dismissed as whim or drama, hormonal or identity instability surrounding a new teen trend.

Gill-Peterson demonstrates that despite claims like Talbot's, medical archives show that trans children have existed for (at least) a century. Grappling with the great harm that has been done to trans and intersex children in the name of normativity and scientific progress, she asserts the need for validating self-knowledge and "actually *listening* to what trans children say about themselves, grounding medical care in their desires, and abandoning binary models of transition and dysphoria that continue to confine children to developmental teleologies ending in heterosexual masculinity or femininity."[77] Talbot uses a binary model of gender and sexuality to further invalidate Skylar, beginning with her description of Skylar's gender presentation and dating history. Though Skylar transitioned to male, Talbot suspiciously remarks that "in his new guise, he doesn't labor to come across as conventionally masculine. Like many 'trans' people of his generation, he is comfortable with some gender ambiguity, and doesn't feel the need to be, as he puts it, a 'macho bro.'" Talbot likewise describes a popular video made by Annette Bening and Warren Beatty's son Stephen, who is FTM, in which he identifies "as a transman, a faggy queen, a homosexual, a queer, a nerdfighter, a writer, an artist, and a guy who needs a haircut."[78]

Halfway through the article, Talbot reveals that Skylar, like Stephen, dates boys. She describes his sexuality, however, as "all a little gauzy and theoretical." Skylar is clear enough about his sexuality in his statements, and so this comment betrays Talbot's struggle to recognize queer ways of being as valid. She explains, using a first-person "we" that exposes who she imagines her readers to be: "It can be hard for some of us to imagine a sexuality that is not inextricably linked to our gender." Skylar's decision to transition does not make sense to her since he continues to date boys; in her mind his gender and sexuality, then, must not be linked. She cannot conceive of the myriad of gender identifications that might "feel right" in their connection to the equally myriad, equally nonnormative possibilities for sexuality and desire. Skylar's queerness troubles Talbot because his narrative does not conform to the gender binary projected in popular stories of trans children, and she deploys common assumptions about the instability of adolescence to undermine his agency and self-knowledge.

Queer possibilities for identity do not anticipate or require points of arrival, nor are arrivals understood as fixed in themselves. Such arrivals are not fixed moments of identity but identifications occurring in the ordinary movement between fluidity and fixity over time. This is not the version of postmodern fluidity referenced by Talbot, which poses as the "freedom" to choose who we are when in fact it is precisely that which is deemed desirable by normative cultural standards that has been scripted ahead of time, without our input or consent, by this neoliberal capitalist version of selfhood.[79] What we find in this version of postmodern fluidity, rather than greater acceptance of variation, are even more rigid boundaries around the normal, right, and good way to occupy the binary of man or woman. What we find are even greater imperatives to strive to occupy these standards, to occupy an ideal imagined and sold to us by someone else. This is merely another version of developmentalism deployed to maintain existing social norms. Transgender and queer theories of selfhood, on the other hand, put pressure on the developmental narrative of adolescence, speaking instead of the queer child who might grow sideways, or the reordering or rejection of developmental sequence itself, or the liberatory potential for naming the self at any point in the prescribed sequence.[80] Trans

chapter two

embodiment likewise reveals the possibility of reconstruction, revision, and remaking outside the developmental imperative.

We can resist the normalizing functions of developmentalism through the analytic reversal posed by Julia Kristeva, in which we understand "the adolescent, like the child," as a "mythical figure of the imaginary that enables us to distance ourselves from some of our failings, splittings of ego, disavowals or mere desires, which it reifies into the figure of someone who has not yet grown up." We might understand this theory as one of an individual mind, full of the peculiarities of emotion, memory, and history accessible through the figure of oneself as an adolescent, but it is also a theory of the cultural imaginary and its shared meanings and disavowals over time. We can see this psychic function played out at the turn of the twentieth century with proclamations about the "discovery" of adolescence, confirming beliefs in Western superiority and fulfilling the promise of science to direct the future. At the same time Hall and Dunn managed their fears of a racialized Other through the developmental logic of adolescence. Early twentieth-century sex education pamphlets projected uncontrollable sexual desire onto the adolescent body while constructing a fantasy that such energies might be directed toward eugenic aims. Talbot uses adolescence to contain the trans phenomena that permeate all human experience, in which adolescence serves to distance nonnormative gender feelings, expressions, and identifications as temporary, part of growing up, or a sign of adult immaturity. Reading the figure of the adolescent for patterns of disavowal and desire reveals the limits of the visible, the possible, the real, and, according to Kristeva, "allows us to see, hear, and read these subjective fluctuations."[81]

Returning to Margaret Lowenfeld's 1934 lecture on "Youth and Health" discussed in the opening of this chapter, Kristeva's theorization provides a lens through which to deconstruct these claims about adolescence. Though Lowenfeld distances herself from the adolescent, she also imagines the adolescent in terms she might use for an adult, even one such as herself. "The adolescent has two main hungers," she says. "The first is the hunger for knowledge, and the second the hunger for power." In the same breath Lowenfeld offers a validation and dismissal of these desires, which are "very real to the girl and boy themselves" but "looked at very differently by the outside world."[82] This phrasing suggests an evasion—we do not know where Lowenfeld stands on the issue, with the girl and boy themselves or with the outside world. Ironically, the distance she constructs between herself and the adolescent is what establishes her own claim to knowledge and power, her authority to speak about adolescents in the first place, and yet she imagines them as like herself, struggling to be recognized as legitimate in a new field of expertise and in a medical field dominated by men. The distance she has constructed between herself and the adolescent is fragile, barely holding that distance at bay, threatening to dissolve. In the copy of this lecture in Lowenfeld's papers at the Wellcome Library, these lines are typed in all capital letters, signaling the importance of these remarks, the way they might have been emphasized in the style of her delivery.

Between the lines of these projections, Lowenfeld appears to simultaneously recognize and deny that the adolescent is a person, someone who wants knowledge and power, just as she does. The solution to these hungers further reveals how the figure of the adolescent in her lecture is reflective of her own subjective fluctuations, as she suggests that they learn about science and medicine, how to become doctors and researchers. She confidently declares that the "science of health" offers the "satisfaction we need." She explains, "There is nothing so delightful at times as to talk to children on the microbe-hunters, to give them the life stories of Pasteur and Koch, and the men who cleaned the Panama Canal from yellow fever, and the men who pursued and destroyed the sleeping sickness germ in Africa. There is enough material in all that for sheer adventure and excitement and heroism, far better than anything in the cinema. The facts stand for themselves. They carry the *feeling* that there is in this progress of science."[83] Lowenfeld names the hungers of the adolescent in such a way that they mirror her own desires and thus give her the knowledge and power to grant these desires, to bring full circle the fulfillment of her own hungers. Thus, it is *her* participation in the "science of health" that carries this feeling—her feeling—in the progress of science. Despite her sympathetic portrayal of young people, Lowenfeld must stop short of acknowledging that, by her own description, adolescents are much like adults. The authority of this emerging discourse requires that adolescents function as an object of study and not the source of self-knowledge. Lowenfeld cannot deny the validity of this discourse without reevaluating the importance of her role in the lives of her patients, a role that was still under tenuous construction in 1934. She must distance the adolescent as a queer creature, an unknown, a perpetual object of scientific study, because she cannot give over to adolescents themselves the power to say who they are without also calling into question the social need for her institutional authority. The active construction of her authority depends on *her* hunger for knowledge, *her* hunger for power, suggesting her projection of desire in these constructions. And yet, Lowenfeld cannot be reduced to the operations of an institutional discourse but is caught in a complex system of institutional authority and expertise in which she is negotiating for her own voice, her own desires, her own power as a person. However, in these systemic relations the adolescent of Lowenfeld's discourse is not a person but a figure conjured from memory and experience to fulfill her own needs.

Doris Odlum, on the other hand, more successfully deploys a conception of adolescence much like Kristeva's to deconstruct the category entirely, at the end of her 1931 pamphlet, *The Psychology of Adolescence*. At first she cautions parents about attempting to reproduce images of themselves in their children: "Are we so successful and happy in the conduct of our lives that we wish their lives to be a replica of our own? Even if children could see and experience life second-hand through adults, would this even be good for them?" Odlum goes one step further, reversing the logic of developmentalism to shift adolescence into the temporal space of adulthood, unraveling both categories at once: "Are we, in fact, much more than adolescents ourselves? Is it even doubtful whether anybody can be said to be wholly grown up, if by that we mean that we have struck a perfectly satisfactory balance between the primitive urges of our nature and the requirements of reality, so that we are harmoniously functioning organisms, balanced to withstand stresses from without or assailings from within; beings whose judgment is not clouded by emotion, whose orientation is firmly established in relation to our fellows and the life here, and to the infinite and the hereafter."[84] In this moment Odlum grapples with the degree to which the expectations she has just established for

adolescents—the requirements for achieving a "normal" maturity—
are impossible even for adults, even for someone such as herself. The
struggles that Odlum has just outlined as belonging to adolescence
are in fact the very struggles that belong to adulthood, the very struggles of life itself.

As Odlum acknowledges, adolescent struggles are human struggles, and they require human solutions. Can there be institutional
practices of care and knowledge-making that are not driven by hierarchy and control? Thinking of identity as an active and ongoing process of self-determination might support such an ethical relationality
between institutional expertise and human subjects, if such a concept
were to extend to children and adolescents in the first place. However,
identity more often constructs childhood as a blank space shielded by
innocence and adolescence as an unpredictable and unknowable instability *before* self-determination is imagined as possible. The temporal slide enabled by developmentalism only retroactively attributes the
process of successful identity formation in adolescence once a normative adulthood is achieved. During adolescence any act of self-determination can be interpreted as temporary, experimental, misguided, or
disordered. And in adulthood marginalized identities continue to be
interpreted as underdevelopment or immaturity. A queer conception
of identity, however, would not be predictive, would not anticipate or
wish for certain outcomes. It would emphasize nonlinear movement
to conceptualize growth outside developmental narratives of progress.
If the actual, phenomenological world is itself queer already, and it is
our language that defines, stabilizes, constructs, shapes, and biases it,
then we might attend more fully to the queerness and variation of the
world we live in, the queerness of the human body, and the queerness
of identity, human development, and growth.

chapter 3

PERVERSE READING AND THE
ADOLESCENT READER

I stayed at my desk reading some lugubrious volume—usually *The Mysteries of Udolpho*, by the amiable Mrs. Radcliffe. A translation of *The Sorrows of Werther* fell into my hands at this period, and if I could have committed suicide without killing myself, I should certainly have done so.
> —Thomas Bailey Aldrich, *The Story of a Bad Boy*

It was a very good book. I'm quite illiterate, but I read quite a lot.
> —J. D. Salinger, *The Catcher in the Rye*

Lifting the pages of the book, I let them fan slowly by my eyes. Words, dimly familiar but twisted all awry, like faces in a funhouse mirror, fled past, leaving no impression on the glassy surface of my brain.
> —Sylvia Plath, *The Bell Jar*

Illiterate reading. Words that leave no impression. Ideation of suicide without dying. These are some of the queer consequences depicted in fictional representations of adolescent reading. Scenes of reading appear with frequency in fictional texts, and the collection of scenes I assemble here reveal patterns of uncertainty, nonconformity, and risk. These diverse representations of self and text illuminate tensions surrounding adolescent reading and interpretation, tensions that surface questions of agency, identity, and power. They surface unexpected readerly acts, strategies of interpretation, and constructions of self. These scenes of reading also expose the problem of reading itself, the troubling relation between reader and text that reveals our uncertainties about what happens in these unobservable and unsettling acts of interpretation. The act of reading itself cannot mean one thing, and in these pages it moves between notions of the known and unknown. In this chapter I bring together a range of specific, located instantiations of the "adolescent reader" to expose the logics and assumptions that underpin deployments of adolescence as a concept over the course of the twentieth century. The discourse around the topic of adolescent reading points to the social functions of adolescence as a category, whereas fictional representations provide an opportunity to theorize adolescence differently. I use fictional scenes of adolescent reading from late nineteenth-century children's literature, twentieth-century classics, and contemporary young adult fiction as a way to begin unraveling the logic of adolescence. I do not find meanings inherent in fictional texts themselves but rather make meanings at these rich and interpretively supple sites of theorization.

Making meanings that resist accepted forms of knowledge is part of what Eve Kosofsky Sedgwick calls "perverse reading."[1] Nat Hurley explains, "Reading perversely has been central to the work of queer theory, and I would suggest that we can do more with perversion in our theorizations of young people and their texts than we have yet dreamed of." She argues that perverse reading "can thus take us an even greater distance toward thinking impossible things and for refusing the demands of normativity in our theorizing young people and their texts."[2] Perverse reading acknowledges the unstable relation between reader and text to make room for queer possibilities. Reading fiction perversely allows me to illuminate that which otherwise would not be visible or articulable. Kenneth Kidd suggests that "if queer theory is to function as theory, it needs also to theorize (not just interpret) children's literature and children's literature studies." He asks, "What if we were to think of children's literature not simply as a field of literature but also as a theoretical site in its own right?"[3] In the spirit of this suggestion, the fictional scenes I draw from provide a launch point, becoming the occasion for theory. They demonstrate how adolescence functions as a performative category enmeshed with conceptions of childhood and adulthood. I use closely related queer and psychoanalytic schemas to elucidate adolescence as a hermeneutic of self, an interpretive framework shaping subjectivity. I overlap representational layers of world, self, and text in order to stretch the limits of the real and unreal, the possible and impossible, the normal and perverse ways of making sense of our experiences and ourselves.

At first glance adolescence appears to be a queer category, po-

Figure 3.1. James Dean on the set of *Rebel without a Cause*, 1955. Courtesy of Wikimedia Commons.

sitioned interminably outside adulthood.[4] While some identity categories (such as "woman" or "adult") offer the illusion of stability, adolescence is conceptualized as unstable, as transitional, as a time when heterosexuality is practiced but not yet achieved. Adolescence functions as a temporary state of being that one is expected to move through and eventually leave behind. This very instability is part of what produces anxieties about adolescence. Adolescence appears to be queer in that it is often linked with rebellion—and we might consider both "queer" and "rebel" to describe those who act against accepted norms. But these connections suggest that adolescence is queer only in the sense that, like childhood, it serves to contain queer phenomena. We need only to conjure up an image of James Dean, leaning nonchalantly against the wall on the set of *Rebel without a Cause*, to recognize that adolescence also functions as an idealized state (see fig. 3.1). In this sense adolescence can be conceptualized as normal and universal even as it represents distance from normativity.

If we take James Dean as our representative example, however, we face the troubling fact that this idealization of adolescence does not signify the livability of adolescent lives but instead recapitulates risk and death.

Theoretically speaking, the conceptual relation between queer and identity is one of negation. If identity describes kinds of social legibility, discursive forms that both represent and produce subjects, then queer describes that which is rendered invisible, impossible, unthinkable, or unreal. As a theoretical term, "queer" is useful for its ability to describe what language often renders indescribable. Sedgwick writes, "That's one of the things that 'queer' can refer to: the open mesh of possibilities, gaps, overlaps, dissonances and resonances, lapses and excesses of meaning where the constituent elements of anyone's gender, of anyone's sexuality aren't made (or *can't be* made) to signify monolithically."[5] The term "queer," then, suggests a richness and complexity of experience that exists in excess of language, in the profound failure of language to *be* the material world and our experiences of it. And yet, as language fails to be who we are, it also stands in for us, calls us into being. Adolescence calls us into being, structuring subjectivity, instructing us as to which of our feelings belong to the past and which to our future, which of them we should disavow and which we should own. Adolescence sustains cultural beliefs about what childhood was and what adulthood should be, submerging queer ways of being while maintaining social norms. The fictional representations I examine serve to expose these functions of adolescence as contingent and open to fracture.

Bad Readers, Good Readers

Who is the adolescent reader? How is this category imagined to be different from the child reader, whose instruction and delight the children's book industry has made its object? Certainly, the adolescent reader presents contradictions that the child reader presumably does not when professionals are speaking about them as separate groups. But the adolescent reader is not simply a "reader" either, the term under which an adult reader might be considered. One might argue that there is no "adult" reader, only a reader imagined by adults who are writers, publishers, librarians, and literary critics. The adults are active, the reader a passive construct. But "adolescent" serves as a qualifier of some kind, denoting another kind of reader, a special kind of reader with specific needs, habits, and challenges. The adolescent reader does not conform to the passive relation often assumed by the term "reader." The adolescent reader is described as a kind of mystery, an unknown, undefined and indefinable.

I begin with J. D. Salinger's 1951 *The Catcher in the Rye*, a book that has an expansive cultural history beyond the text of its pages. The novel was published before the designation "young adult literature" existed and yet significantly influenced the genre as it took shape in the sixties and seventies. At the time of its publication, the book was read by young people and a good many adults too. In the novel Holden Caulfield is simultaneously a certain and an uncertain reader, a reader who both does and does not choose the book he is going to read. He tells us, "The book I was reading was this book I took out of the library by mistake. They gave me the wrong book, and I didn't notice it till I got back to my room. They gave me *Out of Africa* by Isak Dinesen." He never tells us what book he intended to get at the library. Instead, he says, "I thought it was going to stink, but it didn't. It was a very good book. I'm quite illiterate, but I read a lot." He doesn't say why *Out of Africa* is a good book but rather undermines his claim to have read it at all. Holden resists categorization here, talking about his reading only a short while after making a confession of his unreliability as a narrator: "I'm the most terrific liar you ever saw in your life," he announces.[6] What are we to make of Holden's claim of illiterate reading? What do these confessions mean?

His contradictory account of illiterate reading, on the one hand, is a mockery of the impressionability of youth, an account that both confounds and conforms to the imaginary dilemma of the adolescent reader, a reader caught between what is assumed to be the simple reading of childhood and the full agency of adulthood. This binary opposition between childhood and adulthood, between object and agent, describes two oversimplified versions of subjectivity, with adolescence messily straddling the two. Holden claims, "I put on my new hat and sat down and started reading that book *Out of Africa*. I'd read it already, but I wanted to read certain parts over again."[7] We do not know what Holden is *doing* with this book, why he is reading it again, what happens when he reads. He is at once a dutiful reader with the book the librarian has given him, which is a classic, *Out of Africa*; and he is an arbitrary reader who reads even though he has the wrong book, even though he reads certain parts over, even though he is quite illiterate. This uncertainty, which oozes from the gaps and excesses of meaning in his account of reading, is what I want to link to the panic surrounding *Catcher* in the mid-fifties.

Published as a novel for adults, *Catcher* quickly gained wide-spread recognition as a best seller and critical attention as a "modern masterpiece."[8] While the novel had been frequently taught on college campuses as contemporary literature, it wasn't until the mid-fifties that a number of high school English teachers began to use *Catcher* in some advanced English courses in an attempt to expose high school students "to high-quality contemporary writing."[9] Once the novel made it into the hands of nonadult readers, however, it began to cause censorship scandals. Usually these protests cited Holden Caulfield's foul language and sexual innuendo, but, in a number of instances, the book was challenged because of concerns it would make students "susceptible to Marxist indoctrination."[10] Censorship and scandal did not slow circulation. By 1961 *Catcher* was recommended reading for many high school students while simultaneously one of the most frequently challenged or censored books.[11] Linda M. Pavonetti, a professor of education who writes about young adult reading, recalls one of her classmates from advanced English being expelled from school for writing a report on *Catcher* during her senior year of high school in the mid-1960s.[12] Such events indicate a deep conflict and profound anxiety among parents, teachers, and school administrators about adolescent readers, about what they should read and how they should read it. Questions about the content of the book are questions about what might be done with it, how it might impress readers, how it might lead them to act out its imaginary refusals and misbehaviors. The adolescent reader imagined by censors is a contradiction: a *good* reader, someone who will read cover to cover with full understanding, but also a very literal reader, someone who will take Holden as a role model and at his word regardless of the ironies that unfold line by line. In this sense the adolescent reader is a passive reader, someone deeply susceptible to indoctrination. The reader imagined by censors is at once a fantasy and a nightmare—someone without agency, someone who can be overpowered by a book and thus someone who can be overpowered by them.

One concept necessary for maintaining the social division between childhood and adulthood is agency—it is agency that distinguishes the child from the adult. The child's agency is usually assumed to be limited, even as children are given free reign of themselves in the protected spaces of the backyard or among playmates, whereas the adult's agency is assumed to be full agency, regardless of the ways in which adults are constrained by outside circumstances like the necessity of making a living. Agency, in this sense, describes a mental capacity, where the child is not fully aware of their choices and actions, but, presumably, the adult is. The logic of adolescence, as seen in the objections to young people reading *Catcher in the Rye*, casts the adolescent in a more ambiguous space, one that more closely resembles the various and contradictory ways agency is ever possible within the constraints of language and culture.[13] Any available course of action is already defined within a social and institutional context as positive or negative participation in family, school, and state. However, because the adolescent is granted limited authority in these social institutions, the consequences for nonparticipation or negative participation appear to be—though this is not necessarily the case—less severe than they are for an adult; that is, for some adolescents, the consequences of nonparticipation do not always come to bear on one's ability to live, work, feed oneself, and so on. This creates the contradictory and temporary condition of subjugation to and freedom from the institutions of family, school, and state. The adolescent is both bound to these institutions and under very little obligation to them until the future moment when they are expected to "grow up." This condition feeds the contradictory mythology of adolescence as something to loathe and to long for, idealizing the adolescent rebel while blaming the ills of society on wayward youth; it is a space of both disempowerment and freedom at the same time.

While this contradictory space is assumed to belong to adolescence, and therefore to be a temporary fluctuation of agency, I want to emphasize the ways that agency is always unstable, fluctuating, and contradictory. The idea of adolescence as a turbulent, unstable, transitional state allows for this ambiguity. The adolescent might at once be understood as unable (like the child) and also as unwilling (like the adult) to use their own agency and judgment. Censors deploy both of these conceptualizations, sometimes simultaneously. Of course, social and cultural contexts determine how adolescent choices are viewed. The perception of *Catcher* as dangerous reading is specific to the fears and expectations circulating in the United States in the 1950s, but the logic of adolescence deployed by censors persists to this day.

We can find echoes of the unpredictable adolescent reader in another midcentury novel that, like *Catcher in the Rye*, has a cultural life of its own, considered both a classic and an adolescent classic, Sylvia Plath's *The Bell Jar*.[14] Its status as an adolescent novel is a contradictory description in itself, signaling both a dismissive or devaluing gesture and a positive investment in reclaiming this example of "classic literature" for adolescent reading. The narrator, Esther Greenwood, is in college, having just earned a summer internship working at a New York magazine. The novel dramatizes Esther's perceptions as she suffers a mental breakdown, beginning in New York and then later at home, where she attempts suicide. While Esther could be considered just past adolescence, her postadolescent status does not prevent the cultural inscription of the novel *as* adolescent. It is significant that Plath's mother, Aurelia, has publicly stated how hurt she was by *The Bell Jar*'s "raging adolescent voice."[15] This description is a way for Aurelia to distance herself from what she saw as the "cruel" depiction of the narrator's mother, but it also exposes her simultaneous identification with and disavowal of the mother figure in the novel. Her comments illustrate one of the ways adolescence can function as a distancing mechanism. Whatever the views expressed in the novel—whether they are Esther's alienation from her mother or her disdain for social conventions—such perspectives are held at a distance by thinking of Esther and the novel itself as "adolescent."

Like *Catcher*, Plath's *The Bell Jar* depicts scenes of reading that disturb and disorient the relation between reader and text. Esther Greenwood has decided to read *Finnegans Wake* over the summer and finish her honors thesis. This odd book is depicted as much as an object as it is a text, the words physical, the sounds like shapes: "I crawled between the mattress and the padded bedstead and let the mattress fall across me like a tombstone. The thick book made an unpleasant dent in my stomach." Esther keeps the book with her, pressed into her stomach, as the mattress rests heavy on top of her. She is practicing, eerily, to bury herself in the crawlspace of her mother's house. Her attempt at suicide overlaps with her attempt at reading, the language of these two activities dangerously intertwined:

> My eyes sank through an alphabet soup of letters to the long word in the middle of the page.
> *bababadalgharaghtakamminarronnkonnbronntonneronntuonn-thunntrovarrhounawnshkawntoohoohoordenenthurnuk!*
> I counted the letters. There were exactly a hundred of them. I thought that must be important.
> Why should there be a hundred letters?
> Haltingly, I tried the word aloud.
> It sounded like a heavy wooden object falling downstairs, boomp boomp boomp, step after step. Lifting the pages of the book, I let them fan slowly by my eyes. Words, dimly familiar but twisted all awry, like faces in a funhouse mirror, fled past, leaving no impression on the glassy surface of my brain.

Her eyes sink, the words and the object of the book fall downstairs, the words and images flee past, leaving no impression. In this scene Esther is fixated on one of the one-hundred-letter words invented by James Joyce in *Finnegans Wake*. This feature of the text, among others in Joyce's novel, can be said to intentionally disrupt reading practices. Indeed, Esther seems to be drawn to the book's most disruptive moments, reading aloud the one-hundred-letter word in the middle of the page: "I thought this must be important. Why should there be a hundred letters?"[16] She thumbs the pages like a flipbook with no coherent images, no legible words. Esther is reading *Finnegans Wake*, but not in the ways expected of her by her college thesis director. She is an accomplished student, someone who has won a college scholarship and a magazine prize. But Esther's reading is difficult to account for, even as she narrates it for us. This difficulty might lead one to categorize Esther as a *bad* reader, maybe even as someone who *can't* read because she is losing her mind. Her bad reading, however, suggests her complicated negotiation of agency, her ability to choose what she does with *Finnegans Wake,* to take it with her where she is going, no matter how strange, how dark, or how unknown.

The Nowhere Period

G. Robert Carlsen opens his 1980 edition of *Books and the Teen-Age Reader: A Guide for Teachers, Librarians, and Parents* with a description of adolescence as a state of limbo: "In between there is what has been called for centuries a 'nowhere' period, a troubled, unformed time of being no longer a child and yet not fully mature."[17] The word "nowhere" weighs heavily in Carlsen's description. The kind of person that Carlsen describes, here the adolescent, the kind of person that exists "nowhere," is a kind of person who exists always outside of somewhere, defined against the definable location of adulthood, always arriving but never to arrive. What kind of reading is possible in this "nowhere" period? What kind of meaning can be made in a "troubled, unformed time"? Perhaps it is Holden Caulfield's illiterate reading of *Out of Africa.* Perhaps it is the complete separation of text and meaning that occurs as Esther Greenwood flips through the pages of *Finnegans Wake.* I do not consider these examples failures or aberrations of reading, but places where reading self, world, and text is radically called into question, making visible the very instability of subjectivity and meaning itself. In queer theory such disruption is not understood as a problem to be overcome, as Carlsen seems to suggest, but as an opportunity to open possibilities for knowing and being, possibilities vital to the material conditions of queer lives and arguably of adolescent lives as well. In *The Bell Jar* one might read Esther's disruptions of thinking and sanity as failures, but these disruptions provide the narrative space for her to resist and critique the expectations of compulsory heterosexuality: marriage and motherhood. Likewise, in *Catcher in the Rye,* Holden resists the norms of success and masculinity as he flunks out of another private prep school.

The concept of adolescence functions to distance queer possibilities from adulthood, serving both as a location for desire and as a mechanism for disavowal that distances the queer, the unknown, the anomalous, the abject. This understanding of adolescence relies on two overlapping conceptualizations from Julia Kristeva: abjection from *Powers of Horror* and the theorization of adolescence in *New Maladies of the Soul*. Kristeva explains abjection as that which "disturbs identity, system, order. What does not respect borders, positions, rules. The in-between, the ambiguous, the composite."[18] Already these terms echo stereotypes about adolescents: the endless search for identity, rebellion within systems, disrespect for elders and social order, in-betweenness.[19] In queer theory abjection is closely related to understandings of queer as that which falls outside of accepted definitions and realities, and it has been theorized as both a queer subjectivity and a social condition of queerness.[20] Carlsen's "nowhere" period and "troubled, unformed time" resemble a state of abjection as Kristeva describes it. As a concept and a stage of life, adolescence serves as a mechanism for keeping the abject separate from adulthood and adult subjectivity, as we see in configurations like Carlsen's. This is consistent with Kristeva's view of adolescence as a "mythical figure of the imaginary that enables us to distance ourselves from some of our failings, splittings of the ego, disavowals, or mere desires, which it reifies into the figure of someone who has not yet grown up."[21] Like Rose's assertion that "there is no child behind the category 'children's fiction,' other than the one which the category itself sets in place," the adolescent, like the child, is functioning as a repository for adult desire.[22] The affinity of these two assertions, of course, comes out of Rose's and Kristeva's shared investments in psychoanalysis. Kristeva evokes both the child and the adolescent as mythical figures, but it is worth examining how adolescence functions in excess of childhood, and abjection provides a lens to begin that work.

Kristeva defines abjection as that which can be neither subject nor object but that which is radically denied or cast out. In the psychoanalytic vocabulary of self and other, the adult is figured as a subject, the self that experiences the world, and the child is figured as object, that which is accessible only through recollections that take the past self as its object. The adolescent is left to function as the abject, the self that is nowhere, in-between, neither subject nor object. While Kristeva notes that the adolescent could also function as a recollected self, like childhood, Carlsen's description constructs another meaning. The "troubled, unformed time" he describes does not evoke memories of childhood but "nowhere," a state of complete abjection. This choice of words signals a disruption of identity, meaning, and even the progression of time itself. Reading Kristeva's account of abjection next to Carlsen's description of adolescence, we can align the function of the abject with the function of the adolescent as a cultural figure. Kristeva writes, "If the object" (which we might read here as the recollected child), "through its opposition, settles me within the fragile texture of a desire for meaning" (as something we can name, fix, understand), "what is *abject*, on the contrary, the jettisoned object, is radically excluded and draws me toward the place where meaning collapses."[23] Childhood becomes the location we turn to for simplicity, fantasy, and innocence in our desire for meaning. But it is the disruption of meaning that causes abjection, and so this disruption is radically expelled and relocated outside of what we consider *ourselves* in to a stage we call adolescence. We say that adolescents are confused, unstable, hormonal, rebellious, or uncertain in order to distance these qualities in ourselves. This explains why adolescence might be simultaneously identified with what is lesser, Othered, or trivial and yet also weighted with projections of desire and longing.

This formulation of abjection is not only psychoanalytic but also social and phenomenological, according to David Halperin, "an effect of the play of social power." Halperin considers abjection to be a necessary negotiation for queer survival. Though he is writing specifically about gay male subjectivity, he gestures briefly to the applicability of abjection to other groups: "Indeed, even to recognize oneself as being named, described, and summed up by the clinical term *homosexual* (or *faggot* or *queer*) is to come to self-awareness and to a recognition of social condemnation at the very same instant. Abjection therefore has a particularly precise and powerful relevance to gay men as well as to other despised social groups, who have a heightened, and intimate, experience of its social operations." I do not intend to claim that all adolescents are "despised" but instead to point to adolescence as a location for the despised, a container for what is unknown, strange, or queer and also a place where queerness is imagined to be extinguishable. Abjection is one way to describe the negotiation required when one is interpellated as queer, as adolescent, as Other, against that which is good, right, normal, adult, human. It means that one must refashion the terms of dismissal and disgust as a way of surviving, casting them out and bringing them home again with new meaning. Halperin believes that "the concept of abjection presents [this] struggle in a dialectical, dynamic fashion as an ongoing battle for meaning" rather than as static, one-way, or one-dimensional.[24] And, in this dialectic, the possibilities for redefining and reinterpreting the self allow for livable possibilities outside of normativity, outside of the intelligible choices.

Using a psychoanalytic schema suggests the ways adolescence might function on an individual level and on a collective level as part of cultural mythology. The performative functions of adolescence allow us "to see, hear, and read these subjective fluctuations" in both conceptions of the self and the social.[25] These fluctuations do not belong to the stage of adolescence, but to all of us. And the people called adolescents are people who must also grapple with the functions of this category in their negotiations of self and world. If the adolescent, for the adult person, stands in for the parts of self that disrupt identity, meaning, and stability—that is, disrupt adulthood and thus must be cast out—then what happens is that the people called adolescents are interpellated as lacking characteristics supposedly belonging to adulthood, characteristics such as autonomy and a stable sense of self. I want to suggest that none of these characteristics belong to either adolescence or adulthood but that these ways of knowing and being are endlessly entangled, existing in relation to one another, continually moving in and out of one another, always somewhere and nowhere at once.

Returning to Carlsen, we can see how this theorization works in constructions of the "adolescent reader." *Books and the Teen-Age Reader* aims to describe and quantify a particular kind of reader. But who is the adolescent reader? This is an unanswerable question, but one that illustrates the dynamics at play. For Carlsen the adolescent reader represents a problem that must be solved. Many critical works from the past thirty years in the field of young adult literature begin with a chapter that sets out to explain the young adult or adolescent reader.[26] The recurrence of these discussions demonstrates both the ongoing gesture to define and classify the adolescent and the inability to do so. We cannot know the adolescent reader, and to claim such knowledge would be an inevitably essentializing move. These gestures indicate a desire for meaning, the desire to stabilize definitions of adolescence so that the proper reading materials and environments can be provided, so that *good* readers can be made out of adolescents. For those teachers, librarians, editors, and publishers whose work depends on knowing something about the adolescent reader, this question is not only one of theoretical importance but one of practical implication as well. And yet, as we see in Carlen's description and others, the adolescent often stands in for the unknown. The difficulty lies not in lack of research or effort or uniformity in this field of study but in the fact that the adolescent reader is an idea, and, as an idea, it is a fluid and unstable subject position only temporarily occupied by an ever-shifting set of subjects who get called adolescents and readers at certain times, in certain spaces, and not others.

Marc Aronson illustrates my point in an observation he makes in *Beyond the Pale*, writing about his experiences at the Chicago Midway Airport, where a boy avidly reading a fishing book would paradoxically be considered a nonreader in his field of work: "The most avid reader of all, though, was tucked away in the back, where he could concentrate. This was a boy who looked to be eleven or twelve, and he was studying his book with a concentration I saw nowhere else. His book was *How to Catch Yellow-Fin Tuna*. Ironically, from the point of view of the children's and young adult world, because of what he was reading, that boy passionately learning from those dense, printed pages, is a non-reader."[27] Aronson sees the boy's exclusion from the category "reader" to be a problem with the publishing world, a world that must better understand the needs of boy readers. Aronson is right to point to the disjoint between the category of "reader" constructed in discussions of children's and young adult publishing and the actual reading practices of young people. However, I want to suggest that this category of "reader" was never meant to describe actual readers but instead created to represent an ideal reader. This imagined reader, like the fantasy of censors whose children are reading *Catcher in the Rye*, is continually sought after and advocated for but always just beyond the grasp of the institutions intended to care for them. The trouble occurs when this ideological construction is not recognized as ideology but allowed to function as a reference to the reality of adolescent readers. Because this construction cannot refer to actual readers, who

chapter three

are too contingent in their adolescentness and readerness to be summarized by a stable and unified set of characteristics, the category of "adolescent reader" functions as a signifier used to prop up and justify a whole host of adult projections and desires.

Our Whole Future Life

Kristeva's formulations of abjection and adolescence reveal the ways projections can occur in the direction of the past, in recollections of a younger self or in generalizations about youth. These functions of adolescence also play a key role in the logics of reproductive futurism, in which projections occur instead in the direction of the future. What Edelman calls "reproductive futurism" must be understood as part of the historical phenomenon (discussed in chapter 1) in which categories of age began to be harnessed as the necessary and logical means for directing the future. Whereas the figure of the child is often synonymous with an idealized future, the adolescent comes to represent the ruin we are headed for without institutional intervention. Thus, adolescence and childhood have overlapping but separate functions as sites of intense institutional control. While Edelman is most concerned with how the figure of the child is used against queer adults, the logic of reproductive futurism is also used against the people called children and adolescents. When the logic of reproductive futurism is used on children—as an explanation for why they should take a bath, go to school, become a Christian, do chores, or read a book—their lives appear to hang in the balance. These arguments are ominous in the mouths of parents and teachers who are in positions of power to withhold a child's material comforts, food, shelter, approval, and love—in a word, his or her future.

The logic of reproductive futurism is apparent in Lucy Maud Montgomery's 1908 children's classic *Anne of Green Gables*, published only a few years after G. Stanley Hall's exhaustive two-volume work, *Adolescence*. Both Hall's *Adolescence* and a turn-of-the-century novel like *Anne of Green Gables* are particularly relevant for this analysis, emerging out of the post-Darwinian politics of the late nineteenth century, when distinctions between childhood and adolescence were under construction, both symbolically being harnessed as futurity. *Anne of Green Gables* chronicles the mishaps of a precocious, red-haired hero who, despite her best intentions, continually struggles to achieve what is expected of her. Late in the novel Anne reports to her guardian, Marilla, what she learned at school that day about how she should be thinking of the future: "Miss Stacy took all us girls who are in our teens down to the brook last Wednesday, and talked to us about it. She said we couldn't be too careful what habits we formed and what ideals we acquired in our teens, because by the time we were twenty our characters would be developed and the foundation laid for our whole future life." The words "our whole future life" seem to reverberate, getting fainter and fainter with each repetition, as if this ideal "whole future life" were getting further and further away as each moment passes. Anne Shirley is already different from her peers. Adopted by a bachelor brother and spinster sister, she is always just beyond the grasp of the dignity and privilege afforded her best friend, Diana. Anne recounts for Marilla the advice of her teacher: "And she said if the foundation was shaky we could never build anything really worth while on it. Diana and I talked the matter over coming home from school. We felt extremely solemn."[28] Indeed, feeling the weight of responsibility for the *whole future* could be a solemn moment for a person of any age. But what are these habits we must form? What ideals must we acquire? How are we to know which are the *right* ones? "Habits" and "ideals" take on an amorphous quality. The reasoning of reproductive futurism is adaptable to any purpose, any set of instructions, anything imposed on us "for our own good." Reproductive futurism forecloses the need to know why we are doing what we are doing, forecloses the possibility of deciding for ourselves, forecloses the possibility of offering our consent. The future is too important, too urgent, too critical to risk figuring it out ourselves.

Anne, the well-intentioned but flawed child, student, and adopted daughter, repeats the lesson of the day: "And we decided that we would try to be very careful indeed and form respectable habits and learn all we could and be as sensible as possible, so that by the time we were twenty our characters would be properly developed." The scenes of reading in *Anne of Green Gables* dramatize the conflict between Anne's good intentions—her desire to conform—and the possibilities foreclosed for her reading and, arguably, her life. In another account of her day, Anne declares to Marilla: "I never read any book now unless either Miss Stacy or Mrs. Allan thinks it is a proper book for a girl thirteen and three-quarters to read. Miss Stacy made me promise that." This promise, declared near the end of the novel, arrives belatedly. Anne's speech throughout the book is punctuated by literary references, serving both to undermine this declaration and to highlight the breadth of her reading, her desire for aesthetic pleasures. "She found me reading a book one day called *The Lurid Mystery of the Haunted Hall*. It was one Ruby Gillis had lent me, and, oh, Marilla, it was so fascinating and creepy. It just curdled the blood in my veins." One can hear the impassioned Anne describing this perverse reading, relishing the lurid mystery's effects on her body and her spirit. "But Miss Stacy said it was a very silly, unwholesome book, and she asked me not to read any more of it or any like it, but it was agonizing to give back that book without knowing how it turned out. But my love for Miss Stacy stood the test and I did." This act of love serves to normalize Anne, to curb her appetite for lurid mysteries, to normalize her desire by making it conform to the "proper book" of Miss Stacy's choosing. This act of love forecloses possibilities, forecloses pleasure for Anne. Her achievement of self-control does not come without its irony: "It's really wonderful, Marilla, what you can do when you're truly anxious to please a certain person."[29]

Hall's *Adolescence* is also deeply anxious about the corrupting and stunting influences of reading. Hall cites a number of statistical surveys on reading interests and habits during childhood and adolescence. This research is specifically concerned with reading outside of school, reading habits presumed to reflect the individual interests, choices, and vices of young people. Among others Hall gives details from two separate studies, one by E. A. Kirkpatrick and one by E. G. Lancaster, who both report a "reading craze" among youth. Hall notes that Lancaster, in particular, believes that "parents little realize the intensity of the desire to read or how this nascent period is the golden age to cultivate taste and inoculate against reading what is bad." Hall himself seconds this thought: "For the young especially, the only ark of safety in the dark and rapidly rising flood of printer's ink is to turn resolutely away from the ideal of quantity to that of quality." What is so striking about this section on reading is how quickly the reporting of adolescent habits and interests turns to the regulation of those habits and interests. Equally striking is that Hall does not necessarily specify what he means by "quality," even though the studies he cites frequently name genres and even titles chosen by young people themselves. His point, then, is not *what* to read but how to intervene in the reading habits of others, how to impose regulation, how and when teachers and parents can take advantage of this "golden age to cultivate taste and inoculate against reading what is bad."[30]

After reviewing these detailed statistics and reports, Hall ultimately concludes, "While literature rescues youth from individual limitations and enables it to act and think more as spectators of all time, and sharers of all existence, the passion for reading may be excessive, and books which from the silent alcoves of our nearly 5,500 American libraries rule the world more now than ever before, may cause the young to neglect the oracles within, weaken them by too wide reading, make conversation bookish, and overwhelm spontaneity and originality with a superfetation of alien ideas."[31] Importantly, literature and reading are operating here as a measure of human development, an instrument that either supports "proper" development or hinders it. Literature is constructed in the previous passage as doing one or the other; literature is not neutral, not passive, but essential *and* dangerous. Like the admonishment in *Anne of Green Gables* by Miss Stacy, this narrow understanding of literature and reading closes down possibilities. Anne says, "Miss Stacy made me promise," and with that she gives up the book and its pleasures.[32]

What is at stake here is not merely access to varied reading materials but control over what counts as knowledge. Hall depicts a passive reader, one who will accumulate the proper degree of cultural capital through exposure to great works or, alternately, one who will become corrupted by a "superfetation of alien ideas."[33] This depiction of literature and reading ultimately conceals the power dynamics at play, the power dynamics that enable Hall to imagine the adolescent reader as passive and impressionable in the first place. The word "superfetation" is a fascinating choice. Superfetation describes the fertilization of two or more ova from different ovulation cycles resulting in embryos of different ages in the womb. This phenomenon is extremely rare in humans and occurs only sometimes in animals. Hall uses superfetation as a horrifying analogy, where the intellectual development of a young person *becomes* an embryo, and competing ideologies become a second, belated, alien embryo competing for nourishment and putting the development of the first in danger. Exposure to varied perspectives, to more information, to alternative points of view, is positioned as life threatening rather than potentially enlightening, educational, or even ineffectual. The promise required by Miss Stacy, the advice of Lancaster to parents, the cautions offered by Hall—these mechanisms aim to produce and regulate knowledge through an overdetermined conception of the relation between books and readers. These mechanisms favor a single, fixed, stable definition of knowledge and favor maintaining the dominance of that knowledge, its hegemony.

The idea of impressionable youth has survived to this day alongside notions of youth as unreasonable and uncontrollable. Indeed, such conflicting representations can be found in the same texts. Hall wants to develop mechanisms to ensure that the next generation will share his values, priorities, and morals and so imagines an adolescent reader who can be shaped by reading in predictable ways, in ways that Hall himself is predicting. His fantasy is that, if the proper book is chosen by parents and teachers, then the proper adult member of society will result. This oversimplification is a double bind in that it makes the improper book, the book with *other* perspectives, all the more threatening. Neither Hall's fantasy nor his fears account for queer possibilities when readers encounter texts. Neither accounts for the multiple and varied ways that language and meaning diverge and intersect. Reading self, world, or text cannot be managed in the ways necessary to stabilize queer ways of being and knowing. How telling, then, that the adolescent reader is so often imagined in ways that attempt to resolve all that cannot be known about the relation between reader and text, all that cannot be known about the future.

Reading as Suicide

So who gets to say what counts as knowledge? This epistemological question is pressing when it comes to childhood and adolescence, because these groups are not authorized to say what the truth is, often not even the truth about themselves. Roberta Seelinger Trites argues that "power is even more fundamental to adolescent literature than growth. During adolescence, adolescents must learn their place in the power structure. They must learn to negotiate the many institutions that shape them: school, government, religion, identity politics, family, and so on."[34] These power dynamics are frequently dramatized in adolescent literature, and the suspense and humor of these scenes are contingent on social norms that render adolescents without power to interpret their experiences, regardless of their efforts. One such scene appears in *Anne of Green Gables*. Anne is accused of losing Marilla's amethyst brooch, and, even though Anne tells the truth about the brooch, she is banished to her room and forbidden to go to a highly anticipated church picnic until she confesses that she took it. Put into this position Anne fabricates an elaborate confession about taking and losing the pin but is still forbidden to go to the picnic, *now* because she lost the brooch. No matter what Anne says, she does not get to decide what the truth of the matter is, and it is not until Marilla herself later finds the brooch pinned to her shawl that she absolves Anne.[35] The humor and suspense of a scene like this depends on the power dynamic between adult and child. If *Anne of Green Gables* seems old-fashioned, the frequency of these generational misunderstandings in contemporary young adult fiction suggests that they are a cultural trope, one worked and reworked but never resolved.

Joyce Carol Oates dramatizes these power dynamics in her young adult novel *Big Mouth and Ugly Girl*, in which a nerdy, overachieving high school student named Matt Donaghy is accused of threatening to blow up the school. "The detective with the glasses regarded Matt now with a look of forced patience. 'Son, you know why we're here.'"[36] But, of course, Matt has no idea why. Oates plays off the climate of paranoia following the Columbine shootings, depicting school administrators and police officers who cannot relinquish their responsibility to "protect" the school until they can prove that Matt is innocent. None of the other high school students remember Matt's threat, but none can remember his not making one either; caught up in the paranoia themselves, they refuse to defend him against these accusations. There is only one person, an outcast named Ursula Riggs, who remembers the incident in the cafeteria being misconstrued, but even her testimony is not enough to clear Matt's name. The stigma of the accusation remains until the accusers and their motives are exposed.

Over the course of the novel, Matt never has the power to clear his own name, to tell the truth, to say what the truth is.

We find a similar scene in Frank Portman's *King Dork*, in which the narrator, Tom, recounts a mix-up with his parents. He comes home from school one day to find his mother and stepfather disapprovingly waiting for him at the kitchen table, "the entire contents of [his] room" spread out before them, including some unusual reading material.[37] The items on the table include an assortment of gun magazines Tom carries around at school to appear troubled and dangerous so that bullies will avoid him. His parents assume the gun magazines reflect his interests. Tom narrates the scene, but there is very little dialogue. Tom does not even try to offer his parents an explanation, driving home the impotence of his words, his truth.[38] Instead, he stands mute as they say ominous things: "I don't know what to say. Your mother and I hoped to set an example so you would respect and share our values."[39] In this scene, Portman humorously takes the parent-child power dynamic to an extreme, exaggerating its absurdity. The parents enact the scene, interpret the items spread out on the table, and extract a lesson for their adolescent son while he silently accepts the image of him they are constructing at that moment, an image conveyed to the reader as obviously mistaken.

This scene in *King Dork* echoes a dynamic articulated by Hall's *Adolescence* in very different terms, in which these silencing effects are naturalized as developmental symptoms of adolescence itself: "Plasticity is at its maximum, utterance at its minimum. The inward traffic obstructs outer currents. Boys especially are dumb-bound, monophrastic, inarticulate." In his preface he writes, "Character and personality are taking form, but everything is plastic." Later Hall overlaps his discussion of physiological development and character: "Normal muscle tensions are thus of great importance during these plastic, and therefore vulnerable, years." In a discussion of the development of mind and body, "youth" is an agent and an abstract generalization: "It is plastic to every suggestion; tends to do everything that comes to its head, to instantly carry out every impulse; loves nothing more than abandon and hates nothing so much as restraint."[40] One notable aspect of Hall's writing is his tendency to overlap both literal and figurative plasticity, the physiology of the body and the psychology of the mind, as if these two always reflect each other. The connection Hall makes between plasticity and utterance does not serve to explain or excuse the adolescent's silence; rather, it becomes an agent of the adolescent's silencing, an ideological mechanism that prevents the adolescent from being heard, from being recognized. It is a mechanism that makes impossible or irrelevant the adolescent's naming and knowing. Fictional scenes often portray these power dynamics in ways that simultaneously undermine and reinforce common assumptions about adolescence.

In a scene of reading from a late nineteenth-century children's novel, Thomas Bailey Aldrich's 1869 *The Story of a Bad Boy*, which was published in serial form the same year as Louisa May Alcott's *Little Women*, there is another playful, ironic dramatization of adult fears about young people.[41] The main character, Tom Bailey, is an unreliable narrator like Holden Caulfield, except that his exaggerations are more obviously being played for laughs. In a chapter titled "I Become a Blighted Being," Tom recounts the loss of his first love, Miss Nelly, whom he was not old enough to marry. He enacts a parody of adult fears about the naive, overly literal, and impressionable reader. He says, "For a boy of a naturally vivacious disposition, the part of a blighted being presented difficulties." But he tries on the part anyway: "I neglected my hair. I avoided my playmates. I frowned abstractly. I did not eat as much as was good for me. I took lonely walks. I brooded in solitude. I not only committed to memory the more turgid poems of the late Lord Byron—'Fare thee well, and if forever,' etc.—but I became a despondent poet on my own account."[42]

Literature and reading model for Tom how to enact the part of a blighted being, the part of a scorned lover, the part of a despondent poet. The artificiality of this enactment is emphasized by the step-by-step instructions, the absurdity of purposefully neglecting one's hair or taking lonely walks, and these acts are set in opposition to the normal state of being a "naturally vivacious" boy. Literature enables Tom to resist nature, to resist the natural inclinations of boyhood, to "overwhelm originality and spontaneity" with reading.[43] Tom is not depicted as projecting his lovesick feelings onto his reading but rather as being vulnerable to the influence of a book and getting absorbed, swallowed whole by Lord Byron. He *becomes* a blighted being: "I stayed at my desk reading some lugubrious volume—usually The Mysteries of Udolpho, by the amiable Mrs. Radcliffe. A translation of The Sorrows of Werther fell into my hands at this period, and if I could have committed suicide without killing myself, I should certainly have done so."[44] The irony of this scene, in which Tom is not literally at risk for suicide, works as a critique of anxious nineteenth-century social discourses about the negative influence and consequences of adolescent reading. While adult fears about adolescent reading are made to seem overblown and absurd by Aldrich, this scene also undercuts the authenticity or truth of adolescent actions and intentions. Tom's experiences and knowledge of himself are cast as artificial, temporary, and unstable. Tom's consideration of suicide both mocks and confirms the dangers of reading as imagined by the educator and the censor, as imagined by Hall. Tom dramatizes the figure of the passive reader vulnerable to literal interpretation, vulnerable to the invasion and "superfetation of alien ideas" that could derail development altogether and end the young reader's life.[45]

The irony of The Story of a Bad Boy resonates uncomfortably with the irony of The Bell Jar, where the issue of suicide takes on a very different character both in the novel itself and in the cultural mythology surrounding Plath's own suicide a month after The Bell Jar's publication. The queer possibilities suggested by The Bell Jar—Esther's resistance to marriage, to having children, to giving up writing poems—are subsumed by suicide and take on the quality of a cautionary tale. Reading perversely, however, one can interpret Esther's fictional suicide attempt as a representational strategy used by Plath to critique and reject social norms. Michel Foucault writes about suicide in The History of Sexuality as "one of the first astonishments of a society in which political power had assigned itself the task of administering life." Whereas a sovereign ruler (God or monarch) had previously held the right to condemn one to death, biopower reverses this entitlement, claiming instead the right of the nation "to ensure, maintain, or develop its life."[46] The problem of suicide, then, becomes a problem for the nation, a sign that it has failed at its purpose, a sign that it does not in fact have the power to ensure life.[47]

Foucault's formulation of a political power with the "task of administering life" makes possible what Edelman refers to as reproductive futurism. Likewise, Edelman's queer refusal of the future is a refusal of the "life" implied by that future, a life that is not his own but a heteronormative ideal imagined by the institutions charged with fostering life. Foucault understands this institutional power as one that "exerts a positive influence on life, that endeavors to administer, optimize, and multiply it, subjecting it to precise controls and comprehensive regulations."[48] This "positive influence" resembles Hall's intentions as he stated them, his desire to establish "true norms" by which "to both diagnose and measure arrest and retardation in the individual and the race."[49] Foucault describes suicide from the perspective of the nation and its institutions; hence it is *their* astonishment and not the suicidal person's. He does not attempt to account for the intentions of any individual suicide but nevertheless suggests that suicide is a resistance or, more precisely, a refusal, of this power over life: "Now it is over life, throughout its unfolding, that power establishes its domination; death is power's limit, the moment that escapes it; death becomes the most secret aspect of existence, the most 'private.'"[50] Suicide, in this formulation, does not necessarily represent the desire to die or the refusal of life, but a refusal of *the life* intended for the individual by the institutions of family, school, and state. It represents the last available means of resistance when one cannot imagine oneself outside the mechanisms of regulation and control operating under the logic of reproductive futurism.

In *The Bell Jar* Esther recalls something her boyfriend has said to her, something she accepts to be true without question: "I also remembered Buddy Willard saying in a sinister knowing way that after I had children I would feel differently, I wouldn't want to write poems anymore." Even though Buddy's prediction clearly contradicts what Esther knows about herself, she accepts what he says as true because she has heard it before, heard it everywhere, heard it without ever having to remember hearing it. His sinister knowing comes from a much larger institutional and cultural knowing, one that says who a woman is supposed to be and how she is supposed to feel when she is a mother. She has seen it in her own mother, in books and magazines, at engagement parties and weddings, at all the rites of passage presumed to be good and right and normal. Her resistance offers her few alternatives: "So I began to think that maybe it was true that when you were married and had children it was like being brainwashed, and afterward you went numb as a slave in some private, totalitarian state."[51] She does not know if married women are brainwashed or even unhappy, but for her it would feel like being brainwashed, like numbness, like death. Esther says she is never getting married, and this declaration can be read as a form of queer resistance. However, the cost of her resistance—the ways that it may render her illegible in the narrative coherence defined as *life*, illegible as a woman, and therefore as a person—calls into question the very viability of her life.

The cost of resistance is of particular concern when it comes to queer lives. Resistance is the inevitable condition of falling outside of normative conceptions of life, what counts as life. Resistance implies willful choice, but from the outside, from the perspective of power, resistance is the name given to the subject who resists guidance, regulation, and control; resists despite efforts to shape and influence; resists because this queer subject cannot be shaped in the desired ways. Resistance, then, is also the condition of being *unable* to conform; unable to achieve the life that is good, right, and normal; unable to achieve what is understood as human. Even though Esther says she is never going to get married as if this is her conscious choice, these words imply that she *cannot* be made to fit the image of wife and mother Buddy Willard refers to, cannot make herself feel differently, even though that is exactly what is expected of her. The association of adolescence with resistance—or rebellion—sets adolescence in perpetual conflict with adulthood and comes to represent the critical moment of institutional intervention, the moment before it is too late. Rebellion does not describe the actual behaviors of adolescents but instead speaks to the powerful inscription of adolescent agency as inherently resistant, rebellious, and nonconforming regardless of their behavior. Adolescence exists in a curiously contradictory relation to conformity as the place where resistance belongs and is expected and yet where it can still be managed, guided, and, ultimately, grown out of. Adulthood *needs* adolescence to maintain the illusion of stability, the illusion of fixed meaning, the illusion of arrival at these sites of institutional control, normative identity, and reproductive future.

The Unlivable Life

The word "survival" in the cliché *I survived my adolescence* does not suggest that living through adolescence is a given. James Dobson, the founder of the antigay Christian organization Focus on the Family, frames the adolescent years starkly in life or death terms in his 1978 self-help book for teens, *Preparing for Adolescence.*[52] The book begins with a preface directed at parents, using the metaphor of a football game to talk about the "game of life," in which parents are coaches. Dobson explains, the coach "knows there will be little opportunity to teach or guide once the game has begun," and so "his final words are vitally important, and in fact could even change the outcome of the game." The phrase "final words" is somewhat ominous, along with the phrase "vitally important," evoking life-and-death stakes. The preface concludes by reiterating this point, using a degree of condescension one might expect Dobson to save for his younger readers: "Do you get the message? If you have a youngster in the preadolescent age, you should capitalize on this final 'coaching session' prior to the big game. You must take this occasion to refresh his memory, provide last-minute instructions, and offer any necessary words of caution. But beware: if you let this fleeting moment escape unnoticed, you may never get another opportunity."[53] Like the early twentieth-century figures of the child and adolescent (discussed in chapter 2), the "preadolescent age" is imagined by Dobson as pliant and receptive, whereas adolescence is imagined as inaccessible to the parent-coach, the moment when it is too late. The rhetorical question, "Do you get the message?" and the warning, "but beware," play on parental fears. The preface is anxious for parents to do things a certain way, to enact a particular type of control over their children, to reinforce particular ways of being at this so-called critical moment of intervention. Parents are called on to play a vital role in shaping the future of their children and thus the future of society through the management and control of adolescence.

Like the preface for parents, the chapters addressed to adolescent readers continually use language that suggests their very lives are at stake, advocating for specific kinds of behavior and self-regulation to stay safe. But this threatening language also constructs an adolescent reader who is resistant to the book's message or at least likely to be unimpressed by it without the peril implied by its life-and-death stakes. For example, the first chapter introduces another extended metaphor for life: "Imagine yourself driving alone down the highway in a small car." On the highway of life, Dobson explains, the reader has just driven through a town called Puberty and is headed toward one called Adultsville. As if being *alone* and in a small car were not frightening enough, Dobson intensifies his account of the risk involved in this journey:

> But as you round a curve, you suddenly see a man waving a red flag and holding up a warning sign. He motions for you to stop as quickly as possible, so you jam on the brakes and skid to a halt just in front of the flagman. He comes over to the window of your car and says, "Friend, I have some very important information for you. A bridge has collapsed about one mile down the road, leaving a huge drop-off into a dark canyon. If you're not careful, you'll drive your car off the edge of the road and tumble down that canyon, and, of course, if you do that you'll never get to Adultsville."[54]

In this metaphor a young person does not safely, consensually, or calmly sit down to read Dobson's book about how to prepare for adolescence. Instead, the book is a "red flag" and a "warning" that requires the adolescent reader to "jam on the breaks" and "skid to a halt" just before running over Dobson, as if the default status of adolescence is equivalent to speeding down a highway with poor visibility. The stage of adolescence is made equivalent to imminent death with the images of driving off the edge of a bridge and tumbling down a dark canyon in a small car.

If the reader were inclined to interpret the canyon as merely a dark time, perhaps even as a metaphor for adolescence itself as a difficult stage of life, Dobson heads off this possibility by asserting that falling into the canyon means "you'll never get to Adultsville." Likewise, he explains that the reader can't back up (does this mean reverse time?) and so needs to drive slowly, exit the highway, and go around the "ruined" bridge. The possibility of driving around the canyon further suggests that Dobson means the driver's literal life is at stake on the highway, but he further muddles the differences between the ordinary challenges faced by adolescents and the literal risk of death, explaining that the road is life and that he is the flagman: "I want to warn you about a problem that lies down the road—a 'canyon' that *most* teenagers fall into on the road to adulthood." If most teenagers fall into the canyon, it stands to reason that he is not talking about a literal death. And yet, he asserts that "many young people have wrecked their lives by plunging down this dark gorge, but I can show you how to avoid it—how to go around the danger."[55] The phrase "wrecked their lives" overlaps with the language of wrecking the small car by tumbling down the canyon. Like the danger implied by Hall's "superfetation of alien ideas," the ambiguity remains between a literal or metaphorical death for the adolescent reader, overlapping threats to one's bodily safety with ways of being that Dobson merely disapproves of. Thus, the metaphor suggests that teenagers might choose to live in such a way that they are "wrecked"—that is, in ways that Dobson views as equivalent to death. Queer possibilities figure the social's death drive.[56]

Dobson's metaphor does not empower the adolescent reader with a safer car, a map of the road, or the possibility of skilled driving. The danger is not located in the realm of the driver's agency, in which a teenager might be capable of making good decisions or learning from challenging situations. The danger is instead on the road of adolescence itself, which is in disrepair and lacks a detour sign. This metaphor constructs the need for adult control in order for teenagers to survive. In 2009 Allstate Insurance ran a series of full-page ads about teenage driving that appeared on the back covers of the *Economist*, the *New Yorker, Time*, and *Newsweek* magazines as part of a campaign to pass stricter graduated licensing laws at the national level.[57] These ads resurface disabling narratives about adolescent faculties found in Hall's work at the turn of the twentieth century. What for Dobson was an ambiguous metaphor—driving on the road of life—is for Allstate a literal threat wielded to prevent teen driving.

One advertisement features a drawing of an expansive graveyard full of tombstones. The years denoting births and deaths etched on the tombstones indicate that all the graves belong to teenagers. An empty road runs through the middle of the many rows, and the headline reads, "Last Year, Nearly 5,000 Teens Died in Car Crashes." Below this headline, in all capital letters, it reads, "MAKING IT SAFER

Last year, nearly 5,000 teens died in car crashes.

MAKING IT SAFER FOR A TEEN TO BE IN A WAR ZONE THAN ON A HIGHWAY.

Figure 3.2. Allstate Insurance, "Last Year, Nearly 5,000 Teens Died in Car Crashes," advertisement, October 12, 2009, *Newsweek*.

FOR A TEEN TO BE IN A WAR ZONE THAN ON A HIGHWAY" (see fig. 3.2).[58] Another ad in the series reads, "Two Out of Three Teens Admit to Texting While Driving: Some of Them Will Never Be Heard from Again."[59] These ads were part of a campaign for government legislation, the STANDUP Act of 2009, a bill that would create national criteria for graduated driver-licensing laws. Below, in bold, the ad reads, "Let's make sure the STANDUP Act doesn't get buried, or nearly 5,000 more teens could."[60] Like Dobson's message to parents, these ads are aimed at adults—who are potential voters and buyers of insurance—making an appeal to parental concern with the threat of death presumably posed by adolescence.

One of the most insulting of the ads features a headline that reads, "Why Do Most 16-Year-Olds Drive Like They're *Missing a Part of Their Brain?*" What seems like a joke takes a serious turn when this question is answered in all capital letters: "BECAUSE THEY ARE." Be-

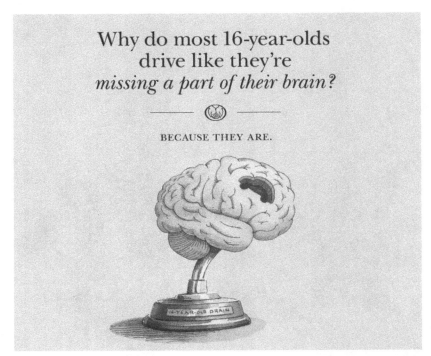

Why do most 16-year-olds drive like they're *missing a part of their brain?*

BECAUSE THEY ARE.

Figure 3.3. Allstate Insurance, "Why Do Most 16-Year-Olds Drive Like They're *Missing a Part of Their Brain?*," advertisement, March 2, 2009, *New Yorker.*

neath these words is a cartoon drawing of the human brain with a car-shaped hole, on a display pedestal labeled "16-Year-Old Brain," as if to (humorously?) indicate the scientific validity of Allstate's claims. The small print below the illustration explains, "Even bright, mature teenagers sometimes do things that are 'stupid.' But when that happens, it's not really their fault. It's because their brain hasn't finished developing. The underdeveloped area is called the dorsal lateral prefrontal cortex. It plays a critical role in decision making, problem solving and understanding future consequences of today's actions. Problem is, it won't be fully mature until they're in their 20s. It's one reason 16-year-old drivers have crash rates three times higher than 17-year-olds and five times higher than 18-year-olds" (see fig. 3.3).[61]

Since most states allow full driving privileges at the age of sixteen, it is strange to correlate these crash rates primarily with brain development rather than with inexperienced driving. Likewise, the claim that the dorsal lateral prefrontal cortex is underdeveloped until after adolescence—a claim resembling nineteenth-century developmental theories—has been challenged by recent studies in neuroscience.[62] Along with these spurious uses of neuroscience, the ads feature some misleading statistical support for their position, declaring that "when states have implemented comprehensive GDL programs, the number of fatal crashes among 16-year-old drivers has fallen by almost 40%."[63] Another ad cites a specific state: "Since North Carolina implemented one of the most comprehensive GDL laws in the country, it has seen a 25% decline in crashes involving 16-year-olds."[64] The fact that both figures specify declines only among sixteen-year-olds suggests that the data has been skewed specifically to promote GDL laws. One of the consequences of GDL laws is the postponement of driving privileges, which means that in states where stricter laws have been passed, there would be fewer sixteen-year-olds on the road. North Carolina's GDL laws, in particular, require a year of supervised driving *after* having completed drivers' education classes and written exams at fifteen years old or later, followed by six months of restricted driving before full driving privileges are granted, thus delaying full driving privileges to at least sixteen and a half years of age. A report on the effects of GDL laws in North Carolina shows a 29 percent decline in crashes among sixteen-year-olds between 1997 and 1999 and only a 1 percent change in crashes involving older drivers, which at first glance appears to confirm that GDL laws are working. However, later in the report we find that the control group of older drivers included only drivers over twenty-one, leaving seventeen- to twenty-year-old drivers out of these figures entirely.[65] If inexperience is the biggest predictor for accidents rather than age, fewer sixteen-year-old drivers would merely shift the majority of accidents to seventeen-year-old drivers in their first year on the road. Much like the fears expressed about adolescent reading throughout the twentieth century, the ad campaign by Allstate hinges on the dangers of adolescence to disempower teenagers rather than framing the problem as one that can be solved through increased competence and skill.

Likewise, Dobson's *Preparing for Adolescence* demonstrates conflicting investments in the capabilities of adolescents, on the one hand characterizing them as incompetent and unpredictable, while on the other hand seeming to need readers to be capable of self-knowledge and self-direction. This conflict is particularly evident in Dobson's chapter on conformity:

> The word "conformity" refers to the desire to be just like everyone else—to do what they do and say what they say, to think what they think and wear what they wear. A conformist is someone who is afraid to be different from the majority; he feels a great need to be like everyone else. To conform means to accept the ideas, the fashion, the way of walking, and the way of talking that is popular at the time. In our society, there is a *tremendous* pressure on all of us to conform to the standards of the group.

In what follows we find out that the dangers of conformity are succumbing to drugs, sex, and secular culture and that "the pressure to conform is at its worst during adolescence," which is why "teenagers often move in 'herds,' like a flock of sheep." Ironically, Dobson's most pressing concern is the risk conformity poses to Christianity. He hopes his readers will have the strength to say, "I'm not going to let *anything* keep me from living a Christian life. In other words, 'I will not conform!'"[66] Dobson does not acknowledge that the "Christian life" he refers to requires another degree of conformity, one that may be even more totalizing than the one he is guarding against. The Christian life requires conformity on the level of behavior, thoughts, feelings, and desires. Dobson encourages his readers to think for themselves so that they will not unthinkingly do as their friends do. But on the other side of this empowering message is an enormous pressure for readers to live as he prescribes, to conform to the norms of the Christian life, and to suspend thinking when it comes to his prescriptions. Dobson's adolescent reader is much like the reader imagined by Hall or by censors in the mid-twentieth century, someone easily manipulated by a book or by "alien ideas," someone who can be led like a flock of sheep.[67]

Dobson calls his book *Preparing for Adolescence*, but what this book is purporting to do is prepare adolescent readers for life, operating under the assumption that adolescence is the crucial moment at which such preparation must take place. Understood this way, the book makes a pretty bold claim. But the category of adolescence relieves Dobson of the need to make a case for his credibility to speak to such matters. Dobson can claim that he knows how to prepare for adolescence because of the cultural assumption that adolescence is an experience we all go through, that anyone who has been through it knows what it's like, and that this experience is transferrable in some way. This is another one of the ways in which the category of adolescence creates the illusion of knowledge about others and the illusion of control over an unpredictable future. Adolescence allows Dobson to presume that he knows how to prepare others for life through careful interventions during this developmental stage. But adolescence is not a preparation for life, as if such preparation were even possible, as if there were a stage before *life*. Adolescence *is* life.

Queer Possibility

When twentieth-century evocations of the adolescent reader, from Hall to Dobson, are read alongside fictional representations of adolescent reading, they speak to the necessity of naming and knowing the self—the urgency of having this power of naming and knowing—not to settle meaning once and for all but to make space for the inevitably unpredictable, unanticipated, and queer ways of being and knowing that surface over the course of a human life. This proposition is not simply a matter of making queerness more "normal" or recognizable within privileged structures, a strategy that will always reinscribe an inside and another queer outside. Rather, we must disrupt the developmental logics that create the *inside* and the *outside* in hierarchical relation in the first place. Kate Bornstein disrupts developmental sequence this way: "I have this idea, that every time we discover that the names we're being called are somehow keeping us less than free, we need to come up with new names for ourselves, and that the names we give ourselves must no longer reflect a fear of being labeled outsiders, must no longer bind us to a system that would rather see us dead."[68] For Bornstein new names are a matter of survival. We appear in the world, seen by others, in part through the identifications made possible by a language that inevitably precedes our arrival. Bornstein's approach to the problem of identity is to destabilize it through an endless, playful, and empowering revision of the names we call ourselves.

Likewise, Judith Butler theorizes this process in creative, productive terms as "practices of instituting new modes of reality," which "take place in part through the scene of embodiment, where the body is not understood as a static and accomplished fact, but as an aging process, a mode of becoming that, in becoming otherwise, exceeds the norm, reworks the norm."[69] Butler's "aging process" does not demarcate a developmental sequence but suggests that aging is a "mode of becoming" marked by moments of fluidity and fixity, but never static, a mode of becoming that "in becoming otherwise" disrupts normative notions of adulthood.

One of the performative effects of categories of age is that they are conceptualizations of human life and developmental sequence imposed on our subjectivity through the process of meaning-making and cohering the self. While the work of critique is primarily concerned with the oppressive functions of language and culture, we can also consider meaning-making from a feminist and queer psychoanalytic perspective in a therapeutic sense—that is, as needed and necessary even if that meaning is always contingent and unstable. One of the insights of feminist psychoanalysis and queer theory is that the meanings we make to understand ourselves are not stable or locatable in an essential self even if it is important that they *feel* right and true. This perspective departs from a social constructivist mode that might position discourse and meaning-making as inherently oppressive. Meaning-making is regulatory in the sense that it cannot help but shape what we see and experience as real and true, but it is not inevitably oppressive even if my analysis has lingered on moments when it *is*. Even Rose acknowledges, "All subjects—adults and children—have finally to take up a position of identity in language; they have to recognize themselves in the first-person pronoun and cohere themselves to the accepted register of words and signs. But it is the shift of that 'have to' from a necessity, which is shared by both adult and child, to something more like a command, which passes from one to the other, that seems to find one of its favourite territories in and around the writing of children's books."[70] This tendency toward command is also what scholars in queer theory and transgender studies expose in the oppressive functions of gender and sexuality, even as gender and sexuality remain foundational to queer and trans subjectivities. Butler explains, "when we speak about *my* sexuality or *my* gender, as we do (and we must) we mean something complicated by it."[71] Like gender and sexuality, categories of age can at once be essential to self-understanding and also subject to self-reflexive analysis and revision. All meaning is constructed, all of what we understand as "the self" is assembled out of projection and fantasy and thus subject to disruption, shifts, and changes. We cannot live without our constructed selves. I think the key is recognizing this—not so that we can do away with fantasy— but so that we can participate more consciously in these meaning- making activities. My analysis is invested in understanding the discur- sive and narrative functions of categories of age while also mobilizing our capacities to shift them in ways that serve us better individually and collectively. This is criticism with a therapeutic function.

I want to end this chapter with a scene from E. R. Frank's *America*, a young adult novel that I read as one writer's compact, interpre- tively rich negotiation of being in the world. On the first page of this young adult novel, we meet a teenager named America, the narrator, who has grown up in foster care and, when we first encounter him, has found himself living in a psychiatric hospital following a suicide attempt. The novel opens with this telling advice from America: "You have to watch what you say here because everything you say means something and somebody's always telling you what you mean."[72] In these lines we can imagine the series of doctors, therapists, nurses— the voices of the institution—telling him what he means, what his words say according to their textbooks, manuals, and procedures. In the institution his words can be made to speak their language.

Everything one says *does* mean something; he's right. "You have to watch what you say" because his words already belong to a language that is not his, a language that is part of discourse, that is part of the shared meanings we use to make sense of one another. But America doesn't speak and instead tells us, "So, I take their medicine and walk around in socks the way they make you, and stay real quiet."[73] In his *not* speaking America does something else. The people around him, perhaps, believe that their words are their own even as they are a part of discourse, part of the institution, part of medicine and psychology, part of culture. But America feels this fraught relation to discourse in a way that they do not. They speak the language of the institution to exercise its power. As the one walking around in socks, America feels these power dynamics and the paradox of his own agency. America knows that "everything you say means something" and that he is not the one who gets to say what it means. It is his relation to discourse that makes him aware of this gap, this fissure of meaning, this excess. And, in that space, he finds the possibility of meaning something else. He finds the queer possibility of not meaning something at all, the queer possibility of meaning *nothing*. His advice to us—and to the adolescent readers of this book—renders this gap visible and suggests both his and our own paradoxical agency to remake meaning or to take pleasure in no meaning at all. His words open to the unknowable, generating meaning and withdrawing from it. It is perhaps no coincidence that Frank's narrator shares a name with the nation, an overlap we might see as a literal and symbolic investment in the fate of both, like the one made by Hall at the turn of the century. The author, a practicing psychotherapist, has written four young adult novels based on her experiences with her patients. In writing an adolescent novel, she mobilizes Kristeva's theory of adolescence to inhabit the subject positions of both doctor and adolescent patient simultaneously.

Kristeva, another practicing psychotherapist, suggests that writing is useful for both patient and analyst during therapy. She does not consider "adolescent" to be a "developmental stage" but an "open psychic structure" accessible at any age through the act of writing. Kristeva overlaps novel writing with the historical conception of interiority and selfhood first manifested in the "nineteenth-century psychological novel." "More real than a fantasy, fiction generates a new living identity," she explains. And, she suggests, "the solitary economy of writing protects subjects from phobic affects."[74] For Kristeva this solitary and realized exercise of fantasy creates the space for a patient to work through problems and to make changes through its access to the open psychic structure she calls "adolescent." Kristeva offers us both adolescence and the novel as fluid spaces that might be read and interpreted, that enable the reconstruction of identity and self, and that sustain the instability of meaning long enough for something else to take shape.

What we invest in the meaning of adolescence, as writers or readers of these texts, is really for ourselves. What makes Kristeva's theory so useful is the overlap of self, text, and world in which we are situated as a kind of reader. But there is no place within psychoanalysis to finally settle on meaning. If meaning is not inherently stable, the question ceases to be what do things mean, but why do we continue to find certain meanings and not others? What do we desire? Even, what do we need? My analysis of the adolescent reader in this chapter focuses on locations where meanings seem to have stabilized to fulfill a desire or need over the course of the twentieth century. What we find in fiction are meanings also subject to cultural patterns, but they are also open to interpretive flexibility, both reading and writing available to us as complex negotiations of being in the world. Whether adolescent, child, or adult, we are all pressing at the limits of language and culture, all bound by institutional discourses and yet full of queer possibility; we are all dutiful and unpredictable, impressionable and rebellious readers.

chapter 4

TOWARD AN ETHICS OF RELATIONALITY

The child has a primary need from the very beginning of her life to be regarded and respected as the person she really is at any given time.
> —Alice Miller, *The Drama of the Gifted Child*

The strongest lesson I can teach my son is the same lesson I teach my daughter: how to be who he wishes to be for himself. And the best way I can do this is to be who I am and hope that he will learn from this not how to be me, which is not possible, but how to be himself.
> —Audre Lorde, *Sister Outsider*

This chapter undertakes a deeply personal task—thinking through the ethical stakes of relationality through categories of age. On the one hand, this task is motivated by and for the people called children and adolescents who are mistreated and exploited without recognition within the structures of the family and society. I am interested in articulating the logics that shape this mistreatment as well as exploring ethical alternatives for being with and relating to young people. On the other hand, this task is also about imagining ethical alternatives for relationality more broadly and for the particular patterns of hierarchy and domination that have shaped social and material relations since at least the nineteenth century. One of the difficulties in conceptualizing and practicing a relational ethics with regard to young people is that varying degrees of dependency can work to eclipse perceptions of autonomy, personhood, and worthiness of respect. And yet, physical, legal, or financial dependency describes the social condition of children and adolescents today, as well as the social condition of many adults, rather than the natural condition of any particular stage of life. Projecting the condition of dependency onto the figure of the child denies the profound degree to which *all* relationality involves interdependency and mutual entanglement. Anna Mae Duane notes that it is our cultural and political "investment in autonomy that renders the child's dependence and vulnerability a block to full engagement and full humanity."[1] Thus, recognizing the interdependency and vulnerability of childhood provides the opportunity to reshape ethical considerations for all human relationships.

Karen Sánchez-Eppler makes this point another way, arguing that children may "offer a more accurate and productive model for social interaction than the ideal autonomous individual of liberalism's rights discourse ever has."[2] John Wall calls for a similar ethical restructuring through a methodology he calls "childism," arguing that a "fuller understanding of children's lived experiences in the world can transform basic ethical assumptions and norms, regardless of whether one is considering particular issues concerning children or not." He explains that just as "feminism has reconstructed ethical ideas, for both women and men, around new understandings of gender, agency, voice, power, narrative, care, and relationality," the methodology of "childism should similarly rearrange the ethical landscape around experiences such as age, temporality, growth, difference, imagination, and creativity."[3] This chapter participates in this ethical project with particular attention to the category of adolescence. Though I have shown how the logic of adolescence is one we would be well to do without, the category of adolescence persists, organizing the psychic structure of adult subjectivity while also naming persons within relational and institutional contexts. Categories of age organize the relation between self and other, urgently requiring new logics for thinking about relationality and our ethical responsibilities to one another and the world.

One strategy deployed in identity politics for the purpose of achieving social justice is to lay claim to the human, to say that those who have been oppressed and excluded *are* human and thus deserving of rights, dignity, and respect. This rhetorical strategy can be temporarily effective insofar as the category of human works to achieve social justice aims in specific contexts, but the exclusionary functions of the category of human itself persist, despite such efforts. Judith Butler considers this effect in relation to sex and gender, which operate "through exclusionary means, such that the human is not only produced over and against the inhuman, but through a set of foreclosures, radical erasures, that are, strictly speaking, refused the possibility of cultural articulation."[4] We saw how these exclusions work on the level of gender, race, class, and sexuality in late nineteenth- and early twentieth-century categorizations of the criminal, homosexual, ethnic, savage, prostitute, deviant, primitive, queer, and delinquent in chapter 2.

Critical race studies, trans and queer theory, and feminist materialism approach this problem through an interrogation of the human, seeking to redefine ethical relations to bodies, world, and matter beyond the logic of the human and the subject. We might be tempted, upon recognizing the ways that children and adolescents are disenfranchised by categories of age, to argue that *they* are human and thus deserving of rights and respect. This strategy does not escape the exclusionary functions of the human, and it so often falls short as a rhetorical strategy because categories of age have a paradoxical relation to the construction of the human in the first place. The human is made possible by childhood while simultaneously locating the achievement of human status beyond childhood and adolescence. Thus, it is the child's status as an "adult in the making" and "not yet that which it alone has the capacity to become" that Claudia Castañeda argues is where its "availability—and so too its value as a cultural resource—lies."[5] The child exists both as the definitional locus of the human—representing its values, investments, and belief systems—and as a malleable form that is not-yet-human.[6] The adolescent sometimes shares in this figuration and at other times becomes the embodiment of degeneration, the failed-to-become human, both childhood and adolescence working together to manage and contain a range of fantasies and fears.

Rebekah Sheldon argues that the figure of the child epitomizes and reinforces the human, standing in "as a figure for life-itself" in its most durable forms, and yet it makes visible "the autonomy and vitality of the nonhuman and the nonliving" while binding "the realization of nonhuman vitality back into the charmed circle of the human." Resisting this binding effect, Sheldon finds the potential to see the "emergent energies of posthumanity" in figurations of the child.[7] Sheldon's work suggests a posthuman vision of the world that the figure of the child has the potential to make visible. The usual ways of thinking about categories of age function as a trap in which we can't imagine ethical relations to someone or something other than human, in which we can't conceptualize agency as something other than entirely absent or belonging exclusively to an autonomous subject. But what if we remove "human" from the criteria determining who (or what) is and is not deserving of ethical consideration?

This chapter frames ethical considerations for relationality most commonly between one person and another, primarily concerned with the question of what should we as people should *do* and *not* do, but the pathway to our most ethical engagements with one another and the world requires a posthuman frame. Karen Barad writes, "What is needed is a robust account of the materialization of *all* bodies—'human' and 'nonhuman'—including the agential contributions of all material forces (both 'social' and 'natural'). This will require an understanding of the nature of the relationship between discursive practices and material phenomena; an accounting of 'nonhuman' as well as 'human' forms of agency; and an understanding of the precise causal nature of productive practices that takes account of the fullness of matter's implication in its ongoing historicity."[8] Sheldon offers the increase in earthquakes caused by fracking in Oklahoma as an example of "life's autonomous agency," in which bedrock imagined to be passive and inert demonstrates the "responsiveness of stone."[9] For Sheldon a posthuman awareness invites more ethical relations to the world as well as a reckoning with the agency of matter. One of the problems with conceptualizing the agency of young people is not the fact that they have varying degrees of it—whereas adults presumably have full agency—but rather our inability to imagine forms of agency beyond the bounds of the human.

Castañeda describes what this recognition of the "agency of nature" can do for our understanding of even an infant, "a natural-cultural body, always already formed through the semiotically and materially specific processes of conception, growth, and birthing that are constitutive of its particular making." She explains, "The new-born's existence cannot be known fully by adults because that existence is the effect of an agency that is excessive to adult knowledge." Like Sheldon's example of Oklahoma's bedrock responding to fracking with an exponential increase in earthquakes, the embodied and relational responsiveness of an infant is imagined to be inert and passive even in the presence of the radical changes infants can make to their surroundings. Castañeda writes, "To 'theorize' this subject is to inhabit a different mode of knowing, necessarily partial and situated, that works always in and through the fact of not knowing, of not being able to know fully. This not knowing does not entail a refusal to make claims in and to the world. Instead it establishes the existence of plural 'real' worlds, and also of ontic politics as the form of politics through which these pluralities become intelligible, and can be more effectively negotiated."[10] In Castañeda's reformulation what is necessary is an understanding of nature and materiality itself as agentic, an insight drawn from feminist science studies.[11] This insight shifts our understanding of adult agency in addition to acknowledging that even an infant has agential capacities that should not be denied or repressed. It has never been the case that infants did not have agential capacities but rather that our ability to recognize those capacities has been routinely eclipsed by the usual ways of thinking and talking about agency and autonomy in the first place.

Exposing the functions of categories of age allows us to reconceptualize not only what a child or adolescent is but also the complexity, vibrancy, and queerness of the world that categories of age serve to manage and contain. Rather than attempting to elevate the child or adolescent to the status of the human or the autonomous liberal subject, these analytic reversals attempt to pry open childhood and adolescence to reconceptualize subjectivity itself as an ethical entanglement of meaning, matter, and world. This analysis takes as a starting point that *all* our ways of making meaning are radically contingent and unstable, even as we *need* the illusion of cohesion and stability to survive. There is no essential truth or reality that I aim to uncover, only the mechanisms of that meaning-making activity around a particular set of historically locatable logics. This is the goal of the therapeutic exercise: to see ourselves more clearly, to shift narratives that no longer serve us, to construct meaning anew.

The "Good" Child

At the start of Alfie Kohn's self-help parenting book, *Unconditional Parenting*, he tells the story of riding on a plane with a small child. He noticed that when the flight was over, many other passengers praised the child's parents with compliments like, "He was so good during the flight!" Kohn explains that, in this context, the word "good" referred to how little the child was noticed, how quiet he was, and how little trouble he was to the adults around him. Kohn reflects on this moment: "I realized that this is what many people in our society seem to want most from children: not that they are caring or creative or curious, but simply that they are well behaved. A 'good' child—from infancy to adolescence—is one who isn't too much trouble to us grown-ups." The "good" child reflects cultural assumptions about the presumed passivity and lack of agency in childhood. The child's actions on the environment are presumed to lack purpose or direction and thus justify suppression and adult control. In the past, Kohn explains, this control was often achieved through authoritarian means—using threats, violence, and punishment, including physical violence—whereas today "good" behavior is more likely to be elicited through rewards and praise. But Kohn warns, "Do not mistake new means for new ends. The goal continues to be control."[12]

Kohn poses the question to parents: Do we really want children who are simply obedient or compliant? And what kind of adults will these strategies produce? He describes the effects of "compulsive compliance," in which "children's fear of their parents leads them to do whatever they're told—immediately and unthinkingly," as well as the "emotional consequences of an excessive need to please and obey adults" at the cost of a secure and independent sense of self. Certainly, from the perspective of institutional projects of control, the traits of obedience and compliance have been desirable in children *because* they produce dutiful, productive adult citizens, adults who respect the social order and the status quo, who do what they "should." But Kohn appeals to parents: "The critical question is what kind of people we want our children to be—and that includes whether we want them to be the kind who accept things as they are or the kind who try to make things better." He acknowledges, "This is subversive stuff—literally."[13]

The relational strategies Kohn proposes require adults to see children as whole people even when they are small—whole people impacted by their environment and who seek to have an impact. Children are *not* the whole people they will become, but whole people *now*.

In *The Drama of the Gifted Child*, the renowned psychologist and writer Alice Miller describes accomplished, ambitious, productive adults, who as children were praised for being advanced beyond their years, who toilet-trained early and easily, who competently took care of younger siblings, and who didn't cry or complain or become a problem for parents. Miller writes, "According to prevailing attitudes, these people—the pride of their parents—should have had a strong and stable sense of self-assurance. But the case is exactly the opposite." Such people excel at all that they do, but they report feelings of depression and emptiness as soon as the grandiosity of each new accomplishment wears off: "Then they are plagued by anxiety or deep feelings of guilt and shame. What are the reasons for such disturbances in these competent, accomplished people?"[14] Perhaps many academics, like myself, see themselves in Miller's description. Certainly, it seems that academia was designed to both soothe and perpetuate such a cycle, anxiously working toward the next rung of achievement only to find that there are more after it, that one never arrives at the end, that one is never just enough as they are.[15] We might also consider the dynamics Miller describes as an adult form of "compulsive compliance," the result of the parenting strategies of praise and rewards that Kohn criticizes in *Unconditional Parenting*, particularly when those strategies are most successful at eliciting "good" behavior from children.[16] However, Miller also theorizes a subtler relational dynamic between parents and children. Miller finds that as children, these high-achieving adults had a primary caregiver "who at the core was emotionally insecure and who depended for her equilibrium on her child's behaving in a particular way."[17] She describes a conditional form of relational attachment that relies on the *use* of the child to meet the parent's emotional needs. Though more personal, more intimate, this form of exploitation is not so different from the use of the figural child or adolescent throughout the twentieth century to stand in for society's deepest needs or fears about itself—the promise of futurity, the limits of our control, the embodiment of a true origin, or the edge of unknowability.

Miller explains that these gifted children were able to intuit and adapt their behavior to the emotional dysregulation and projections of their primary caregivers, becoming what the parent needed at the expense of developing and inhabiting an authentic sense of self. The authentic self should be understood not as a stable or originary source of identity but rather as an ongoing narrative self-determination or state of becoming that is possible under conditions of entanglement and dependency but repressed when survival is at stake. Though few parents might go so far as to actually starve or kill their children, the threat of spanking or being sent to bed without dinner are common and still socially accepted forms of punishment. Likewise, Kohn finds that giving and withholding love as behavioral modification strategies are no less threatening to a child's very survival than authoritarian methods. For the "gifted child" described by Miller, becoming what the parent needed "secured 'love' for the child—that is, his parents' exploitation" and being needed in this way "guaranteed him a measure of existential security."[18] As adults, this skill is "then extended and perfected," intuiting the needs of others and seeking to be "good," successful, admired, or needed to secure love. In a moment of self-implication, she remarks that it is "no wonder they often choose to become psychotherapists later on," dedicating their lives to intuiting the needs of others.

The depression and feelings of emptiness that result from living this way are caused by the repression of an authentic sense of self, one necessary to feel truly loved and connected to others *as oneself*. Miller writes, "What would have happened if I had appeared before you sad, needy, angry, furious? Where would your love have been then? And I was all these things as well. Does this mean that it was not really me you loved, but only what I pretended to be?"[19] Lindsay C. Gibson describes the emotional neglect from being raised by what she calls "emotionally immature parents," who "may look and act perfectly normal, caring for their child's physical health and providing meals and safety" but who are not capable of seeing their children as they are or creating an emotional connection with them: "The loneliness of feeling unseen by others is as fundamental a pain as physical injury, but it doesn't show on the outside. Emotional loneliness is a vague and private experience, not easy to see or describe. You might call it a feeling of emptiness or being alone in the world."[20] What is troubling to me is that these forms of abuse described by Kohn, Miller, and Gibson are built in the very definition of a child as the fulfillment of parental or societal needs. Thus, the "good" child is not a bother to anyone, does not appear to even have a "self" to be sacrificed to others, but is imagined as there *for* others from the beginning.

These accounts, however, reframe the actions and personhood of children themselves against accepted societal norms. The child is recognized as intelligent, intuitive, and adaptable to the adult's unconscious needs in sophisticated ways. But the child is not a fully independent agent either. These interactions are not reducible to simplistic power dynamics, in which adults have power and children are disempowered, but rather illustrate our entanglements in the ethics of relationality. Relating to another person should not be conditional upon someone becoming what you need them to be but rather should constitute the attempt to see and respond to who is really in front of you at any given moment. Miller writes that "the child has a primary need from the very beginning of her life to be regarded and respected as the person she really is at any given time." That is, the child is not potentiality, the not-yet-adult, or the promise of the future. For Miller the child is a person. And she understands this basic requirement to apply even to an infant, whom she sees as a being both worthy of regarding and able to respond, even in a nonverbal state of complete dependency: "This is beautifully illustrated in one of Donald Winnicott's images: the mother gazes at the baby in her arms, and the baby gazes at his mother's face and finds himself therein . . . provided that the mother is really looking at the unique, small, helpless being and not projecting her own expectations, fears, and plans for the child. In that case, he would not find himself in his mother's face, but rather the mother's own projections."[21]

As I have shown throughout the critiques in this book, this form of exploitation, the *use* of the child to meet adult needs, is built into the social conception of what a child is in the first place. If such a relation appears natural and justified according to the definitional bounds of what a child is, then we must reckon with the degree to which exploitation is foundational to the Western idea of childhood itself. Miller's analysis takes us beyond a critique of the figural child as a repository for adult desire to theorize an alternative relation, one that accounts for the ethical responsibility we have to regard our entanglement with all beings and the material world alongside who or what they are in their present becomings. What this means is not that such regard will result in an objective or stable truth about others but rather that our gaze is a performative one in which the most ethical practice is to not-know until the moment of contact, to allow each encounter to shift what we think we know, and to acknowledge that the frame of our regard has the potential to change the reality of what appears before us.

Though Miller's books envision an ethical relation between parents and children, her son, Martin, suggests that she was not able to practice this ethical relation in life. *The Drama of the Gifted Child*, Miller's first book, was published nearly thirty years after the birth of her son. Shortly after Martin was born, he was given away to an acquaintance for two weeks before being taken in by his aunt, where he lived for the first six months of his life, and he was later sent away to a children's home for two years when his sister was born, who as an infant was also sent away for a year. Martin explains that his primary attachments were to maids or nannies, who were often fired and replaced, and that his parents primarily spoke Polish to each other when he was in their presence, while he knew only German. His father was cruel, physically and sexually abusive, and his mother preoccupied, emotionally distant, and often away from home. As a young adult, she pursued a close relationship with him, but in a dysfunctional, controlling, and exploitative way that Martin acquiesced to until his late thirties. When he started to break away and establish his independence from her, she became increasingly hostile and manipulative. His book includes a letter from her during this time, illustrating abusive and dysfunctional dynamics she would have condemned in her books. In her letter she uses her theories of childhood on him but turned against him, posturing as care but figuring her son as *her* abuser, accusing him of becoming like his father. The narrative she constructs in this letter removes her from her role as mother and her responsibility toward him, instead condemning Martin for his feelings and scapegoating his father as the source of all his anger and pain. Martin writes, "She effectively made me feel like a monster she wanted to destroy."[22] What are we to make of this great contradiction?

I must confess that reading Miller's letter to her son paralyzed me. *The Drama of the Gifted Child* holds great resonance for me on both a personal and intellectual level, as it has for many people. For this reason I was ready to be skeptical of Martin's version of his mother, but her letter represented her by her own hand, and the gaslighting, shaming, projections, and attacks were familiar to me. For a moment I was not sure if I could write about *The Drama of the Gifted Child* at all anymore. Martin explains how difficult it was to betray his mother, even after her death, how his intentions for writing were his own healing and a sense of justice. Importantly, he says that he does not believe his history with his mother "negates the merits of her books and the importance of her theories." In fact, he deploys her methods in his own work as a therapist, and her methods were used in his own process of healing in his relationship with her. He explains, "Her books, and her paintings as well, were developed in a wide, creative space where Alice Miller could be herself, free from her grievances. Unfortunately, she split off this place from her real existence."[23] Martin believes that the cause of this splitting was dissociation from her own war trauma during the Holocaust. Martin's evaluation of his mother grants her a degree of complex personhood and compassion that she could not extend to him or to her own mother.[24] In her letter to Martin, Miller describes her mother in one-sided language as all bad—"Why did I need sixty years to see how cruel, destructive, exploitative, thoroughly mendacious and loveless my mother was?"—only to then create a parallel with Martin's father and then Martin himself.[25]

Unprocessed trauma means that anyone else can become the symbol of that trauma, even and especially one's own children. Staying in control of one's children, then, becomes symbolic of preventing future trauma, preventing children from becoming what you most fear. Kohn writes that parents do not love their children unconditionally because they believe "acceptance without strings attached will just be interpreted as permission to act in a way that's selfish, demanding, greedy, or inconsiderate," which "is based on the deeply cynical belief that accepting kids for who they are just frees them to be bad because, well, that's who they are." The nineteenth-century evolutionary figurations of the child discussed in chapters 1 and 2 reflect this cynical belief, what Kohn calls a "prejudice" toward children that is not based in evidence.[26] For a parent with unprocessed trauma, difficulty relinquishing control, and discomfort with the emotions of others, any individuation or expression in the child risks triggering a trauma response and thus the desire to contain, control, and dominate the threat. Here we see Miller narrate these effects while projecting them onto Martin: "And in your behavior towards me, you let me experience both, as if I were little Martin and you the big boss, who distributes on a whim alternately 'love' and beatings on me and wishes to remain clueless." Though *she* is the one replaying her trauma with her son, positioning herself as the child and her son as the "big boss," she imagines that *he* is the one replaying his childhood trauma with her. She fights him as she fights her own abusers, transparently projecting her pain on to him: "I cannot and will not accept the role of victim. No longer will I allow myself to be tormented or seduced, not even by my own son." She cannot grapple with her likeness to her mother, who "was a cruel human being," who "destroyed the lives of her two children without any trace of a guilty conscience, while she believed herself to be loving and caring."[27] She cannot tolerate the notion that, as Martin's mother, she might play a role in his pain or have a role to play in his healing. Controlling Martin is necessary for Miller to feel a sense of control over all that was wrong in the world.

For both the categories of childhood and adolescence, we can find histories of degradation and idealization mirroring this pattern of projection. These moves toward negative or positive characterizations operate similarly as two different forms of exploitation, putting categories of age to work for those looking *at* children rather than for children themselves. As for childhood the nineteenth century aligned childlikeness with animality, the primitive, the savage, and the not-yet-human at the same time as figuring the child as innocence, pricelessness, potentiality, and the future. As for adolescence the twentieth century imagined the teen years as out of control, deviant, criminal, and the failed-to-become-human at the same time as it idealized youthfulness, rebellion, and freedom from adult responsibility. Neither the negative nor the positive characteristics in these lists describe categories of age from the perspective of *being* a child or adolescent. These contradictory characteristics emerge out of the shared function of categories of age as a hermeneutic of self, a normalizing technology, a temporal location for adult projections and disavowals. In this capacity the logic of categories of age sustains normativity and existing social hierarchies, sorting desirable and undesirable parts of self between the past, present, and future while mapping the social world onto a temporal slope toward or away from the achievement of human status. To combat these harmful effects of categories of age, the people called children and adolescents, as well as the people who live under any sign of social difference, must be understood as having complex personhood that spans the full spectrum of human experience—including desire, emotion, and will as well as the capacity to do harm, fail, or die. But this alone does not account for the ethical entanglement of human relationality.

The Drama of the Gifted Child suggests that there is a way for parents to see their children as separate from themselves, as they *really* are, as if such a thing exists apart from the child's relationship to the parent in the first place. And, in one sense, I would agree that this is a simple and effective way to correct the usual ways of seeing children. However, this correction assumes a separability that is not possible in the entanglement between meaning and matter. To some degree the entanglement of Miller's own identity and experience with her son *is* inevitable—and to some degree our projections are inescapable. I do not mean to suggest that Miller's emotional abuse of her son is inevitable. However, we define and experience ourselves in relation to others, and others in relation to us, and this acknowledgment is precisely how to reframe our ethical responsibility to one another so that we can do better. Perhaps Miller might have acknowledged the ways she was like her mother through their shared history of generational trauma and, using her own method for healing, return to herself with the love and acceptance that her mother could not give her. Only then could she love Martin *as he was* and not as she needed him to be. What is needed is a radical acceptance of the parts of self and other that have been disavowed, a grappling with the limits of our control, and the healing of trauma, so that when parents see the full range of feeling and human experience in their children (as they inevitably will), they can see them as part of a whole—not as the resurrection of their abusers but as people who are struggling to be heard, who are capable of doing great harm, but who need love and acceptance in the whole of who they are, even imperfect, flawed, or hurting.

The "good" child described by Kohn and Miller suggests a set of relational dynamics that we do not escape even as adults who live apart from our parents. This does not mean that as children or adults we do not have autonomy, but it suggests that autonomy is not a characteristic independently located outside parental perceptions and actions. Autonomy might be better theorized as an ethical principle of relationality itself, created *through* the parent's actions toward the child. It is the recognition of both autonomy and mutual entanglement that creates an ethical practice of autonomy, our obligations to one another, and the limits of our control over others. Likewise, the child's authentic self is not somehow determined outside the perceptions of the parent but within it, made possible by the interpretive space of the parent's regard and respect, a recognition of the entanglement of meaning, matter, and world within an ethical practice of relationality.

The "Bad" Adolescent

Alongside the social construct of the "good" child is the "bad" adolescent, these two figurations working together to contain a range of fantasies and fears. Even when teens are behaving responsibly, they can be perceived as antagonistic, as Florida state representative Elizabeth Porter demonstrated in 2018 with her disparaging comments about the survivors of the Parkland High School shooting. When these young people asked Florida lawmakers to pass stricter gun control measures, she responded, "Are there any children on this floor? Are there any children making laws? Do we allow the children to tell us to pass a law that says, 'No homework' or 'You finish high school at the age of 12' just because they want it so? No. The adults make the laws."[28] Porter at once positions Parkland High School students as rebellious teens and petulant children, using the categories of both childhood and adolescence to discredit them, as if their civic participation were motivated by self-absorbed whimsy rather than legitimate concerns about safety from mass shootings. Granted, many teenagers enjoy good relationships with their parents and other adults despite these functions of adolescence as a category. But I am troubled by the ways that the category, by its very definition, is called upon to deny or erase the complex personhood of young people. Even supposedly well-meaning self-help books for parents deploy similarly dehumanizing tactics, as we see in Michael J. Bradley's *Yes, Your Teen Is Crazy! Loving Your Kid without Losing Your Mind*. The book refers to "groundbreaking research that is finally proving with science what you've come to suspect through your pain: *Your kid is crazy.*" Bradley admits this is just a humorous way (to him and presumably other parents) of saying what "is now becoming accepted more and more as neurological fact," that *"adolescents are temporarily brain-damaged."*[29]

Like the Allstate ads discussed in chapter 3 or the constructions of adolescence in nineteenth-century racial science in chapter 2, the category itself functions to encompass phenomena excluded from the presumed innocence of childhood and the presumed normativity of adulthood. Young people perceived as "good kids" within the category of adolescence appear so only through their proximity to normativity, and the arrival at adolescence is imagined to be fraught with danger even for them. This is how, year after year, we can find claims that today's teenagers are at more risk than ever before, plagued by more drug addiction, crime, gangs, teen pregnancy, STDs, depression and anxiety, antisocial behavior, and suicide than any generation of young people in history.[30] Suicide represents the ultimate fear played out through the category of adolescence—the end of life itself—while at the same time unambiguously marking the absolute limits of our knowledge and control of others.

Countless studies and media reports claim that teen suicide is on the rise and that young people are taking their own lives at younger ages and in greater numbers than ever before. Take, for example, the article "Internet a 'Lord of the Flies': Teen Suicide Rise after Instagram, Snapchat Began" from a three-part series in the *Orange County Register* in 2018. The article focuses on social media as the cause for the increase in suicides, playing on parental fears of the unknown: "High school today is not your mother's high school. It's not even the high school that millennials experienced."[31] The problem is that "friendships cross school boundaries and teens know far more than even the saviest [sic] parents realize," but simultaneously the opposite problem occurs, in which "kids are sitting home alone, disenfranchised and disconnected," according to a Los Angeles psychologist. She states, "It's very dark the way social currency is wielded. They watch the Kardashians and don't know how to respond."[32]

Later the article explains that teens think they need to be perfect and put too much emphasis on getting into the right college and getting good grades, while social media creates a competitive social environment and unrealistic expectations. But also they are binging on the Netflix show 13 *Reasons Why* and trapped in "a victim mentality." Another expert says teens are missing validation, and "the social media plague of staged 'happy' photos creates the opposite of validation."[33] My rehearsal of this contradictory list of reasons for teen suicide illustrates how such speculations are more reflective of the fears, investments, and desires of the people making them than they are meaningful diagnoses of a social problem. Perhaps there is a social problem at the root of some teen deaths, but the generalizations made in this article reflect social fears about adolescents more broadly, framing suicide as further evidence of their *inability* and immaturity, blaming new media and technology as if it had more agency than young people themselves, suggesting that what young people need most is protection *from* themselves. The question of "why are teens killing themselves" is posed exclusively as "what is wrong with teens" and the problem framed as specifically *adolescent*, as if they do not share the same world and live under similar social conditions as adults today. If speculating about larger social problems, one might ask instead, "Why doesn't life feel livable to teens?" or "What social changes would make life more livable?"

That said, what are we to make of the fact that teen suicide may *not* be on the rise? Or that teens take their own lives at a lower rate than any other age group besides children? Philip Graham, drawing on data from western Europe, explains that it "is extremely unusual for a child under the age of 14 to commit suicide. The official figures suggest that less than one in a million children aged 10–14 years end their own lives each year, compared to 60 times that number aged 15–19 years. By the end of the teens the rate of suicide has more or less stabilized and remains the same throughout the whole of adult life, perhaps with a slight increase in the elderly."[34] In the United States, data shows the rate of suicide for children under the age of fifteen at or below 1.0 out of every 100,000 between 2000 and 2016, with a rate of 1.34 in 2017. The rate of suicide is the lowest for ages fifteen to twenty-four, at 14.46 in 2017, for example, showing a trend of steadily increasing with age until it peaks at 20.2 per 100,000 for ages forty-five to fifty-four and then decreasing for ages fifty-five to sixty-four and sixty-five to seventy-four until it peaks again to 20.1 for those over eighty-five.[35] Why is no attention given to the fact that teenagers are the *least* likely to take their own lives than any other age group?

Notice also that the age designation of fifteen to twenty-four includes a significant number of adults in with adolescents. If we split this group into two, the numbers for ages fifteen to nineteen are significantly lower than they are for the ages of twenty to twenty-four, at 11.8 per 100,000 in 2017.[36] The rate for ages twenty to twenty-four is 17.0, which is comparable but still lower than ages twenty-five to thirty-four at 17.53 per 100,000 in 2017 and lower than any other age group besides children and ages sixty-five to seventy-five.[37] Using data from 2000 to 2015, the suicide rate for ages twenty to twenty-four is consistently between 55–65 percent higher than it is for ages fifteen to nineteen.[38] What these numbers suggest is not that teens are more impulsive and out of control than adults but that adolescence marks the beginning of *adult* behavior like suicidality and that increases in the suicide rates of younger people mirror state and national trends among adults. All data on the increasing rate of suicide are based on numbers going back only to the year 2000, when suicide rates were at an all-time low since the 1970s.[39] And a recent study acknowledges that the "observed increase in suicide may reflect more accurate reporting, possibly due to coroners and families being more willing to label the death a suicide."[40] Whether these trends have larger social causes or are due to more accurate reporting, any speculations about suicide should *not* consider teen suicide a separate epidemic somehow distinct from the suicides of adults.

In *Framing Youth* Mike Males documents the repeated false assertions in the media and research studies alike that suicide rates have been increasing among adolescents in the state of California, showing how suicide rates in the mid-1990s were in fact the lowest they had been since the 1960s. Males writes, "If I had to pick the weirdest, most blatant, most obtuse pack of lies top authorities tell about adolescents, it would be the unanimous insistence that California teenage suicide is skyrocketing." Males shows how expert after expert repeatedly made the same claims alongside sensationalistic media reports, despite the fact that "by 1996, California teenage suicide and self-destruction stood at its lowest level in at least 35 years." However, Males notes that these statistics were "not raised to point out that kids were *less* self-destructive, or examine why." Why exaggerate the threat of teen suicide? Males suggests that "the original motive might have been benign: to maintain services in a time of conservative cutbacks." He sees this "expert-fabricated epidemic" as needing an "expert-fabricated teenage psychology to explain," in which "institutional interests were locked into one, unvarying statement about adolescents: they're worse than ever." To shift the blame away from parents or ineffective social policy, Males suggests that nineteenth-century theories about "innate teenage biological and psychological defects" were brought back to life.[41] The threat of teenage suicide confirms the narrative that adolescents are out of control, reckless, mentally unstable, and beyond help. Certainly, the objective here still appears to be a form of social control, threatening parents with the death of their teenage children if they are not watchful enough, careful enough, or loving enough. Much like the sex education pamphlets of the early twentieth century discussed in chapter 2 or self-help books such as James Dobson's *Preparing for Adolescence* and the Allstate insurance campaign for graduated driving laws in chapter 3, adolescents appear to be the object of new measures for social control while parents are being called on to participate in a system of cooperative watchfulness motivated by institutional objectives. The message to parents over and over appears to be: "You need to control teenagers, or they will die."

The need to control teenagers and motivate them to be "good," however, is a highly problematic undertaking with profound psychological costs, as we have seen from Kohn and Miller. The same three-part series from the *Orange County Register* remarks on the recent suicides of four Southern Californian teenagers in 2018 who "appeared to excel." This strange phrasing "appeared to excel" reflects how unthinkable it is to align suicidality with success, as if the suicides of these young people retrospectively negates the fact that they did exactly as they were told, excelled at school and in extracurriculars, and were the pride of their parents—and that these were the very conditions under which their lives became unlivable. Like the sensationalistic reports Males discusses from the 1990s, this article quotes various experts asserting the increase in teenage suicide and speculates that social media and the internet are responsible for the increasing pressure felt by young people to be perfect. The article declares that "what is known is that smart, successful, gifted teens are committing suicide in increasing numbers, and if certain things don't change—and change quickly—many more young lives will be snuffed out." The article challenges the pressures put on kids, seeming to suggest *less* pressure is needed, but directs responsibility for this pressure away from parents or schools and toward causes that "are new, murky and very much 21st century." This is because "parents might as well be on Mars when it comes to understanding the new world of their teens," even though "many don't even know it."[42] Adolescence is synonymous with the unknown, and if parents *think* they understand their teens, the article suggests, they are naively mistaken. Jean Twenge, a professor of psychology at San Diego State University who studies generational trends, is quoted out of context: "It's not an exaggeration to describe iGen as being on the brink of the worst mental-health crisis in decades."[43]

What is missing from this discussion is the acknowledgment that teens are *not* any more suicidal or depressed than adults. Graham writes, "Contrary to popular belief, young people in their teens, if compared to those in their twenties and thirties, are not moodier or more depressed. Rates of low self-esteem, depression, and suicidal ideas increase in the early teens and then remain stable from about the age of 14 years onwards through the rest of young adulthood and middle age. Thus, as far as mood and mood disorders are concerned, those in their teens are very like those in later adulthood, as they are in so many other aspects of life." Graham argues that when depression, anxiety, and other forms of severe distress appear in adolescence that young people are more likely to recover "if they can actively and energetically do something" about the situation causing their distress, and this is not possible unless teens "have control over their lives." What adolescents and adults have in common is the condition of "learned helplessness," in which "they experience simultaneously a sense of power and an incapacity to use their new found competence," resulting in a feeling of frustration and the potential for distress "that will remain with them for the rest of their lives." Graham notes that all people must grapple with feelings of powerlessness at various points, but that adolescence is particularly and unnecessarily burdened with this feeling because of the ways teens are routinely "disempowered in family life, in school, and in the neighbourhood or community" to direct the course of their own lives.[44] Robert Epstein likewise argues that the infantilization of adolescents is the cause of the so-called problems of adolescence.[45] These are the very arguments made by Frank Musgrove in his sociological study of youth in Britain in 1965.[46] Graham, Epstein, and Musgrove all suggest that young people need more independence, more self-direction, and control over their own lives to offset feelings of helplessness and depression, and yet the flurry of news reports on teen suicide suggest the exact opposite, framing this issue as one about teen misuse of technology and the need for more protection and control.

The researcher Jean Twenge does see changes in the most recent generation of young people, those born between 1995 and 2012, as directly linked to technology and the invention of the iPhone and iPad. Unlike the *Orange County Register*, however, she reminds readers that the goal of her research "is not to succumb to nostalgia for the way things used to be; it's to understand how they are now." She finds that teens are more likely to feel lonely, to get less sleep, and to report that they are unhappy than previous generations and that these trends appear to be linked to the amount time spent on "screen activities such as social media, texting, and browsing the web."[47] At the same time her research shows that "today's teens are physically safer than teens have ever been" and that they are "more comfortable in their bedrooms than in a car or at a party," "less likely to get into a car accident," and "less susceptible to drinking's attendant ills." Teens date less than previous generations and have lower rates of sexual activity and the all-time lowest rates of teen pregnancy. Twenge finds that they drive less and are less likely to have a driver's license than previous generations and do not hang out with their friends unsupervised or hold paying jobs like their predecessors. She writes, "The allure of independence, so powerful in previous generations, holds less sway over today's teens, who are less likely to leave the house without their parents." And she finds that "across a range of behaviors—drinking, dating, spending time unsupervised—18-year-olds now act more like 15-year-olds used to, and 15-year-olds more like 13-year-olds." While Twenge acknowledges that "parenting styles continue to change, as do school curricula and culture," she emphasizes that "the twin rise of the smartphone and social media has caused an earthquake of a magnitude we've not seen in a very long time, if ever."

The *Orange County Register* follows this cause-and-effect reasoning, pointing to new technology as the source of new problems. But what if we interpret Twenge's findings in reverse? If her findings are correct, then the most recent generation of teens is the most protected, infantilized, and dependent than any generation prior. These are circumstances of control created by parenting and school cultures that have perhaps achieved the greatest success with the iPhone as a substitute for true independence. If the smartphone might be the reason "rates of teen depression and suicide have skyrocketed since 2011," the smartphone is just as likely the cause for the corresponding rise in teen complacency.[48] While the old myths about the "bad" adolescent continue to circulate, these myths bear little or no resemblance to the lives of the actual people called adolescents.

The Road Less Sanctioned

The emphasis on the problem of teen suicide is another way to distance and disavow the feelings and thoughts associated with the desire to end one's own life. Suicidality is located outside the bounds of the human in adolescence or in the realm of the pathological or insane. Kate Bornstein's teen self-help book, *Hello, Cruel World: 101 Alternatives to Suicide for Teens, Freaks and Other Outlaws*, practices a more ethical relationality to the people called adolescents and to the phenomenon of suicide than the examples discussed earlier. The form of address in the book is explicitly relational, in which Bornstein emerges as a person speaking to another person, acknowledging the situatedness of her thoughts and perspective while taking on a posture of not-knowing when it comes to her reader. The first line of the book is "Hi, I'm Kate Bornstein." She explains, "I wrote this book to help you stay alive because I think the world needs more kind people in it, no matter who or what they are, or do. The world is healthier because of outsiders and outlaws and freaks and queers and sinners. I fall neatly into all of those categories, so it's no big deal to me if you do or don't."[49] The space opened up for the reader to *be* whoever they are is broadened to include queer possibilities, but this space isn't predictive of the reader's identity, feelings, or experiences.

Bornstein shares her own experiences but repeatedly carves out space for the reader: "But that's my life. Your life is a different story." The "Quick Start Guide" goes through a list of conventional recommendations for suicide prevention, such as calling a hotline or talking to a friend or therapist, all of which Bornstein advocates while acknowledging that these steps might not be enough and, for some people, could even make things worse. She writes, "If none of this has worked for you, or if any of it sounded wrong or frightening, there are some options that have not necessarily been sanctioned by therapists and medical doctors." The alternatives in this book are referred to as "the road less sanctioned." They are not meant as a cure but rather a set of strategies to cope with suicidal feelings when they arise as well as a schema for developing new strategies. Suicidality is not ever *over* in this book; in fact, Bornstein explains that "no single alternative I've found to killing myself has ever been enough to keep me alive for longer than a year or so. . . . Some of the methods I've used to stay alive have only worked for a few hours, or a few minutes."[50] By saying this Bornstein creates an ethos of staying alive that requires effort, creativity, and times of reevaluation. Feelings of despair and hopelessness are not pathological but part of being alive, reframed as a cue to engage in this type of work. *Hello, Cruel World* is a life-affirming acknowledgment of the desire to die.

The problem of suicide is often talked about abstractly, as if everyone in the conversation is speaking firmly and securely from the position that suicide is unthinkable. The idea that only mentally ill people would take their own lives is a patent denial of the real struggles *all* people endure and that there are some conditions of life that are worse than death. I lost my brother to suicide in 2015, and, though I did not know when it would happen, his death was not a surprise. I spoke to him nearly every day in the two years before he died. I was not left with unanswered questions or regrets. He was not a teenager—he would have been thirty-two—and I mention him in this context only because he also did not fit any of the existing social narratives about suicide and mental illness. He was hardworking, responsible, and highly intelligent. At the time of his death, he had a psychiatrist, psychologist, neurologist, naturopath, and chiropractor whom he saw regularly. He had tried over fifty combinations of psych meds for severe depression, going through the alphabet twice and graphing his responses with each change to detect subtle patterns of potential improvement. He tried a number of more experimental treatments: diet changes, nutrient therapy, ECT, ketamine, and marijuana. He exercised vigorously every day for an endorphin boost. He was disciplined, systematic, and analytical. He pursued and acquired high-paying professional employment at various points in his life. He had a number of long-term romantic relationships. He did everything he possibly could to stay alive—his life was an endurance exercise. And his decision to die was not irrational or the product of distorted thinking.

The homework his psychologist gave him shortly before his death, which he published online, demonstrated his high degree of self-awareness but also some of the grandiosity described by Miller in *The Drama of the Gifted Child*.[51] On one level he rejected most social standards for success while on another level strove endlessly to meet his own standards for excellence, finding his value in a version of being "good." He did not feel seen or known for who he really was. He suffered from what he called a hallucination of loneliness, what he considered a form of psychosis, a craving for human connection that he could not experience, except only briefly, even when he sought out the presence of other people. Though he considered this emotional experience to be an illusion—and in one sense he was right about that—he was also describing with uncanny accuracy the effects explained by Miller, Gibson, and Kohn on a child who must censor and deny the authentic self for a version that pleases others in order to survive.

Kohn explains that praise is a form of conditional love, one that communicates to the child that "what we're accepting conditionally isn't just a particular characteristic or behavior," so "the child comes to see her 'whole self' as good only when she pleases the parent." Gibson writes, "All they have is a gut feeling of emptiness, which is how a child experiences loneliness. . . . When the children of emotionally immature parents grow up, the core emptiness remains, even if they have a superficially normal adult life." The lack of emotional connection described by Gibson is a feature of the "false self" created by the child to become acceptable to a distant or emotionally dysregulated parent. As Alice Miller describes, "He cannot develop and differentiate his true self, because he is unable to live it. Understandably, this person will complain of a sense of emptiness, futility, or homelessness, for the emptiness is real. A process of emptying, impoverishment, and crippling of his potential actually took place. The integrity of the child was injured when all that was alive and spontaneous in him was cut off."[52]

Bornstein writes about the conditions leading to her first suicidal feelings as "a boy who didn't want to be a boy" in the 1950s: "I worked real hard at being a boy. It was something I was conscious of doing all the time. I watched other boys and did what they did. I did what all the ads and movies and school textbooks told me that boys do."[53] While Bornstein's experience might at first glance appear to exclusively belong to queer and trans childhoods, I want to highlight the normalizing functions of categories of age, and adolescence specifically, to produce particular types of identities and behaviors within a developmental logic, what it means to "grow up." The advice given by Dobson, for example in the conservative teen self-help book *Preparing for Adolescence*, echoes Bornstein's experience. Learning about what is masculine and what is feminine is positioned as something that all adolescents must do. Dobson writes,

> Maybe you too will have to answer some questions about your sexual identity between now and adulthood. If so, the easiest way to learn how to play the role of your particular sex, whether it be a man or a woman, is to watch an adult whom you respect. Try to be like him or her. This is called *identifying* with another person. If it's your mother or your teacher or another adult of your sex, watch and learn how he or she acts. Quietly observe how he walks and talks, and gradually, you will find that it will become natural for you to be something like

your model, even though you're a unique individual. This process comes under the heading of the search for identity, and it is an important part of growing up.

In this passage the trans phenomena Dobson describes—the sense that one's gendered behavior or identifications do not line up with one's assigned sex—is talked about as an ordinary part of adolescence, as the "search for identity" and an "important part of growing up." Likewise, trans phenomena and queer desire are collapsed, both contained by adolescence. Dobson describes adolescence as "stressful" and "threatening" to displace the perceived threat of queer and trans phenomena, or any version of social nonconformity, onto this stage of supposed instability and transition in which personal, therapeutic, or educational intervention appears to be appropriate and developmentally necessary.[54]

Dobson is encouraging young people to make an effort to conform, normalizing such efforts, while simultaneously constructing adolescence as the time when queer or trans phenomena are to be expected. Adolescence bears the ideological weight of all transitory and contingent moments of self-making so that adulthood can represent a final arrival at selfhood. In this sense adolescence itself works as a regulatory and disciplinary tool for both adults and adolescents. The view of adolescence as a time of instability and transition justifies perceptions that young people are rebellious, hormonal, or confused, descriptions that imply that they are not agents of their own actions, desires, or identities. What Dobson advises, however, is that children fashion themselves in a way that is socially acceptable and pleasing to adults. Bornstein explains the cost of this process: "The more I tried to be a boy or a girl, the less I seemed to measure up to *either*, and the less I wanted to stay alive. It finally got to the point where it just didn't seem worth it anymore." Notably, Bornstein describes her efforts to conform in the same terms that Kohn, Gibson, and Miller describe for a child trying to be "good": "I watched for what to do right. I needed other people to validate my effort to be real. It was important that they saw me as one of them. I don't think I ever pulled it off. Their kind of realness seemed always to be out of reach."[55] The issue for Bornstein is not that there is an originary self to be found behind or underneath the self she had fashioned for others, but that such self-fashioning occurred under compulsory conditions in which family relationships, friendships, social success, and her very survival were at stake. Adolescence structures these compulsory conditions not only for gender and sexuality but for all forms of normativity.

One of the high-achieving Southern Californian teenagers mentioned by the *Orange County Register* left a series of suicide letters, published by the paper in 2018. I originally found Patrick Turner's letters for personal reasons rather than in the course of my research for this book, and, like my brother, Patrick and his notes defy the usual narratives around suicide. By all accounts Patrick was a good kid who played sports, got good grades, and was well liked—more than two thousand people attended his funeral. In one letter he writes, "The ongoing stress put on at CDM [Corona del Mar High School] has been inescapable. Putting this much pressure on me has caused me to do what I do." He then details a number of scenarios in which teachers assigned grades for material that they did not teach, said that material not covered in class would be on a final exam, and assigned homework and then left the students to their own devices. These teaching scenarios are unfair, for sure, but mostly mundane. He mentions one teacher (not by name) who was mean, "who made every day I had with this teacher something I dreaded."[56] What exactly was the nature of the "pressure" that he refers to in his letters? Certainly, it was not the problem of too much work, nor was it comparing oneself to others or the feeling of being left out supposedly exacerbated by social media.

The actions of these teachers are devastating only if one feels that one *must* be "good," must follow the rules, and get good grades to survive. Patrick writes, "I want you to know that my parents were not the reason for this. My parents actually don't put almost any stress on me at all. It is purely the school."[57] Reading this, it is difficult for me not to think, *Well, then, fuck the school.* My own capacity to idealize the teen rebel—a figure not based in my own experiences but from being an avid reader of young adult literature—makes this queer response possible for me. What I struggle with the most while reading Patrick's letters is his seeming acceptance of the standards of success—the version of being "good"—that made his life feel unlivable. He writes in a letter to his family, "Do not use this as an excuse to slow down, keep going." To his brothers he adds, "I hope you get that job at Indiana and kill it at whatever you end up doing," and "I hope you have the time of your life wherever you end up going to school." To his sister he writes, "I hope you kick ass on the East Coast."[58] In another letter to friends, he thanks all the teachers who made him feel valued, and he affectionately tells his coaches to "keep winning championships and kicking ass."[59] Why not encourage others to reject the oppressive forms of success and normativity that led him to this point in the first place?

Patrick was a success according to the standards of achievement established by his community, but his letter exposes the emptiness of this success and the troubling consequences of rewards and praise described by Kohn. Patrick writes, "So much pressure is put on kids to do good, and a lot of kids make mistakes. One slip up makes a kid feel like the smallest person in the world. You are looked at as a loser if you don't go to college or get a certain GPA or test score. All anyone talks about is how great their kid is. It's all about how great I am. It's never about the kid who maybe does not play a sport, have a 4.0+ GPA, but displays great character." What this letter describes is the feeling of erasure and isolation resulting from this form of recognition: "It's all about how great I am." Like Miller's "gifted child," the grandiosity of being "great" quickly wears off, only to be replaced by feelings of emptiness, the consequence of not being seen in the wholeness of who we are. Patrick writes, "Nobody seems to understand, they only see people on the outside."[60] Ann Cvetkovich theorizes "depression as a cultural and social phenomenon" with the objective "to depathologize negative feelings." She sees the feelings associated with depression as an effect of neoliberal capitalism, explaining that "depression, or alternative accounts of what gets called depression, is thus a way to describe neoliberalism and globalization, or the current state of political economy, in affective terms."[61] Kohn likewise indicts neoliberal capitalism in his critique of conditional parenting, how "we are taught that good things must always be earned, never given away" and thus how "the laws of the marketplace—supply and demand, tit for tat—have assumed the status of universal and absolute principles" in which "every human interaction, even among family members" is viewed "as a kind of economic *trans*action."[62]

Within the logic of the marketplace, the child must give the parent, the school, and the institution what it wants to earn safety, care, and love. Henry Giroux describes the psychic consequences of neoliberalism another way, echoing the very terms outlined in Patrick's letter: "Within this narrow individualism in which all that matters is one's ability to compete and 'win' as defined by the ideologies, values, materials, social relations, and practices of commerce, it becomes difficult for young people to imagine a future in which the self becomes more than a self-promoting commodity and a symbol of commodification."[63] Cvetkovich and Giroux describe an institutionalized form of relation that mirrors the parental relation described by Kohn and Miller. Audre Lorde explains, "The principle horror of any system which defines the good in terms of profit rather than in terms of human need, or which defines human need to the exclusion of the psychic and emotional components of that need—the principle horror of such a system is that it robs our work of its erotic value, its erotic power and life appeal and fulfillment."[64] Neoliberalism creates a society that expects its citizens to ignore and deny the signs of overwork, to dedicate themselves to work without meaning or purpose, to think of their value primarily in terms of labor and professional success. The great irony of writing these words in an academic book for tenure does not escape me. Perhaps I *need* to imagine that Patrick could have rejected the pressures and standards of Corona del Mar and entertained queerer possibilities for a meaningful life. Even now I am not sure if I could do the same. If the pressures of tenure made my life feel unlivable, could I imagine doing something else? Could I walk away from this book and not feel that my life was over? Perhaps the question is not why do some people decide to take their own lives, but how do any of us survive?

The institutional and medical protocols for a suicidal person with a plan, or for someone following a suicide attempt, are designed entirely around restraint and control. The premise behind this idea is that suicidality is a state of insanity, hopefully temporary, in which people need to be protected from themselves. Bornstein says that "people who don't see any way of changing themselves or the world spend a lot of time wishing they were dead." The key, she suggests, is the ability to take that control back: "It came down to this: should I

101 Alternatives to Suicide

FOR TEENS, FREAKS AND OTHER OUTLAWS

HOW EASY IS IT TO DO?

(EACH ALTERNATIVE RATED ON A DIFFICULTY SCALE)

As easy as petting a cow As tricky as riding a cow As difficult as a cow on wheels Real easy and real dangerous

Figure 4.1. Kate Bornstein, "Key," in *Hello, Cruel World* (New York: Seven Stories, 2006), 97.

kill myself or should I make myself a life worth living? And it wasn't so much the question that kept me alive or even my answer. What kept me alive was the notion that it was me who was asking the question." What kind of life is worse than death for one person might not be the same as it is for another, and that is precisely the limit of our knowledge and control over others. Bornstein's approach to suicide prevention does not involve "reasons not to kill yourself" but a set of strategies to cope with suicidal feelings when they arise, ranging from easy and safe to difficult and dangerous, including options like "keep moving" and "ask for help" as well as "tell a lie," "make a deal with the

HOW SAFE IS IT?
(EACH ALTERNATIVE RATED ON A
FOUR HEART SCALE)

HOW EFFECTIVE IS IT?
(EACH ALTERNATIVE RATED ON A
FOUR UMBRELLA SCALE)

Super
Effective

Not So Much

Figure 4.2. Kate Bornstein, "How Safe Is It? How Effective Is It?," in
Hello, Cruel World (New York, Seven Stories, 2006), 98.

devil," "take drugs," and "starve yourself."[65] Each of the alternatives is
accompanied with a rating scale for difficulty, safety, and effectiveness
(see figs. 4.1 and 4.2).

The fact that the book contains controversial alternatives like cutting, illegal drugs, and anorexia might seem counterintuitive. But it
is important not to mistake these alternatives as recommendations or
even endorsements of these activities. They are instead a profound
acknowledgment and acceptance of the fullest range of feelings and
experiences any person might have. Bornstein seems to say, over and
over, there is nothing that her readers have thought or done that is
too bad or scary or illegal for her. The sections on cutting, drugs, and
anorexia serve as an acknowledgment of these possibilities as well as a
guide for thinking through the decision to do or not to do any of them,
including questions the readers should first ask themselves, warnings
about the consequences of these choices, and alternatives to these alternatives. The fear that teenagers will be corrupted by the presence
of these controversial alternatives in the book assumes that if you give
teenagers an inch, they will jump off the (literal or metaphorical) cliff.

This fear reflects again what Kohn calls the "deeply cynical belief" that if young people are given the freedom to be who they are, they will choose to be bad, "because, well, that's who they are."[66]

Conversely, giving control over to teenagers creates circumstances in which they can be competent, capable of good, and empowered to do the right thing, at the same time as recognizing that they are equally capable of harm and bear the weight of their decisions. The familiar social conceptions of the "good" child and the "bad" adolescent constrain opportunities for young people to be in and act on the world as themselves, serving to simplify and disavow the moral ambiguity of all human potential and to deny our ethical entanglement with one another and the world. Wall writes, "The ability for even a child to construct his own world is ethically ambiguous. It is not simply corrupted by outside society or expressive of innate evil. It includes the possibility for most of the horrors of which only humanity seems capable" and is a "testament to moral life's simultaneous fallibility and potential for redemption."[67] Rather than disavow this complexity in herself and her reader, Bornstein speaks from the position of someone who has done it all and does not judge, someone who is validating the capacity of her readers to do great harm while encouraging them to make conscious choices with the awareness that the consequences of those choices are their own. Bornstein's approach to suicide prevention is about giving over control, not restricting it.

Sexual Autonomy

In the preceding chapters I have demonstrated the ways in which categories of age work to problematically disempower children and adolescents. At first glance it might seem that the problem is one of power: adults have the power, and children and adolescents don't have it. And yet, attempts to grant power to children and adolescents—whether to acknowledge their power or to give them power—take us only so far. James Kincaid argues that power, as a conceptual frame, is limited when it comes to analyses of categories of age: "The question is not the redistribution of power but its adequacy in the first place, its limitations as a tool for understanding and for living." For example, if children and adolescents are considered powerful, adults might conclude they are justified in using their power in the usual ways, since the playing field is equal. Certainly, this way of thinking does not address the problems of coercion or exploitation. But if children and adolescents are not considered powerful, then adults might see this status as the justification—obligation, even—to protect them. It is one thing to protect a small child from the stove or the stairs, temporary protections put in place up to the point that one learns to climb stairs and even to safely avoid a hot stove, inevitably through a process of making mistakes involving falls or burns, which are necessary for learning these life skills. It is another thing to attempt to protect children and adolescents from their own preferences and desires. Kincaid puts it this way: "Isn't there a danger of the very protections becoming coercive? Isn't it possible that the need to protect can run amok?"[68] We have seen examples of this in *Anne of Green Gables*, where Anne is forbidden her reading of "lurid mysteries" or when G. Stanley Hall warns against "too wide reading" and exposure to "alien ideas."[69] We have seen the disabling effects of "protection" implied through Twenge's analysis of today's teenagers as the least independent of any previous generation. While I do not think we can or that we should do away with power as a theory for understanding social relations, power is only one apparatus through which to understand the politics of difference and the institutional mechanisms that shape our lives. As a single frame, power makes some things visible while obscuring others.

In 2015 a North Carolina teen was prosecuted for having nude photos of himself and his girlfriend, both sixteen at the time, on his phone. The photos were taken consensually and shared only between the couple, what might have been considered legal "sexting" if they had been over eighteen years of age. But because of a quirk in North Carolina law, both teens were charged as adults for child endangerment under child pornography laws, even though the "child" in question was the same person as the "adult" being charged: "Each was therefore simultaneously the adult perpetrator who is considered a predator and the minor victim who needs protecting by the law."[70] Both teens took plea deals to avoid conviction and lifelong registration as sex offenders. Like the justice of the peace in Louisiana who refused to marry an interracial couple—"I do it to protect the children," he said—the power of the law operated here to protect a "child" who did not exist.[71] The hypocrisy of these legal actions illustrates the ways childhood and adolescence function as temporal rather than simply ontological categories, in which developmental time can be shifted in the present embodiment of a person to achieve particular ends. These North Carolina teens were punished as *adults* under the law for failing to protect themselves as *children*, a temporal slide used to deny them their rights as people in the present. Kincaid describes the cultural mechanisms at work: "Adolescents are stuffed back into childhood when it serves our purposes, as it often does when we are talking of molestation or crime. Victims of crime as old as eighteen or nineteen can be thought of as children, whereas perpetrators as young as six can be thought of and treated as adults." We do not often see these logics enacted simultaneously in one person. Power, Kincaid says, "allows us to overlook both contradictions and cruelties in our logic, in our family structure, and in our social system at large."[72] Power, as a conceptual frame, suggests that ethical considerations involve only more or less action on the part of adults. In this model all power originates from adults. As adults under the law, the North Carolina teens have the power to exploit children. But, under the law as children, they can only be exploited. According to this logic, they cannot simply be children who wanted to take nude photos of themselves and share them with each other. They cannot be the owners of their own bodies or the agents of their own desires. However, it is clear that reversing the adult-child dynamic under the terms of power does not clarify matters. It does not make any more sense to see children as the "real" predators and adults as victims. We need another way of conceptualizing sexual autonomy through the ethics of relationality.

Bornstein sees gender and sexuality as essential to the project of imagining, and thus making possible, a livable life. Queer possibility is a reason to stay alive. She writes,

> Try this: Imagine the world as a place where anyone can safely and even joyfully express themselves the way they've always wanted to. Nothing about the bodies they were born with or what they choose to do with those bodies—how they dress them, or decorate, or trim, or augment them—would get people laughed at, or targeted, or in any way deprived of their rights. Can you imagine a world like that?
>
> Stay with that image for a moment and envision yourself as the kind of person who lives happily and contentedly in that world. What

gives you pleasure? What are the components of your identity that allow for that pleasure? How many components of that envisioned identity can you put in place in your *real* life in order to achieve real pleasure?

The self-making she advocates is not the individualism of neoliberal capitalism but a conscious enactment of ethical relationality: "Everyone consciously or unconsciously changes who they are in response to their environment or to some relationship that they are negotiating in any given moment. Every life form does that." She frames this capacity in terms of survival and as a skill that can be practiced and honed but explains that "the less consciously we evolve our identities—who we are and how we're seen in the world—the better the chances that one day we're going to wake up and not know where we are or how we got there."[73] Consciousness is Bornstein's cure for the demands of normativity that make so many lives feel unlivable. Her suggestion should not be mistaken as an anything-goes form of relativism but rather the exposure of normativity as a false system of value for whose life is worth living. Bornstein substitutes the oppressive constraints of normativity with an alternate principle for ethical relationality: "DON'T BE MEAN. Anything else goes, anything at all." Our entanglement with others and our environments is unavoidable, and so what matters most is that we consciously choose, and that we feel we are *allowed* to consciously choose, our identities. Bornstein practices and elaborates an ethics of relationality for her reader that acknowledges the entanglement of meaning, matter, and world.

To see this ethical relationality practiced in another context, I want to turn to Cory Silverberg and Fiona Smyth's 2015 sex education comic book, aimed at seven to ten year olds, called *Sex Is a Funny Word*. Children's books written for the purposes of sex education are frequently conservative in approach, aiming to stabilize and control sexual knowledge while guarding sex and reproduction within narratives that produce and maintain heterosexuality. As discussed in chapter 2, the social project of sex education in the early twentieth century began as an explicit means of state control and regulation, a way of harnessing sex and reproduction for state purposes. Desire and consent were obscured by a preoccupation with controlling sexual behavior and directing it toward particular ends that created a coercive relation to sex, whether it manifested in the direction of heterosexuality, abstinence, or marital obligation. *Sex Is a Funny Word* engages with sexuality education in a different way, one that emphasizes the reader's own process of inquiry and discovery and opens up queer possibilities for gender and sexuality. This book might be read as an enactment of Jen Gilbert's suggestion to "imagine sex education as a place of questions rather than answers."[74] In the author's note by Silverberg, he writes, "Most books about sex are full of answers. Answers can be helpful and reassuring, but they also tell us what to think and even how to think instead of encouraging us to think for ourselves and to honor our own knowledge and experience."[75]

Like Bornstein's *Hello, Cruel World*, this book emphasizes questions, ending each chapter with questions for the reader to think about and talk about with someone they trust. The pedagogical structure of teacher-student is disrupted by the comic book formatting, featuring four child characters shown engaging with the book's content in different ways. The questions at the end of each chapter come from these characters rather than the seemingly "objective" and factual text of the book itself. The book contains information about the word "sex," the human body, gendered ways of being, and touch, including masturbation and body autonomy. This information is layered with comic book scenes featuring the four characters interacting with the material, with one another, and with other people in their lives. This layering effectively exposes the information as subject to context, relationships, and individual engagement rather than as rule or law. The book emphasizes the characters' questions and process of inquiry rather than its own answers, modeling for readers the process of discovering and being present with gender and sexuality rather than arriving at, controlling, or directing it.

On the first page of the book, we learn about each of the four characters, including their ages, favorite foods, and likes and dislikes that include lists such as "candy, math, swimming" and "climbing on things, music, shy people."[76] These lists suggest a process of identity formation and self-understanding that exceeds the bounds of gender identity or is based on alternative logics altogether. Cat Fitzpatrick explains that the book "holds itself open to diversity by always being particular. The four characters aren't blank every-kid stand-ins—they are distinct and weird people who do things like collect antique cell-phones or develop opinions about climate change."[77] This particularity continues throughout as we get to know the characters and see them interact with the information of the book. There is a student in a wheelchair as well as one wearing a hijab. The book depicts skin tones and hair color as a rainbow rather than in earth tones, acknowledging that we live in a world in which race is significant, but avoiding visually referencing racial or ethnic stereotypes. There isn't even a discernible norm, which works to imagine a world in which a multitude of differences coexist. The book is attempting to represent diversity as a lived experience of particularity, what it means to be different from others (which we inevitably are) as well as exist alongside others who are different from us. It does not represent existing standards of value to affirm them or push against them. It represents a set of ethical practices, ways of being in relation to gender, sexuality, and bodies.

One of the characters, whose name is Zai, does not immediately appear to be male or female, judging by the illustrations and Zai's dialogue. However, the great diversity of the other characters in terms of race, ethnicity, ability, and gendered expression creates the effect of incorporating Zai's androgyny as not especially noticeable or notable to a reader. Early in the book Zai is shown with a question mark thought bubble while watching two girls say to another child: "You can't wear pink! You're a boy!" The question mark does not indicate anxiety or concern but rather Zai's puzzlement at why anyone would make such a rule. In a subsequent frame we see Zai shopping with a parental figure, holding a shirt on a hanger and insisting confidently, "But, Mom, I like the color pink!"[78] These frames suggest that Zai's sex was assigned male at birth but that the social meaning of this assignment doesn't necessarily fit Zai's self-conceptions. *Sex Is a Funny Word* practices what Jules Gill-Peterson calls an "ethical aperture of relation," one in which adults see "trans children's growth and flourishing as ends in themselves" and where we understand "what it means to wish that there *be* trans children, that to grow trans and live a trans childhood is not merely a possibility but a happy and desirable one."[79] Trans phenomena are represented in the book as a process of inquiry without a predictive outcome, just like any of the characters' processes of learning about themselves.

On the title page of the chapter "Boys, Girls, All of Us," Zai is shown asking, "Only boys and girls? What about the rest of us?" This chapter explains that babies are called boys or girls when they are born, even though there are more than two kinds of bodies. One of the characters, Omar, asks the reader, "What did they call you when you were born?" while Zai asks, "Why do you think people want to know if a baby is a boy or a girl?" On a subsequent page the text explains, "As we grow into being a kid and then an adult, we get to figure out who we are and what words fit best. Most boys grow up to be men, and most girls grow up to be women. But there are many ways to be a boy or a girl. And there are many ways to grow up and become an adult. For most of us, words like boy and girl, or man and woman, feel okay, and they fit. For some of us, they don't." If developmental sequence—the very idea of growing up—implies the arrival at a normatively gendered adulthood, this book disrupts developmental sequence by representing growing up as a process of change and of contingent learning about oneself: "Growing up can mean learning about your outside, what your body can and can't do. Growing up can also mean learning about your inside: the stories, memories, and feelings that make you who you are."[80] This distinction between inside and outside doesn't privilege one or the other as the stable or originary source of gender but rather creates the space for trans phenomena to be experienced and explored not as a bodily contradiction but as an embodied understanding of the relationship between inside and outside, one that all people must explore and negotiate.

Sex Is a Funny Word does not deal directly with sex acts (though a book for older readers that does is in the works), but it has profound implications for thinking about what it might mean to practice and pass along a concept of sexual ethics to children. Michael Warner contrasts his conception of sexual ethics to what he calls "moralism," a false morality based on judging others, feeling superior, and controlling others: "Most people cannot quite rid themselves of the sense that controlling the sex of others, far from being unethical, is where morality begins." We might hear an echo of Kohn's argument that the dominant cultural paradigm of "good" parenting constitutes the control of children—one might say it is the point at which good parenting is presumed to begin. Warner says that our "culture has thousands of ways for people to govern the sex of others—and not just harmful or coercive sex, like rape, but the most personal dimensions of pleasure, identity, and practice." He asks, "Shouldn't it be possible to allow everyone sexual autonomy, in a way consistent with everyone else's sexual autonomy?" Importantly, this is not a call for relativism—"some shame may be well deserved," he says—but rather "the goal of sexual ethics would be to constrain coercion rather than shut down sexual variance."[81] Autonomy is evoked as an ethical value here, a relational practice negotiated between oneself and others, rather than as a definitional fact or a belief in the separateness of the autonomous liberal subject. Warner's conception of autonomy is a relational one, an attempt, as Butler puts it, "to redescribe autonomy in terms of relationality."[82] Sexual ethics *are* relational ethics. One of the things *Sex Is a Funny Word* does is create a safe and legitimized space for the sexual autonomy of children, for every person to acknowledge, explore, and accept the most personal dimensions of their "pleasure, identity, and practice" as they go through the process of discovering and experiencing them.[83] The structure of the book emphasizes that this work belongs to child readers themselves rather than to adult authority figures, subverting notions of childhood innocence and suggesting an alternate relationality among the generations. Rather than enacting mentorship that is an investment in the future becomings of its readers, the role of the book (and thus adults) is to crack open the potentiality of the present for readers who are here now. Denying the sexuality of children, as the notion of childhood innocence suggests we do, or attempting to control sexuality through shame or to obscure sexual knowledge through exclusion or isolation—these are unethical practices that close down possibilities for a livable life.

Gender and sexuality are relational ways of being oneself and being with others. Bornstein writes, "Sexuality is more than who we're attracted to. It is more than what we like to do in bed. It is a social identity. It is the way we experience the world around us in a positive, life-affirming way." Queer possibilities for being are not formed in isolation or even *valuable* in isolation but rather conceptualized as life-sustaining vehicles for connection with others. This principle is explained through another imaginative exercise the reader is invited by Bornstein to undertake:

Imagine sweet sex with a really great person or persons, and it's making both or all of you feel great. . . . Think about every kind of sex you can think of . . . even if some people say it's not right for you to think about it.

Can you imagine being the kind of person who has that kind of sweet sex and relationship? If you can imagine it, you are completely capable of taking steps to realize it. It's a matter of trusting someone enough to let them know who you really are. Trust yourself first.[84]

Bornstein's self-reflexivity and vulnerability elsewhere in the text suggest that this exercise is one that she has used for her own survival, and she shares with the reader her own process of negotiating a trans identity in relation to desire and cultural prohibition. Identity is theorized as a conscious process of becoming that enables the feeling of connection to others as we truly are.

There are similarities between Bornstein's exercise and a moment in *Sex Is a Funny Word*: "Part of being a kid is learning what you like, what you don't like, and who you are. That's part of being a grown-up, too. We never stop learning or changing."[85] The emphasis on self-knowledge and discovery is described in relation to process and change rather than identity formation or points of arrival, resembling what Gilbert describes as a "cautious theory of development in sex education" that is "grounded in psychoanalysis and the interpretive possibilities that are opened up when a good life is measured not by one's proximity to norms but by one's capacity to love and work."[86] Likewise, Bornstein's notion of being "who you really are" is not essentialist or stable. She writes, "Keep in mind that the you that makes life worth living today probably won't be the same you that makes life worth living this time next year." Bornstein accounts for the usefulness of identities while theorizing their subjective function as moving one through life: "Identities aren't mean to be permanent. They're like cars: they take us from one place to another. We work, travel, and seek adventure in them until they break down beyond repair. At that point, living well means finding a new model that better suits us for a new moment."[87] Transition here is not the movement from one stable identity to another but the very condition of inhabiting multiple identities that take us where we want to go. We might hear an echo of Bornstein's exercise in Butler's articulation of the psychoanalytic notion of fantasy: "The struggle to survive is not really separable from the cultural life of fantasy, and the foreclosure of fantasy—through censorship, degradation, or other means—is one strategy for providing for the social death of persons." Butler explains that fantasy exposes the definitional limit of what can be considered "real" and possible. "Fantasy is what allows us to imagine ourselves and others otherwise; it establishes the possible in excess of the real; it points elsewhere, and when it is embodied, it brings elsewhere home."[88] Essential for the survival of queer and trans young people, and for all of us constrained by normative definitions of success and growth, Bornstein's exercise is an open invitation, a process of being and becoming that transgresses the bounds of what language and culture deem real or possible.

Ethical Entanglement

Graham argues that "the evidence strongly suggests that the best outcomes for children's personalities occur when parents begin by carefully observing the way their children feel and behave in different circumstances when they are infants and toddlers, responding to them as individuals." And then "if they then go on to consult them and respect their views in the primary school years, and move to sharing decision-making with them when they reach their teens, the chances that their children will enter adulthood in good mental health are further increased."[89] As I have argued earlier, this relational dynamic does not consist of a separable autonomous parent and an autonomous child acting alongside each other but is created through the acknowledgment of our ethical entanglement with one another. Attempts to theorize child agency in childhood studies have led to a number of thorny problems, summarized by Marah Gubar this way: "If we as scholars want to claim that children have agency, then, we must concede that the kind of agency they have is not synonymous with autonomy." Gubar suggests that acknowledging the differences between children and adults, as well as the limited capacities of children, means that "adult paternalism toward children" is not "ipso facto oppressive" and that, unlike other oppressed groups, "some form of paternalism is not only justified but ethically required." On the one hand, Gubar is right to recognize that dependency, and indeed relationality itself, is a form of ethical entanglement. On the other hand, this formulation reinscribes an adult-child hierarchy of power relations that makes thinking about ethics difficult or impossible except under authoritarian terms like "paternalism." Gubar worries, too, that such an acknowledgment reinscribes what she calls a "difference model" of childhood that "too easily produces prejudice and injustice, condescension and dehumanization." Instead, she proposes a "kinship model" which "highlights likeness and relatedness" at the same time as "it also makes room for difference and variation," inviting us "to regard all human beings, regardless of age, as full subjects."[90] Like Gubar, I think that regarding children as more like adults than different from them is key to shifting the harmful effects of categories of age. But this involves a rethinking of the opposition between "child" and "adult" along with their attendant assumptions about autonomy, agency, and subjectivity.

What Bornstein and books like *Sex Is a Funny Word* enact is a relationality that redefines the concept of agency through imagining the child or adolescent reader as not as a passive recipient of information or a fully independent agent but rather an embodied person with an ethical obligation to oneself and others, enmeshed in discourse and capable of moving in and through it in creative, unpredictable, and unknown ways. Wall describes a child who, "like us all, belongs to a complex circle of interdependent relations which she is both shaped by and shapes for herself." Wall contends that "babies in particular show that each of us is and has been shaped by many layers of surrounding persons, communities, and histories."[91] Castañeda, grappling with the challenge to subjectivity posed by the infant, asks, "Must a subject be able to represent itself in order to be a subject? Must agency take the form of self-representation?" To ask these questions necessitates a rethinking of agency itself: "What kind of agency?" Castañeda aims to "re-theorize the subject in terms that do not make use of the child as the adult's pre-subjective other," which means contending with and accepting unknowing as the "condition of knowledge itself." She explains, "The theory I am imagining suggests that subjects cannot be known in advance. Instead, knowing comes to apprehend the singularity of all subjects, the complexity of their histories, and the modes of their subjection as these change over time and place."[92] This theory takes as a given the unknowability of ourselves and others while establishing relational encounters as the place in which a contingent, contextual knowing might take place.

Barad also theorizes subjectivity as inherently relational: "Subjectivity is not a matter of individuality but a relation of responsibility to the other. Crucially, then, the ethical subject is not the disembodied rational subject of traditional ethics but rather an embodied sensibility, which responds to its proximal relationship to the other through a mode of wonderment that is antecedent to consciousness." Likewise, for Barad, agency is relational, realized through the actions of bodies in proximal relation to one another: "*It is enactment, not something that someone or something has.* It cannot be designated as an attribute of subjects or objects (as they do not preexist as such). It is not an attribute whatsoever. *Agency is "doing" or "being" in its intra-activity.*"[93] Thus, the agency of children is not located in their intentionality, as if the autonomous liberal subject extends to childhood, but rather in the desires, emotions, and physicality of our connective and relational interactions with the world and others. The idea that an adult "has" agency is a myth; it is a belief in the autonomous human subject and the separability of individuals, self, and world. As Gubar demonstrates, the attempt to include children in this myth of privilege, to claim they have this type of agency or that they are autonomous actors in the world, inadequately addresses the questions of ethics and social justice at stake in the treatment of the people called children. What is needed to fully engage these ethical questions is a relational understanding of subjectivity and agency that nuances and resituates the agential capacities of both adults and children.

Normative conceptions of subjectivity privilege the idea of rational consciousness as a prerequisite for ethical action. This idea figures the adult as an interiorized consciousness rather than an embodied being and conversely figures the child in opposition to consciousness or as preconsciousness. If subjectivity is always relational, then it is less important to establish the difference between adults and children than it is to understand the ethics of all relationality, or what Barad refers to as the entanglement of materiality: "We (but not only 'we humans') are always already responsible to the others with whom or which we are entangled, not through conscious intent but through the various ontological entanglements that materiality entails."[94] Barad is writing about the world—all of nature, matter, the universe—and theorizing a posthuman agency that accounts for the ethical relationships that can occur, those including humans and those relationships that might not involve humans at all. But we might also hear a version of Barad's ethical entanglement in Bornstein's "don't be mean" or in Warner's conception of sexual autonomy. I find Barad's theory particularly useful for rethinking categories of age because it makes the varying capacities of children and young people irrelevant to their recognition as agents. And it brings ethical considerations to the forefront, whether we are speaking about infants, children, adolescents, atoms, stone, or planets. If the child epitomizes the ideal of the human at the very same time as actual children are excluded from the privileges of the human, then a humanist understanding of agency will continually perpetuate these exclusionary functions. Children are granted the privileges of the human only at the moment they cease to be children. Castañeda's retheorization of subjectivity also accounts for the preverbal state of infancy in terms that further illuminate the ethics of relationality implied by Alice Miller's contention that even an infant has a "primary need from the very beginning of her life to be regarded and respected as the person she really is at any given time":

> An infant is not simply the raw natural material of the future adult subject it will become but rather an entity that is the effect of the agency of nature and the discursive matrix through which it is formed and reformed. The infant "is" a subject and has subjectivity that is particular to this interaction, such that everything from culturally specific birthing practices to particular modes of embodiment, including racialization, gendering, sexualization, and so on, are constitutive of this entity *as* an infant. What might be called the absence of language here, or rather the presence of particular modes of embodied communication that do not include language per se, does not constitute this entity as presubjective in this formulation, and as such it cannot be occupied by adult fantasies or desires. Instead, this entity's existence, and its embodiment are the ground of its subjectivity, where "subjectivity" signifies embodied experience.[95]

Like the infant, an adult's subjectivity is similarly embodied, contextual, and relational. The example of an infant does not introduce a special kind of subjectivity but rather makes visible the instability and

chapter four

unknowability of all encounters—all entanglements—of matter and meaning.

Barad explains, "agential separability is not individuation." What this means is that ethics is "not about right response to a radically exterior/ized other, but about responsibility and accountability for the lively relationalities of becoming of which we are a part." When Barad speaks of the "relationalities of becoming," this involves the relationality between one person and another, such as a child and an adult, but it refers to a much larger acknowledgment of performativity, the ways that beingness and reality itself become visible in specific, contextual ways. This reformulation of agency and meaning-making within performativity, far from the oppressive discourse of Michel Foucault's *History of Sexuality*, instead brings to light our ethical responsibilities to one another and to the world in the construction of meaning. The sense of ourselves as "adult" depends on the construction of the "child" as separate from adulthood: their meanings and very existence are enmeshed. Barad uses the example of "able-bodied" and "disabled," in which the privileged status of able-bodiedness "is not a natural state of being but a specific form of embodiment that is co-constituted through the boundary-making practices that distinguish 'able-bodied' from 'disabled.'" She proposes, "How different ethics looks from the vantage point of constitutive entanglements. What would it mean to acknowledge that 'able-bodied' depend on the 'disabled' for their very existence? What would it mean to take on that responsibility? What would it mean to deny one's responsibility to the other once there is a recognition that one's very embodiment is integrally entangled with the other?"[96] This ethical acknowledgment of relationality that produces "adult" and "child" as interdependent categories would make adult projections of desire more conscious and more visible, because it destabilizes the capacities of these categories to produce this reality in the first place. Rather than adult and child producing the illusion of knowledge about the other, they would instead illuminate the challenge they pose to each other.

Butler works through some of these questions with regard to the performativity of gender, describing the entanglements of matter and meaning that gender itself exposes when we look at its role in the production of the real. Butler suggests that the work of queer theory to underscore the instability of gender also has the potential for achieving this ethical awareness and thus a less oppressive social world. The work of queer theory

> is precisely to underscore the value of being beside oneself, of being a porous boundary, given over to others, finding oneself in a trajectory of desire in which one is taken out of oneself, and resituated irreversibly in a field of others in which one is not the presumptive center. The particular sociality that belongs to bodily life, to sexual life, and to becoming gendered (which is always, to a certain extent, becoming gendered *for others*) establishes a field of ethical enmeshment with others and a sense of disorientation for the first-person, that is, the perspective of the ego. As bodies, we are always for something more than, and other than, ourselves.[97]

Both Butler and Barad move away from conceptions of the autonomous liberal subject, emphasizing instead the interdependency of our existence. What Butler describes is the condition of being an adult or an infant, and the "porous boundary, given over to others" that both experience in relation to each other, to becoming gendered, to being in the world. Butler's theory of performativity highlights the production of reality in these relational processes. Barad writes, "The nature of the production of bodily boundaries is not merely experiential, or merely epistemological, but ontological—what is at issue and at stake is a matter of the nature of reality, not merely a matter of human experience or human understandings of the world."[98] What this means is not that adults and children or children and adolescents or mothers and infants are somehow all the same but rather that recognizing their separateness also means grappling with their entanglement, what Butler describes as a "field of ethical enmeshment," within which the child and the adolescent must be allowed to matter as themselves at any given moment. This mattering is not an interpretive act but a performative one, productive of the real.

In my introduction I made the statement, at the risk of stating the obvious, that we cannot control other people. In the context of my work exposing institutional projects of control, this claim might be read as a comment on the ineffectiveness or incompleteness of such projects, their inability to shape the future toward their particular aims. And this interpretation is not wrong—there will always be a queer outside to the regulatory mechanisms of any institution. What I really want to say, though, is not that we cannot control other people but that we *should* not. The attempt to control others, however one justifies it, is unethical. But the ethical responsibility to allow others control over themselves does not leave us only with a form of relativism in which anything goes or in which we allow ourselves to be exploited or abused. Butler explains that the fact "that we cannot predict or control what permutations of the human might arise does not mean that we must value all possible permutations of the human; it does not mean that we cannot struggle for the realization of certain values, democratic and nonviolent, international and antiracist." But she argues that an ethical relationality is one in which we must grapple with the limits of our own perspectives and positionality and "enter into a collective work in which one's own status as a subject must, for democratic reasons, become disoriented, exposed to what it does not know."[99] The ethics of relationality asks the question of how to be with the earth, the environment, children, other people, or animals rather than how to dominate or control them. An ethical relation requires that we become aware of how norms are shaping or constraining the imagined outcome of any encounter and let go of predetermination. An ethical relationality involves acting within the world to create the possibility for all to be who or what they are in the present moment of their becoming.

epilogue

QUEER THEORY IN THE AGE OF ALTERNATIVE FACTS

It is comforting, however, and a source of profound relief to think that man is only a recent invention, a figure not yet two centuries old, a new wrinkle in our knowledge, and that he will disappear again as soon as that knowledge has discovered a new form.

—Michel Foucault, *The Order of Things*

The world we find ourselves in today is not the same world of the turn of the twentieth century, when stabilizing notions of scientific truth were under construction in new institutions negotiating for their authority to speak the truth about human beings. The defensiveness of those constructions in the early twentieth century exposes the fragility of medical and scientific discourses rather than their dominance. In 1904, the same year that G. Stanley Hall's *Adolescence* was published, a newspaper printed the following editorial, offhandedly dismissing the authority of emerging institutional discourses: "The psycho-pathologists claim to have discovered the anatomical cause for every intellectual and ethical defect, and there is even talk of converting bad boys into good ones by means of surgery, the cauterization of the turbinated bone and a judicious application of the knife to the pharyngeal region being suggested as effective methods of dealing with juvenile depravity. The lack of any suggested method of restricting boy's capacity for noise, during childhood and adolescence shows that these learned psycho-pathologists have not yet sounded the depths of this profound subject."[1] The tone is overtly sarcastic, calling into question the claims of the "psycho-pathologists" and their delusions "of converting bad boys into good ones." The last line, rather than expressing a literal and sincere desire to silence young people, expresses a realistic skepticism about the power of institutions to know and to control people.

The British novelist Rose Macaulay includes a similarly snide re-mark about the scientific study of youth in a 1923 novel, doubting that the "number of years lived" somehow indicates that people share a "temperamental bond," in which "people of the same age are many minds with but a single thought, bearing one to another a close resem-blance." Thus, "the young were commented on as if they were some new and just discovered species of animal life, with special qualities and habits which repaid investigation."[2] Here Macaulay resists the types of generalizations made by Hall and others about adolescence as an object of study. She suggests that young people are *not* general-izable in such a way but that they are instead as various in feeling, per-sonality, and thought as adults. In 1929 the British philosopher Francis Herbert Bradley suggested in the *London Times Literary Supplement*: "We are bound to ask how far any of the abstract generalizations of science can be declared in an absolute sense more factual than that of Religion. Would it not be truer, and more conducive to the widest freethinking, to regard both as metaphorical, not as strict and literal but figurative and analogical expression of experienced reality?"[3] Bradley complicates faith in scientific knowledge to direct the future and emphasizes the situatedness of all knowledge production, a po-sition we might identify with later poststructuralist views. These ex-amples illustrate that institutional discourses expressed the desire for authority and expertise more so than the realization of it in the early twentieth century.

Belief in the objectivity and "truth" of science was not taken for granted until the mid-twentieth century, and within a mere few de-cades poststructuralist theory began to expose the social constructed-ness of science and institutional knowledge. From this standpoint the insights of poststructuralism were not exactly *new* but instead in part a renewal of the epistemological complexities that by midcentury had been forgotten.[4] We might say the same for the ways that subjectivity and identity were understood, in which previously obscured old ideas and old ways of knowing resurfaced with new functions. For example, John Dollimore explains,

> Of the few central beliefs uniting the various post-structuralisms (and connecting them with post/modernism) this is one of the most im-portant: human identity is to be seen as constituted as well as consti-

tutive; constituted (not determined) by, for example, the pre-existing structures of language and ideology, and by the material conditions of human existence. Thus is the subject decentered, and subjectivity revealed as a kind of subjection—not the antithesis of social process but its focus.

In the early modern period also the individual was seen as constituted by and in relation to—even the effect of—a pre-existing order. To know oneself was to know that order.

Carla Freccero puts this another way: "If early modern European textuality foregrounds the status of the subject as linguistically constructed, contingent, textual, and fragmented, then early modern subjectivity has more in common with psychoanalytic and poststructuralist notions of the subject than it does with the modernity that appears in the intervening period."[5] The difference between poststructuralist and early modern understandings of the self has to do with the acceptance or rejection of the social order within which one is entangled. *To know* for the early modern is to accept one's place. *To know* for poststructuralism is to question the social order and subvert it. If "knowing oneself" prior to the nineteenth century meant knowing one's place within an established social order; in contrast, one of the most powerful mythologies of adolescence from the twentieth century is that "knowing oneself" emerges from an authentic sense of individuality that takes place before one finds one's place in the world, concealing the social structures that script the search for identity in the first place. This is not to uphold any one time period as superior but rather to notice that all thought cycles through at various times for various purposes, and when that thought no longer serves us, we shift again. These are the necessary processes of making meaning in the world.

As the epistemological ground shifts once again, we find ourselves in another moment of forgetting, in which the present is lamented as proof of our decline, a "Post-truth Era" in which facts do not seem to matter anymore. Lee McIntyre explains that "the word 'post-truth' is irreducibly normative," "an expression of concern by those who care about the concept of truth and feel that it is under attack."[6] The *Oxford English Dictionary* named "post-truth" the word of the year in November 2016—the same month Donald Trump was elected president. It defines "post-truth" as "related to or denoting circumstances in which objective facts are less influential in shaping public opinion than appeals to emotion and personal belief."[7] McIntyre believes that "what is striking about the idea of post-truth is not just that truth is being challenged, *but that it is being challenged as a mechanism for asserting political dominance.*"[8] Between 2016 and 2018 at least six books on post-truth were published in Britain and the United States, pointing to phenomena like Brexit, Trump's election, and climate-change denial as the sad results of people being unable to discern what is true and what is not.[9] In January 2017 Kellyanne Conway appeared on *Meet the Press* and defended the spurious claims that President Trump's inauguration had the largest attendance in history, insisting that White House press secretary Sean Spicer was not *lying* about attendance numbers but that he was instead providing "alternative facts."[10] Certainly, something has changed. But what, exactly? And what should be done about it?

Conway's phrasing "alternative facts" has an unsettling resonance with queer theory, where the word "alternative" has a counterculture connotation nearly synonymous with antinormativity. Queer theory is a practice of thinking outside what is generally presented to us as thinkable or knowable. Queer, in this sense, is an epistemological alternative to the institutions and social norms that function as the "truth" about lives, bodies, and the world. The work of queer theory, as with other poststructuralist methods, has been traditionally understood as engaged in disrupting notions of truth within a culture that has believed in capital-*T* truth. But, in her interview on *Meet the Press,* Conway seemed to position *herself* and the White House as the agents of radical resignification against the tyranny of the so-called liberal news media. What is the value of queer theory in a world in which disrupting truth claims has become the work of an autocratic political power? Have the methods of queer theory been co-opted for evil?

Bruno Latour poses a similar question about poststructuralism, but as early as 2004, after he read in the *New York Times* about a Republican strategist who openly admitted that science proved the existence of climate change but stated that Republicans should "continue to make the lack of scientific certainty a primary issue" to promote special interests over protective legislation. Latour writes, "Do you see why I am worried? I myself have spent some time in the past trying to show the 'lack of scientific certainty' inherent in the construction of facts. I too make it a 'primary issue.' But I did not exactly aim at fooling the public by obscuring the certainty of a closed argument—or did I? After all, I have been accused of just that sin. Still, I'd like to believe that, on the contrary, I intended to *emancipate* the public from prematurely naturalized objectified facts. Was I foolishly mistaken? Have things changed so fast?"[11]

As I discussed in my introduction, this reevaluation of critique has occurred in multiple fields of study, in Eve Kosofsky Sedgwick's *Touching Feeling* in 2003 and in Rita Felski's *The Limits of Critique* in 2015, for example. In the field of children's literature, Marah Gubar, speaking about the deconstructive trends of the 1990s and the first decade of the 2000s, writes, "Why have so many of us working in childhood studies been content to dispose, not propose?"[12] McIntyre, a research fellow at the Center for Philosophy and the History of Science at Boston University and an instructor in ethics at the Harvard Extension School, feels that poststructuralist methodologies are to blame for post-truth, writing, "It is embarrassing to admit that one of the saddest roots of the post-truth phenomenon seems to have come directly out of colleges and universities."[13] He names Jacques Derrida and Michel Foucault as the cause, and he interprets Latour's 2004 article as an admission of culpability in the politics of climate-science denial. At moments in his 2004 article, Latour appears to admit that he is to blame:

> Entire Ph.D. programs are still running to make sure that good American kids are learning the hard way that facts are made up, that there is no such thing as natural, unmediated, unbiased access to the truth, that we are always prisoners of language, that we always speak from a particular standpoint, and so on, while dangerous extremists are using the very same argument of social construction to destroy hard-won evidence that could save lives. Was I wrong to participate in the invention of this field known as science studies? Is it enough to say that we did not really mean what we said? Why does it burn my tongue to say that global warming is a fact whether you like it or not? Why can't I simply say that the argument is closed for good?[14]

McIntyre agrees, writing that those who use poststructuralist methods "must accept some responsibility for undermining the idea that facts matter in the assessment of reality, and not foreseeing the damage this could cause."[15] Ironically, this is the very same argument found on conservative blogs about "postmodernism" and academia.[16] McIntyre admits that a close reading of Derrida and Foucault might not legitimately support right-wing ideology, acknowledging "the irony that in a few decades the right has evolved from critiquing postmodernism—for example, Lynne Cheney's *Telling the Truth*—to the current situation." McIntyre's solution is "respecting truth," "to stand up for the notion of truth and learn how to fight back."[17] But I am not so sure.

Perhaps I am hesitant to embrace again a stable and objective notion of "truth" because, less than a century ago, scientists and doctors claimed that it was a "fact" that homosexuality was unnatural and pathological. They also claimed that the white European male was superior to all other human beings based on flimsy evidence like skull measurements. The problem has always been that what circulates as the "truth" is so often used to confirm existing social norms and uphold existing social hierarchies. Two examples from the twentieth century, the tobacco industry and the sugar industry, demonstrate how this happens, having been exposed as using their influence to *pay* for scientific research from experts that supported their interests while suppressing research that was bad for business.[18] That is, only the powerful get to say what the truth is. People were deceived by these industries in much the same way that climate-science denial is motivated by special interests, but I don't see anyone calling the 1950s the "Post-truth Era." The type of faith in objective truth that McIntyre wants to go back to is fairly recent in origin—we can trace it back to the late nineteenth century when faith in science began to operate alongside (or in place of) the capital-*T* truth that was God's Truth. This epistemological shift in the nineteenth century enjoyed a degree of acceptance and even dominance for not even half a century before poststructuralist theorists like Foucault started exposing the cultural dynamics at play in the production of scientific knowledge.

I have yet to discover a poststructuralist theorist out there deceiving the masses for political gain. And I think it goes without saying that Trump did not read Foucault or Derrida and that Trump supporters or Brexit voters are not made up of university graduates who got the wrong idea about poststructuralist theory and now think that facts don't matter anymore. What is so troubling about our world today is that Trump seems to be able to say anything he likes while everyone around him protests, and what he says still circulates as "truth" even when it is a "provable falsehood," as Chuck Todd put it to Conway on *Meet the Press*.[19] Real people are disenfranchised, imprisoned, lost, or killed because of his words. Poststructuralist theories anticipate these abuses of power by having claimed all along that institutional power determines what functions as "true" or not. And never is that insight more apparent than right now. Queer theory is not complicit in the postmodern crisis of knowledge-making. It diagnoses it. I think Kemi Adeyemi gets at this point another way in her article "Donald Trump Is the Perfect Man for the Job." She talks about how the language used to make sense of what happened in Trump's election frames all possible causes as the result of individual actions rather than accounting for institutional structures, preventing our recognition that "the United States was founded on a violent colonial encounter, and that the job of the president is itself emergent from and dependent on the racism, sexism, misogyny, homophobia, and xenophobia of this encounter. In other words, the president's 'job' is to uphold and protect racism, sexism, misogyny, homophobia, and xenophobia, as they are core virtues of the U.S. American constitution."[20] Trump merely exposes this history and flaunts it without remorse or shame.

I wonder too if the term "post-truth" and its *Oxford English Dictionary* definition isn't very useful for describing the epistemological norms of the present moment.[21] As McIntyre notes, people have *always* been prone to confirmation bias, prone to trusting information that appeals to their emotions and personal beliefs, and this has been exploited by politicians since the beginning of politicians. Racism, sexism, misogyny, homophobia, and xenophobia run deep and are powerful motivators. Likewise, the people spreading false information—whether it is from the White House or clickbait from Russian bots—are not confused about what is true and what is not. They are purposefully attempting to manipulate people (or in the case of bots, maybe just trying to make money through clicks). Neoliberal capitalism is based on the principle of exploitation. I am wary too of the charge that all social ills of the present are caused by the internet and by social media. It isn't the internet as a technology or how individual users isolate themselves and create echo chambers of self-validating information. The algorithms of Facebook and YouTube do this, not users themselves, pointing to a systemic problem in which echo chambers are the best method of exploiting users' online activity. The post-truth phenomenon is caused by how capitalism exploits the internet, profiling users with an incredibly specific level of detail, how companies like Cambridge Analytica can target voters with content specifically designed to persuade them for or against particular candidates. Post-truth is not caused by individual failure to discern the truth but instead by the incredible sophistication of today's social-manipulation technologies—an intensification of the mechanisms of power already in place before the internet was invented.

These dynamics are explained by what Rebekah Sheldon calls somatic capitalism, which has much in common with but "differs from eugenic biopolitics in its mode of address (moving from population and demography to algorithmic incitement and capacity extraction)" and which "merely deepens and intensifies the paramount biopolitical project of the twentieth century: the elicitation and management of surplus vitality." At the heart of somatic capitalism, Sheldon finds "the literal and material conjunction of the child and capital," "the intervention into and monetization of life-itself."[22] As such, the child is a form of capital available for exploitation rather than a latent subjectivity in need of shaping or directing, and the body is a set of capacities more so than a unified subject.[23] Importantly, "the child serves as the switch gate for somatic capitalism, giving smooth flow, shape, and circuit to several knotty problematics." Sheldon powerfully illustrates the slide from familiar representations of the child as the future of the nation to the present neoliberal context of deregulation, environmental exploitation, and profit-driven risk: "Somatic capitalism operates above and below the level of the individual subject to amplify or diminish specific bodily capacities. It siphons vitality rather than exerting discipline, swerves and harnesses existing tendencies rather than regulating their emergence."[24]

As Foucault predicted, "man" is receding as the form in which knowledge production must take place. Thus, "the present formation shifts from knowledge to *technē*, from the human as the subject and object of knowledge to the human as a biologically vulnerable, biologically exploitable resource, from totality to systematicity." People are no longer valuable as "whole persons" within the disciplinary mechanisms of identity and modern subjectivity, as they were in the twentieth century, but now valued as "subindividual, modular, and extractable parts" within a "new biopolitics" under neoliberal capitalism. The figure of the child serves to reincorporate this dehumanization as well as "the realization of nonhuman vitality back into the charmed circle of the human." It is at this juncture that Sheldon finds "the child has become more available and more pervasive even as economic and legislative policies undermine the very social vitality the child supposedly indexes." Through the figure of the child, Sheldon "points to the drag of the retreating *epistēmē* but also to the pull of the one approaching," in which the dynamics of what I have called the logic of adolescence, based in the developmentalism (or historicism) that emerges over the course of the nineteenth century, are giving way to another logic for knowing and understanding ourselves and the world.[25]

In his article from 2004, Latour does not take back the idea that knowledge is constructed (despite McIntyre's interpretation), but he does begin to reevaluate the tools of critique and how they might be used better in a context that has changed significantly since he began his work in the 1970s. In a recent article in the *New York Times*, he explains, "I think we were so happy to develop all this critique because we were so *sure* of the authority of science. And that the authority of science would be shared because there was a common world. Even this notion of a common world we didn't have to articulate, because it was so obvious. Now we have people who no longer share the idea that there is a common world. And that of course changes everything."[26] We might understand the loss of a "common world"—another way to describe post-truth phenomena—within the context of somatic capitalism, in which a shared culture of stable and unified meanings around what constitutes reality are no longer necessary for mechanisms of power to operate effectively. Instead, the operation of multiple, even infinite, ideological planes work simultaneously to extract and maximize profits from discrete bodily capacities, like clicks or votes.

Henry Giroux describes the waning of the "social contract," where now "the state gives minimum guarantees of security," as people are no longer "bound together as citizens but as consumers, while the neoliberal values of self-interest, personal advancement, and economic calculation" have "rendered ornamental 'the basic principles of and institutions of democracy.'" Giroux finds a widespread social abandonment of youth and, like Sheldon, remarks on the ways that the early twentieth-century narratives of reproductive futurism have given way to discussions of youth as an expendable resource available for profit. He writes, "Social problems become utterly privatized and removed from public consideration," while "communal responsibility [is] derided in favor of individual happiness, largely measured through the acquisition and disposability of consumer goods." Neoliberalism "is not only a system of economic power relations but also a political project, intent on producing new forms of subjectivity and sanctioning particular modes of conduct." The spectacular cruelty played out in the media and in the everyday lives of actual children and adults is accomplished through "rituals" that "legitimate its norms, values, institutions, and social practices." Giroux refers to neoliberalism as a theater of cruelty "reproduced daily through a regime of common sense" that "has become normalized—even celebrated by the dominant media—and now serves as a powerful pedagogical force that shapes our lives, memories, and daily experiences."[27]

While I depart from Giroux in his characterization of the past as a time when "democracy was linked to the well-being of youth," when "how a society imagined democracy and its future was contingent on how it viewed its responsibility toward future generations," I find his observations about the present to be quite urgent and pressing, illustrative of the epistemological "ground that is once more stirring under our feet."[28] He writes, "White wealthy kids may labor under the narrow dictates of a commodity culture, but they are not incarcerated in record numbers, placed in schools that merely serve to warehouse the refuse of global capitalism, or subjected to a life of misery and impoverishment."[29] In this book I have described forms of harm that take place under the guise of care, but what we have seen in recent years with the Trump administration's policy of separating refugee families at the border—mothers and babies—and indefinitely holding children in concentration camps while the world looks on, speaks to this spectacular theater of harm that no longer requires the justification of idealizing narratives of a universalizing humanity.

I think Sedgwick anticipates this present moment when she writes, "Why bother exposing the ruses of power in a country where, at any given moment, 40 percent of young black men are enmeshed in the penal system? In the United States and internationally, while there is plenty of hidden violence that requires exposure there is also, and increasingly, an ethos where forms of violence that are hypervisible from the start may be offered as an exemplary spectacle rather than remain to be unveiled as a scandalous secret." Along these same lines, she remarks, "I'm a lot less worried about being pathologized by my therapist than about my vanishing mental health coverage—and that's given the great good luck of having health insurance at all." Like Latour's comment from the *New York Times*, she notes that the work of critique "is a far different act from what such exposures would have been in the 1960s," when the solidity of these institutions, the "common world" Latour refers to, could be taken for granted.[30] It is worth continuing to think through what *has* changed and how our tools might be put to the best use in the present context. Latour describes how the Enlightenment used a "very powerful descriptive tool, that of matters of fact, which were excellent for *debunking* quite a lot of beliefs, powers, and illusions," but by the mid-twentieth century "matters of fact" required the "same debunking impetus" and have now left us temporarily in "some sort of darkness." At this critical moment Latour asks, "Can we devise another powerful descriptive tool that deals this time with matters of concern and whose import then will no longer be to debunk but to protect and to care, as Donna Haraway would put it? Is it really possible to transform the critical urge in the ethos of someone who *adds* reality to matters of fact and not *subtract* reality?" Toward this end Latour proposes that "the critic is not one who debunks, but the one who assembles. The critic is not the one who lifts the rugs from under the feet of naïve believers, but the one who offers participants arenas in which to gather."[31] Likewise, what Haraway calls "staying with the trouble," the practices Sedgwick puts forward as "reparative reading," or what Karen Barad calls the "ethics of entanglement"—these are all gestures toward grounded, ethically oriented, creative, and constructive practices coming out of poststructuralist theory.[32]

The project of this book participates in a similar shift in the fields of childhood studies and children's literature, away from critique and toward questions of ethics regarding children and categories of age, both present and historical. Marah Gubar's "kinship model" of childhood, John Wall's *Ethics in Light of Childhood*, and Jules Gill-Peterson's "ethical aperture of relation" toward trans children are all suggestive of the types of constructive, imaginative, and world-making work that comes after deconstruction.[33] The chapters collected in Anna Mae Duane's *Children's Table*, as well as the articles in recent special issues such as *WSQ*'s "Child" and *GLQ*'s "The Child Now" also speak to the growing importance and recognition of this methodological work.[34] The Children's Literature Association Annual Conference in 2019 themed "Activism and Empathy" featured many papers with explicitly ethical stakes and goals. In many ways our field has never been far from ethical concerns in the first place. At its heart this is a shift away from the exclusive focus on cultural ideas about the child in the work of scholars like Jacqueline Rose and Karín Lesnik-Oberstein and toward scholarly approaches that consider the lives, texts, and matter of actual children.[35] However, the turn toward ethics in the field does not represent a pre-Rose orientation toward texts and culture or a return to simplistic questions that reconstruct a passive Other, like, "Is this book good for children?" In fact, I do not see the ethical turn as a departure from Rose or poststructuralist theory so much as an elaboration of the stakes of deconstruction and critical analysis, work that fields like feminism, critical race studies, and queer theory have brought to the center of their intellectual practices since their inception. After all, what is the purpose of rethinking the category child if not to imagine a better world, a better way of seeing and relating to the people called children?

My aim has been to put pressure on institutional knowledge of adolescence, to unravel its categorizations and certainties, but I acknowledge also that there are fields of study that require generalizations, require the reiteration and stabilization of categories as part of their disciplinary practices. This leaves us with a question: Can we build on institutional knowledge without requiring this displacement of authority away from young people themselves? This is a fundamental relation of dominance in the act of constructing knowledge about others, and this is the ethical problem with early twentieth-century categories of age and the categories of difference produced by institutional discourses during this time. Can the institution function, with all its benefits, without requiring the sacrifice of self and other to its management and control?

These questions require us to grapple with queer theory's role both outside and within institutional contexts to conceptualize a transformative, radical resistance. Queer theory's antinormative methods are necessary not only for questioning existing power structures but also for creating a more ethical world. And this means being able to do both deconstructive and constructive work. Queer knowing is not arbitrary, not a version of relativism or so flimsy as to change with each passing moment. Queer epistemologies, for example, allow for a profound recognition of *what is real* about the body and about desire even when the cultural norms of gender and sexuality or the limits of language make such recognition seem unthinkable or impossible. And such forms of knowledge can be based on *feeling*, on forms of knowing that necessarily exist beyond the grasp of language, which is why I am so hesitant to accept the definition of post-truth or its diagnosis of our present. The value of queer theory is not in its ability to seize power and rule the world. It is about survival when the conditions of survival seem impossible, unthinkable. It is about a pathway through trauma and violence. It's not about lies or truth; it's about being able to move one's subjectivity out and away with new tools, new words, and new concepts, as the old ones are taken away, absorbed into the system, normalized, or weaponized. It is about the ability to imagine systemic and institutional alternatives beyond our present logics of individualism and capitalist exploitation. The logic of adolescence emerges out of and naturalizes these features of late modernity while obscuring ethical alternatives as unthinkable or unknowable. We must imagine adolescence otherwise if we are to both live and work through what is to come.

notes

Preface.

1. Philip Graham is a professor emeritus of child psychiatry at the Institute of Child Health in London.

2. Graham, *End of Adolescence*, 1.

3. Epstein, *Case against Adolescence*, xix.

4. See also Giroux, *Youth in a Suspect Society*.

5. Musgrove, *Youth and the Social Order*, 1, 2, 3.

6. The idea that young people are reaching puberty at younger and younger ages might itself be a popular myth about adolescence, one usually deployed to disenfranchise young people through narratives of societal decline.

7. Musgrove, *Youth and the Social Order*, 58, 3–6.

8. Cohen, foreword to Musgrove, *Youth and the Social Order*, ix, xi, x, xix.

9. See Sheldon, *Child to Come*, 118.

Introduction.
Queer Theory and Categories of Age

1. Butler, *Undoing Gender*, 29.

2. Lorde, *Sister Outsider*, 53–59.

3. For ghosting the gay child, see Stockton, *Queer Child*. For scenes of social ridicule, the movie *Tomboy* (2011) is a recent example. There are countless examples of suicide, but one is *Lost and Delirious* (2001).

4. Sedgwick, *Tendencies*, 1, 3, 4.

5. Rose, *Case of Peter Pan*, 10, 1.

6. Sedgwick, *Touching Feeling*, 123–51; Sedgwick, "Paranoid Reading and Reparative Reading," in Sedgwick, *Novel Gazing*, 1–37; Felski, *Limits of*

Critique; Gubar, "Risky Business"; Gubar, "Hermeneutics of Recuperation."
See also Rudd, *Reading the Child*.

7. This phrase is often attributed to Ricoeur's book *Freud and Philosophy* but was actually coined by him much later to describe his work as a whole. See Felski, *Limits of Critique*, 31.

8. Sedgwick, *Touching Feeling*, 130.

9. Felski, *Limits of Critique*, 8.

10. Gubar, "Hermeneutics of Recuperation," 305.

11. Felski, *Limits of Critique*, 5.

12. Sedgwick, *Touching Feeling*, 128, 124.

13. Barad understands "the apparatus" in scientific experimentation as crucial in shaping what becomes visible and knowable, what is able to emerge as *matter* within phenomena and thus is productive of reality (*Meeting the Universe Halfway*, 148).

14. See Foucault, *History of Sexuality*.

15. Freud, "Psychogenesis of a Case," in Strachey, *Standard Edition*, 18:147; Krafft-Ebing, *Psychopathia sexualis*.

16. Kristeva, *New Maladies of the Soul*, 135.

17. I am using the phrase "hermeneutic of the self" as an elaboration of Foucault's conceptualization of sexuality as a hermeneutic of self (*History of Sexuality*).

18. This question echoes a psychoanalytic notion of childhood and adolescence as constitutive of adult subjectivity. See Rose, *Case of Peter Pan*; and Kristeva, *New Maladies of the Soul*.

19. Queer theory has productively questioned this sequencing of development and identity. See Halberstam, *In a Queer Time*; Freeman, *Time Binds*; and Edelman, *No Future*.

20. See Hacking, *Historical Ontology*.

21. Sánchez-Eppler writes that her focus on childhood necessarily entails a broad and flexible range of ages, "from infancy to adolescence, treating childhood not as a specific period of years but as a set of social conditions" (*Dependent States*, xxi). See also Steedman, *Strange Dislocations*; Kincaid, *Erotic Innocence*; and Bernstein, *Racial Innocence*.

22. Gubar, "Risky Business," 450, 451.

23. Gubar, *Artful Dodgers*, 31.

24. Bernstein, *Racial Innocence*, 28–29.

25. Kincaid, *Child-Loving*, 5; quoted in Bernstein, *Racial Innocence*, 24; Kincaid, *Child-Loving*, 12; Kincaid, *Erotic Innocence*, 16; quoted in Bernstein, *Racial Innocence*, 6.

26. Kincaid, *Child-Loving*, 73.

27. Kincaid, *Erotic Innocence*, 16; Rose, *Case of Peter Pan*, 2.

28. Sánchez-Eppler, *Dependent States*, xxii.

29. Kincaid, *Erotic Innocence*, 19.

30. Edelman, *No Future*, 3.

31. Kincaid, *Child-Loving*, 5.

32. For example, Kincaid's emphasis on discourse and the cultural mythologies that construct the "pedophile" and the "child" as figures and roles is still misunderstood in both nonacademic and academic contexts as a defense of child molesters, despite Kincaid's clear statements about the great harm of denying our culpability in the circumstances leading to child abuse. That is, he is misunderstood as justifying or upholding the very discourse he aims to critique. Kincaid does not defend child abuse but rather describes the elaborate ways our culture avoids acknowledging the reality of it. See *Erotic Innocence*.

33. Edelman, *No Future*, 11.

34. Rose, *Case of Peter Pan*, 2.

35. This is referred to as representationalism, which Barad defines as "the belief in the ontological distinction between representations and that which they purport to represent; in particular, that which is represented is held to be independent of all practices of representing" (*Meeting the Universe Halfway*, 46).

36. Rose, *Case of Peter Pan*, 7, 10.

37. In some cases the emphasis on language in critical analysis has become a totalizing view, in which, as Barad remarks, "Language has been granted too much power" (*Meeting the Universe Halfway*, 132). Lesnik-Oberstein's (mis)interpretations of Rose, for example, illustrate a view of language in which no material world or bodily phenomenon is retrievable (*Children's Literature*). This is an opposite trend to the one I am addressing. Scholars such as Lesnik-Oberstein and Stephen Thomson, for example, find Sedgwick, Edelman, and Stockton not too distant from the matter of real lives but rather to be risking "impending collapses of post-structuralist self-reflexivity" ("What Is Queer Theory Doing?," 37). See also Lesnik-Oberstein, "Childhood, Queer Theory, and Feminism."

38. Prout, *Future of Childhood*, 2.

39. Edelman, *No Future*, 29, 49.

40. Giffney, "Queer Apocal(o)ptic/ism," in Giffney and Hird, *Queering the Non/Human*, 73.

41. Sedgwick, *Tendencies*, 163, 164.

42. Gubar, "Hermeneutics of Recuperation," 292.

43. Sánchez-Eppler, *Dependent States*, xv, xxii.

44. Gubar, "Hermeneutics of Recuperation," 292.

45. Sánchez-Eppler, *Dependent States*, xxiii, xxv.

46. See Gubar, *Artful Dodgers*.

47. Bernstein, *Racial Innocence*, 212.

48. Duane, "Questioning the Autonomous Subject," in Duane, *Children's Table*, 15.

49. Steedman, *Strange Dislocations*, x.

50. Steedman's historical analysis in *Strange Dislocations* draws heavily on psychoanalysis and cites Foucault, and she has been taken up by poststructuralist approaches to childhood in recent years; for example, see Sheldon, *Child to Come*; and Gill-Peterson, *Histories of the Transgender Child*.

51. Sedgwick, *Touching Feeling*, 11.

52. Gubar, "Hermeneutics of Recuperation," 291; Sedgwick, *Touching Feeling*, 13.

53. Sedgwick, *Touching Feeling*, 6.

54. Barad, *Meeting the Universe Halfway*, 133.

55. Ibid.

56. Butler, *Bodies That Matter*, 2.

57. Barad, *Meeting the Universe Halfway*, 152.

58. Sedgwick, *Tendencies*, 163.

59. See Mead, *Coming of Age in Samoa*.

60. For an example of this phenomenon, see Libby Anne, "We Don't 'Do' Teenagers," *Love, Joy, Feminism* (blog), September 12, 2011, https://www.patheos.com/blogs/lovejoyfeminism/2011/09/we-dont-do-teenagers.html.

61. Butler, *Gender Trouble*, xxiv.

62. Barad, *Meeting the Universe Halfway*, 152, 49, 55.

63. Freccero, *Queer/Early/Modern*, 2, 4.

64. Barad, *Meeting the Universe Halfway*, 55.

65. Warner, *Trouble with Normal*, 56–58. Likewise, Hacking describes "the avalanche of numbers that begins around 1820" as being "obsessed with *analyse morale*, namely, the statistics of deviance," including "suicide, prostitution, drunkenness, vagrancy, madness, crime, *les misérables*." This striking trend of accounting for deviance leads him to ask, "Is making up people intimately linked to control?" (*Historical Ontology*, 104).

66. Goldberg and Menon, "Queering History," 1616.

67. Freccero, *Queer/Early/Modern*, 5.

68. Steedman, *Strange Dislocations*, x.

69. Sedgwick, *Touching Feeling*, 130.

70. Chinn, "'I Was a Lesbian Child,'" in Duane, *Children's Table*, 161.

Chapter 1.
G. Stanley Hall and the Logic of Developmentalism

1. For example, Springhall remarks, "The modern concept of adolescence as an autonomous age group was created almost singlehandedly in America by G. Stanley Hall (1844–1925) and his colleagues at Clark University" (*Coming of Age*, 28). Spacks notes, "Adolescents have always existed, but the myth of adolescence has thrived most richly since G. Stanley Hall invented it" (*Adolescent Idea*, 228). In a chapter titled "The Invention of the Adolescent," Kett writes, "The era of the adolescent dawned in Europe and America in the two decades after 1900" (*Rites of Passage*, 215). Springhall, Spacks, and Kett do not dismiss the importance of the nineteenth century, and their books include significant historical context leading up to 1900. These older histories, however, have given way to an emphasis on the start of the twentieth century as an origin point—a key moment, for sure—but one that might be further nuanced. Neubauer, for example, claims "adolescence 'came of age' in the decades around 1900, not only because the term had little currency earlier, but, as I shall show, because interlocking discourses about adolescence emerged in psychoanalysis, psychology, criminal justice, pedagogy, sociology, as well as in literature" (*Fin-de-Siècle Culture of Adolescence*, 6). Moran writes, "At the dawn of the twentieth century, a sixty-year-old man invented adolescence" (*Teaching Sex*, 1). Likewise, Baxter argues, "The notion that adolescence is a twentieth-century invention is supported by the fact that the term had little currency before 1900 and made a sudden and pronounced appearance in a wide variety of discourses at the century's beginning" (*Modern Age*, 3).

2. These numbers are taken from full-text searches for the word "adolescence" in Readex's *Early American Newspapers*, 1690–1922, series 1–3; Gale's *British Library Newspapers*; and the *Times Digital Archive*. As of this writing, I did not have access to Readex's *Early American Newspapers*, series 4–16, collections that would dramatically increase the number of sources found in U.S. papers. Additionally, there are 667 references to "adolescence" in Gale's *Nineteenth Century U.S. Newspapers*, though some of these overlap with the references in the Readex database, so I did not combine the number of results from the two databases.

3. There is a notable overlap in the articles reprinted in British and U.S. newspapers in the nineteenth century. Because my argument is concerned with the ways language and meaning move over time, the wider the archive, the more useful it is for tracking these types of shifts in usage and meaning. Likewise, Hall's educational and professional background span both sides of the Atlantic. There are differences in how adolescence took shape in different countries; however, "the simultaneous development in different nations of the institutions and psychology of adolescence had some common characteristics and sources" (Kett, *Rites of Passage*, 215).

4. Because I am interested in broad patterns of usage and meaning, a medium like newspapers serves my purpose better than novels or parenting manuals. Cordell explains, "The composition and circulation of texts among antebellum newspapers offers a model of authorship that is communal rather than individual, distributed rather than centralized" ("Reprinting," 418). My project is different from Cordell and Smith's at the Viral Texts Project in that I have analyzed patterns of usage and meaning for an individual word across databases of nineteenth-century newspapers, whereas the Viral Texts Project is mapping instances of whole article reprinting among multiple newspapers and periodicals to theorize which factors caused some articles to "go viral" (Cordell and Smith, "Viral Texts Project").

5. *London Times*, February 14, 1862; "The United States," *London Times*, May 25, 1865; "Visit of the Prince of Wales to Australia," *London Times*, December 20, 1860.

6. See "For the Oracle: From Simon," *Harrisburg (Pa.) Oracle of Dauphin and Harrisburgh Advertiser*, December 29, 1804; and "For the Enquirer," *Richmond (Va.) Enquirer*, January 21, 1812.

7. Walkerdine, "Beyond Developmentalism?," 453, 462.

8. Castañeda, *Figurations*, 13.

9. See Mandelbaum, *History, Man, and Reason*, 41; and Foucault, *Order of Things*, xxiii.

10. Steedman, *Strange Dislocations*, 7.

11. Foucault, *Order of Things*, xxii.

12. The word "adolescence" comes from Latin and appears in French in the late thirteenth century and English in the fifteenth century, meaning the "period of life between childhood and young adulthood, youth, youthfulness" (*Oxford English Dictionary*, s.v. "adolescence," accessed September 15, 2019, http://www.oed.com). The newspaper databases together show only 9 uses of the word before 1800 and only 20–30 a year between 1800 and 1840, tripling in number in the 1840s and beyond. The word "adolescence,"

however, was not frequently used in the nineteenth century. A side-by-side comparison in Gale's *Nineteenth Century U.S. Newspapers* shows 667 references to "adolescence" compared to more than 350,000 references to "youth," suggesting that "adolescence" was not a common term of reference for categories of age until the late nineteenth century, when it begins to appear more frequently in medical and scientific discourse.

13. "The Use and Abuse of Time," *New York Chronicle*, June 29, 1769.

14. Philologer, "Pompous Reflections No. 1," *Vancouver (Wash.) Columbian*, April 9, 1811. This article was reprinted as "Pompous Reflections" in the *New-York Weekly Museum* a few weeks later, on April 27, 1811.

15. *Middletown (Conn.) Constitution*, December 6, 1848. The wording varies in reprints from paper to paper, suggesting the variations of oral circulation.

16. *San Antonio Express*, May 20, 1870.

17. "Sculpture," *New York Commercial Advertiser*, October 6, 1798.

18. "Robert Smallpiece," advertisement, *Boston Columbian Centinel*, August 23, 1806.

19. "Amicable Controversy, or Politics beneath an Oak," *Washington (D.C.) Monitor*, June 2, 1808.

20. "Sachem's Head: A Story of the Seventeenth Century," *Middletown (Conn.) Middlesex Gazette*, April 12, 1826.

21. "The Past," *Norwich (Conn.) Courier*, September 26, 1827.

22. "Simple Annals from the 'Remember Me,'" *Bridgeton (N.J.) Washington Whig*, December 27, 1828.

23. "Joanna of Lewardeen," *Boston Daily Atlas*, January 14, 1848.

24. Springhall, *Coming of Age*, 34.

25. Kett, *Rites of Passage*, 6.

26. My encounters with the phrase "infancy and adolescence" were often coincidental in my reading of newspaper references to adolescence. As of this writing, the Readex and Gale newspaper databases are not very effective when searching for a phrase because of the ways the newspaper images must be tagged and coded with searchable text.

27. The earliest instance I could find of this piece appeared in the *Barnstaple (U.K.) North Devon Journal* in 1824, under the title "Phisiology," and it also circulated in various papers in Ireland, Wales, and England in 1824 and 1825 as well as in later years.

28. E. G. Wheeler, "Periods of Human Life," 396.

29. Foucault, *Order of Things*, xxiii.

30. Ibid., 129.

31. Foucault, *Order of Things*, xxi.

32. See Chamberlain, *Child*, 70.

33. Ariès, *Centuries of Childhood*, 23, 25.

34. "The Periods of Human Life," *Newburyport (Ma.) Herald*, April 29, 1825.

35. "Master Burke," *Baltimore Patriot*, May 6, 1831. The title refers to child prodigy Joseph Burke (1818–1902), an actor and musician also known as the "Irish Roscius," who came to the United States in 1830. He would have been thirteen years old at the time of this review.

36. "Dr. A. L. Warner's Lecture," *Richmond (Va.) Enquirer*, November 25, 1834.

37. "Laugh Where We Must, Be Candid Where We Can," *New Hampshire Patriot*, January 13, 1840.

38. Emma C. Embury, "Willfulness, or The Wife's Tale," *Salem (Ma.) Gazette*, June 4, 1841 and *Pennsylvania Inquirer* (Philadelphia), June 18, 1841.

39. "The Illumination at New York," *Baltimore Sun*, May 10, 1847.

40. *Texian Advocate* (Victoria), May 1, 1851.

41. "The Poacher," *Boston Daily Atlas*, February 15, 1853. This story was reportedly translated from the French periodical *Revue des Deux Mondes*.

42. Joel Barlow, "Oration, Delivered at Washington City on the 4th of July Inst," *Boston Daily Advertiser*, July 14, 1809. This speech was also printed in the *Richmond (Va.) Enquirer* and the *Philadelphia Democratic Press* in July and in the *New-Hampshire Patriot* in August 1809.

43. "Debate on Saturday, January 28," *Washington Federalist* (Georgetown), February 18, 1809. The war in question is the Peninsular War, 1808–14, between France and the allied powers of Spain, the United Kingdom, and Portugal for control of the Iberian Peninsula during the Napoleonic Wars.

44. "Address from the Washington Association to the Young Men of Pennsylvania," *Philadelphia Poulson's American Daily Advertiser*, August 19, 1813.

45. "From the Winchester Advertiser," *Washington (Ky.) Union*, September 1, 1815.

46. "City Hall," *Washington (D.C.) Daily National Intelligencer*, August 23, 1820. This article was also printed in 1820 in the New York papers the *American*, the *Mercantile Advertiser*, and the *New-York Gazette*; the *Norwich (Conn.) Courier*; the *Pittsfield (Mass.) Sun*; and the *Providence (R.I.) Patriot*.

47. "The Presidential Election," *Washington (D.C.) Daily National Intelligencer*, February 6, 1816.

48. "The Life of Napoleon Bonaparte," *Washington (D.C.) Daily National Intelligencer*, August 10, 1841.

49. "Our Relations with Mexico: The Prospect a Little Stormy," *New York Herald*, August 14, 1845.

50. "Mr. Knowlton's Resolutions," *Wisconsin Patriot* (Madison), March 8, 1856.

51. In the newspaper databases I accessed, there were no examples of negative descriptors like this prior to 1856, and these phrases are somewhat idiosyncratic themselves. The phrase "gangrene adolescence" appears in a scathing "Rotary Biography of the Wisconsin Assembly of 1856," *Wisconsin Patriot* (Madison), April 5, 1856; and the phrase "effeminate adolescence" appears in an equally scathing "Rotary Biography of the Legislature of Wisconsin of 1856," *Wisconsin Patriot* (Madison), October 25, 1856, likely by the same writer: the April article was written under the pseudonym "Gov. Rotary Pump, Esq" and the October article was published anonymously.

52. "Our Relations with England," *Washington (D.C.) Madisonian*, March 31, 1842.

53. "The Progress of the United States: Its Agriculture and Population," *New York Herald*, February 2, 1845.

54. "The New Revolution: Its Character and Tendency," *New York Herald*, April 2, 1845.

55. "Letters of Interest and Importance," *Chicago Pomeroy's Democrat*, September 21, 1870.

56. "In Hoc Signo Vinces, Another Day of Revelry," *New-Orleans Times*, December 4, 1874; "Round about Town" *New-Orleans Times*, December 20, 1874.

57. "L'Homme Qui Rit," *London Times*, October 14, 1869; *London Times*, December 17, 1869.

58. Baxter, for example, writes, "These [negative] attitudes were articulated and justified in the earliest full-length theoretical treatments of what would become popularly known as 'adolescence': G. Stanley Hall's two-volume work . . . and Margaret Mead's three studies. . . . Hall and Mead were also united in the rehabilitative nature of their work, which claimed to provide objective observations of adolescents, but really outlined methods to deal with members of this demographic if they got out of control" (*Modern Age*, 4–5).

59. Foucault, *History of Sexuality*, 43, 102, 43; Hacking, *Historical Ontology*, 99–114.

60. Somerville, *Queering the Color Line*, 3, 4.

61. For example, Castañeda analyzes how the child in nineteenth-century science is "used to establish hierarchies of race, class, gender, and sexuality as 'facts' of the natural human body" (*Figurations*, 9). Similarly, Bernstein argues that "childhood figured pivotally in a set of large-scale U.S. racial projects" (*Racial Innocence*, 3). Lesko further describes how constructions of "white middle-class boys . . . at the turn of the 20th century similarly depended on girls, on working-class youth, and on youth of color, against whom they were defined as masculine, pure, self-disciplined, and courageous." Thus, Lesko argues, "the modern project to develop adolescence was and is simultaneously a construction of whiteness and masculinity as central to the citizen" (*Act Your Age!*, 9). DeLuzio remarks, "notions of gender, race, and class figured into the scientific production of adolescence as a 'universal,' 'developmental' category that privileged maleness, whiteness, and middle-class status as its normative characteristics" (*Female Adolescence*, 5). And Chinn argues that the idea of modern adolescence emerged in 1900 as the result of prejudice toward immigrants and their Americanized teenage children at the turn of the century: "While early discussions of adolescents conflated their urban immigrant circumstances with their age identity, within a few decades the language used about this particular group of young people migrated to the larger class of adolescents, particularly (and ironically) the bourgeois Anglo teenagers who were previously defined in opposition to these working class kids" (*Inventing Modern Adolescence*, 5–6).

62. Mandelbaum, *History, Man, and Reason*, 41.

63. Foucault, *Order of Things*, xxiii, 128.

64. See Taylor, *Sources of the Self*, 288; Moretti, *Way of the World*, 6–7; and Fabian, *Time and the Other*, 8–15.

65. Freeman, "Time Binds, or Erotohistoriography," 58.

66. Freeman, *Time Binds*, 4.

67. Lesko, *Act Your Age!*, 91.

68. Steedman, *Strange Dislocations*, 12.

69. Foucault, *History of Sexuality*, 143. See also Steedman, *Strange Dislocations*, 10–11; and Taylor, *Sources of the Self*, 111–14. Taking her cue from Taylor, Steedman describes "*the thing that happened* in this period was the move from outside to inside" (*Strange Dislocations*, 11).

70. Freeman, *Time Binds*, 4–5.

71. Taylor, *Sources of the Self*, 288–89.

72. It was Erikson, not Hall, who popularized the idea of the "adolescent identity crisis" in *Identity*. For more on these narrativizing functions of ad-

olescence and identity, see Kristeva, *New Maladies of the Soul*, 135–53; and Gordon, "Turning Back."

73. Mandelbaum, *History, Man, and Reason*, 47.

74. Steedman, *Strange Dislocations*, 50, 52.

75. Hall, *Adolescence*, 1:vii.

76. Gill-Peterson explains that metaphor is an essential tool for the theory and practice of science and that "metaphor illuminates the active role of language and form in the production of scientific knowledge *and* their entanglement with the material world." However, children have also been dehumanized and "made into poorly fitted metaphors" to give shape to other concepts. According to Gill-Peterson, the solution is not to do away with metaphors in the construction of scientific knowledge but "to imagine different ones that would reshape the practice of science and the production of biological knowledge from the situated perspective of the long-presumed passive object" (*Histories of the Transgender Child*, 36–38).

77. Hall, *Adolescence*, 1:viii. On Haeckel's law, see his *Generelle morphologie der organismen*.

78. Hall, *Adolescence*, 1:vii, 2:649.

79. Gould, *Ontogeny and Phylogeny*, 2, 3, 4, 3.

80. Many scholars have made this observation. See Mandelbaum, *History, Man, and Reason*, 44; and Walkerdine, "Beyond Developmentalism?," 455.

81. Hall, *Adolescence*, 1:viii.

82. Moran, *Teaching Sex*, 15.

83. Fabian writes, "A failure to distinguish between Darwin's and Spencer's views of evolution is responsible for a great deal of equivocal back-and-forth tracking between biological and sociocultural applications. On the other hand, an admixture of the two cannot simply be dismissed as an error. It stems from a tradition of equivocation fostered by Spencer himself and perhaps by Darwin in his later stages" (*Time and the Other*, 11).

84. Herbert Spencer, "The Development Hypothesis," *Corning, (N.Y.) Leader*, March 20, 1852. Castañeda writes, "Spencer's voluminous writings employed a version of evolution that used individual development as the basis for human evolution, and narrated both as a progressive story" (*Figurations*, 20–21).

85. Darwin, *On the Origin of the Species*, in Wilson, *From So Simple a Beginning*, 532, 505.

86. Castañeda, *Figurations*, 20.

87. Fabian, *Time and the Other*, 12.

88. Ibid., 14–15, 17.

89. Castañeda, *Figurations*, 22.

90. Walkerdine, "Beyond Developmentalism?," 455.

91. Freeman, "Time Binds, or Erotohistoriography," 57.

92. See Walkerdine, "Beyond Developmentalism?," 457–61.

93. See Krafft-Ebing, *Psychopathia sexualis*; and Freud, "Psychogenesis of a Case," in Strachey, *Standard Edition*, 18:145–72. The construction of queer lives and identities as immature continues in homophobic therapeutic practices today. See Sedgwick, *Tendencies*, 154–64.

94. "The Awkward Age," *Cultivator and Country Gentleman*, June 11, 1868, 429. This article contains a header indicating that it was reprinted from the newspaper the *Independent*.

95. Hall, *Adolescence*, 1:viii.

96. Foucault, *History of Sexuality*, 138.

97. Colebrook, "On Not Becoming Man," in Alaimo and Heckman, *Material Feminisms*, 66.

98. Foucault, *History of Sexuality*, 144.

99. Edelman, *No Future*, 2–3. What Edelman identifies as a symptom of contemporary political thought has its roots in the biopolitics of the emerging institutions of medicine, psychology, and education in the late nineteenth century.

100. Edelman, *No Future*, 3.

101. Bernstein, *Racial Innocence*, 1.

102. Don Ellzey, "JP Refuses to Marry Couple," *Hammond (La.) Daily Star*, October 15, 2009, quoted in Bernstein, *Racial Innocence*, 1.

103. Associated Press, "Landrieu: Keith Bardwell Should Be Dismissed for Denying Marriage Licenses to Interracial Couples," *Huffington Post*, October 16, 2009, quoted in Bernstein, *Racial Innocence*, 1.

104. Edelman, *No Future*, 11.

105. Castañeda, *Figurations*, 1.

106. Giffney, "Queer Apocal(o)ptic/ism," in Giffney and Hird, *Queering the Non/Human*, 72.

107. Bernstein, *Racial Innocence*, 2.

108. Baxter writes, "Urbanization, industrialization, and the various social reforms that accompanied these changes in America in the latter half of the nineteenth century had the effect of making teens a more conspicuous presence" (*Modern Age*, 44). John R. Gillis writes, "The problems of the adolescent were gaining public attention by 1900 because an increasingly larger minority of the population was finding itself in the demographic and

economic situation that produced this new phase of life" (*Youth and History*, 118). Springhall writes, "Historical trends in modern British society were also conspiring to bring recognition to adolescence as a clearly demarcated group with its own peculiar problems" (*Coming of Age*, 26–27).

109. Colebrook, "On Not Becoming Man," in Alaimo and Heckman, *Material Feminisms*, 57. Colebrook is not writing specifically about the child but about the idea of potentiality in materialist politics more broadly.

110. Dinshaw et al., "Theorizing Queer Temporalities," 182.

111. See Stockton, *Queer Child.*

112. Muñoz, *Cruising Utopia*, 127, 49.

113. Sedgwick, *Touching Feeling*, 148.

114. Ibid., 149.

Chapter 2.
Temporality, Selfhood, and the Politics of Difference

1. Margaret Lowenfeld, "Youth and Health" (lecture delivered to the British Red Cross Society, London, July 22, 1934), folder 10, box 5, Margaret Lowenfeld, Archives and Manuscripts, Wellcome Library, London.

2. This argument is elaborated further for the second half of the twentieth century in chapter 3.

3. Yoder, [Untitled], 16.

4. "Dr. Hall's 'Adolescence' Considered One of the Most Important in Years," *Philadelphia Enquirer*, July 22, 1904.

5. Castañeda remarks on how the version of childhood described in this context is specifically Western, one that is "constituted in and for the West, or for European, Western, or modern culture" (*Figurations*, 16). What this means is that the figure of the child described here is not just culturally and historically located in the West, but one formulated historically and culturally to support the West's narratives about its own superiority.

6. Upham, *Transactions and Proceedings*, 113.

7. "Majestic Maturity," advertisement for Bradfield's Female Regulator, *Macon Telegraph*, November 19, 1897.

8. Walkerdine, "Beyond Developmentalism?," 452.

9. Hall, *Adolescence*, 1:v.

10. These epistemological concerns reemerge a mere sixty years later in poststructuralist theory and science studies (see epilogue).

11. Hall, *Adolescence*, 1:vii.

12. Fabian, *Time and the Other*, 1.

13. Hall, *Adolescence*, 1:viii.

14. Butler, *Bodies That Matter*, 168.

15. Rose, *Case of Peter Pan*, 10.

16. Kincaid, *Erotic Innocence*, 20.

17. Bernstein, *Racial Innocence*, 4.

18. See Zelizer, *Pricing the Priceless Child*. In an unpublished dissertation titled "Making Children Normal," Huang documents the corresponding, but seemingly opposite, trend to count, measure, and sort children in statistics at the turn of the century: "Zelizer's excellent analysis has inspired many of the questions that I have brought to this work. Yet, on the surface, our conclusions do not necessarily agree. . . . If we assume that we are both right, there is an interesting irony, that society began to esteem children as precious while objectifying them as future resources. Both scenarios led to the conclusion that the nation should pay attention to children and their development. Some reformers at the time made use of both points of view (following heart-rending stories about child suffering with arguments about wasting precious resources). It seems that they did not see a contradiction" (25). I think Huang's observation is correct: these two seemingly opposite trends are enabled by the objectification of children. The idealization of a priceless child is *the same* impulse as the view that children are raw material for the making of the future.

19. "Seeks National Measure," *Philadelphia Inquirer*, January 30, 1904.

20. "Ask Mercy for Texas Cattle," *Philadelphia Inquirer*, November 14, 1903.

21. Stockton, *Queer Child*, 30, 32. Stockton notes that innocence can be conferred to a child of color, but only through a narrative of abuse: "Evidently, this equal-opportunity innocence for the underprivileged, which requires their being brutalized, is worthy of our sight" (33).

22. Breslow, "Adolescent Citizenship," 475.

23. Ibid., 474.

24. Rollo, "Color of Childhood," 310.

25. Breslow, "Adolescent Citizenship," 474, 489.

26. Hall, *Adolescence*, 1:xiii, 1:xvii.

27. Castañeda, *Figurations*, 41–42, 37.

28. Quoted in Castañeda, *Figurations*, 38.

29. The title of chapter 18 of Hall's *Adolescence* is "Ethnic Psychology and Pedagogy, or Adolescent Races and Their Treatment" (2:648–748).

30. Hall, *Adolescence*, 2:748.

31. Gill-Peterson, *Histories of the Transgender Child*, 52.

32. Ibid., 79, 121, 1.

33. Ibid., 182, 183.

34. Doris M. Odlum, *The Psychology of Adolescence* (reprinted from *Mother and Child*, March–April 1931), pamphlet, 1931, folder 4, box 106, Medical Women's Federation, Archives and Manuscripts, Wellcome Library, London, 1. Odlum was an English psychiatrist who specialized in childhood and adolescence. She founded psychiatric divisions at two British hospitals in the 1920s and 1930s and was a founding member of the British Medical Association.

35. Ibid.

36. I did a Google search to find out if people still believe that temperature impacts the timing of puberty, and it seems that this is not a claim made about humans or different ethnic groups any longer. However, the underlying racist belief that non-European people are biologically hypersexualized remains today. In my search I noticed a similar obsession with early puberty (and its negative alignment with people of color, poverty, processed food, environmental toxins, etc.) that resembled the discourses of the early twentieth century, taking for granted that earlier puberty is unequivocally *bad* and somehow representative of the decline of civilization. While it seems quite obvious that better nutrition and lack of environmental stress could result in earlier puberty (whereas hunger and stress might delay it), I could not find any articles willing to entertain this alignment of a positive cause with earlier puberty. Likewise, I found an archaeological study suggesting that medieval skeletons show the age of onset for puberty to have remained unchanged in the present. See a summary here: Mary Lewis, "Children Aren't Starting Puberty Younger, Medieval Skeletons Reveal," *Conversation*, February 12, 2018, http://theconversation.com/children-arent-starting-puberty-younger-medieval-skeletons-reveal-91095.

37. Odlum, *Psychology of Adolescence*, 2.

38. For more on the "arrested development" of the "grown homosexual," see Stockton, *Queer Child*, 22–25.

39. It is telling that, even now, the Wellcome Library's special collections paired the terms "Homosexuality" and "Prostitution" on archive folders, as if these two were conceptually linked in much the same way as the folders I encountered labeled "Children and Adolescents." In many of these archival documents, outward behaviors such as cross-dressing and prostitution were considered identifying characteristics for male homosexuals.

40. *Homosexuality and Prostitution* (London: British Medical Association, 1955), pamphlet, folder N.11/4, box 106, Medical Women's Federation, 11.

41. Albertine L. Winner, *Homosexuality in Women* (reprinted from *Medical Press* 217 (September 3, 1947), pamphlet, folder N.11/9, box 106, Medical Women's Federation, 3–4.

42. Freud, "Letter from Freud," 787.

43. Eugene Talbot, *Degeneracy*, viii, 40.

44. The English translation of Lombroso's *Criminal Man* was not published until 1911. Eugene Talbot's citations of Lombroso would have been from the German translation, *Der Verbrecher in Anthropologischer, Aerztlicher und Juristischer Beziehung*, published in Hamburg by Richter in 1887. The editors of a more recent scholarly translation with multiple editions of the original works remark that Lombroso's theory included sociological causes and humanitarian efforts at rehabilitation for occasional criminals, efforts that more dubious works like Talbot's do not account for. See Gibson and Rafter, introduction to Lombroso, *Criminal Man*, 2.

45. Lombroso, *Criminal Man*, 188, 192.

46. Robert Sutherland, "Sexual Delinquency" (address to the Thirty-Sixth National Conference of the National Association of Probation Officers, 1939), folder N.11/8, box 106, Medical Women's Federation, 3, 1, 2.

47. Patricia J. Williams, "The Auguries of Innocence," *Nation*, May 24, 1999, 9.

48. Breslow, "Adolescent Citizenship," 484, 485.

49. Chinn, *Inventing Modern Adolescence*, 1–2, 3. Research suggests that this observation holds true for adolescents of the 1990s, the first decade of the 2000s, and today. See Males, *Framing Youth*; Graham, *End of Adolescence*; and Twenge, "Have Smartphones Destroyed a Generation?"

50. Chinn, *Inventing Modern Adolescence*, 4.

51. Stout, "Words of Welcome," 16.

52. Russell, "What Constitutes a Secondary School," 529.

53. *The Approach to Womanhood* (London: Central Council for Health Education, 1947), pamphlet, folder N.3/1, box 106, Medical Women's Federation; Mary Scharlieb, *What Parents Should Tell Their Children* (London: British Social Hygiene Council, 1933), pamphlet, folder N.2/6, box 106, Medical Women's Federation; Basil Hood, *Sex Education of Small Children* (London: British Social Hygiene Council, 1937), pamphlet, folder N.2/2, box 106, Medical Women's Federation.

54. Workday Mother, *What Every Mother Should Tell Her Children* (reprinted from *Ladies Companion*), pamphlet, 1938, folder N.2/13, box 106, Medical Women's Federation, 5, 16, 14–15.

55. Ibid., 15.

56. Theodore F. Tucker and Muriel Pout, *How You Grow: A Book for*

Boys (London: Alliance of Honour, 1935), pamphlet, folder N.5/4, box 106, Medical Women's Federation, 32, 33, 34.

57. Odlum, *Psychology of Adolescence*, 8.

58. Ibid., 9.

59. Foucault, *History of Sexuality*, 42.

60. This is not only a strategy of the sex education pamphlets but a common assumption in early twentieth-century medical, psychological, and educational discourse. Take, for example, Starr's *Adolescent Period*, which declares unequivocally, "Parents and teachers are in a marked degree responsible for the faults of children" (139).

61. Sanger, *Woman and the New Race*, 4.

62. Marie Stopes, who is considered one of Britain's most prominent early activists for reproductive rights, was an ardent fan of Hitler and reportedly wrote her own son out of her will for marrying a woman who was nearsighted—an apparently unforgivable genetic flaw that would prevent him from doing his reproductive duty to the nation and the race. The copy of Margaret Sanger's *Woman and the New Race* held at the Wellcome Library was donated from Stopes's personal collection and still contains her original purchase receipt.

63. Sutherland, "Sexual Delinquency," 6.

64. *Adolescence* (London: Mothers' Union, n.d.), pamphlet, folder N.2/1, box 106, Medical Women's Federation, 16.

65. Workday Mother, *What Every Mother Should Tell*, 3.

66. While it is true that the upper and middle classes lost a greater proportion of their young men than the working classes, historians have shown that casualties during World War I did not significantly impact Britain's population. See Winter, *Great War*.

67. Mary Buchan Douie, *England's Girls and England's Future* (London: British Social Hygiene Council, 1932), pamphlet, folder N.3/3, box 106, Medical Women's Federation, 3, 4.

68. See Edelman, *No Future*.

69. Gill-Peterson, *Histories of the Transgender Child*, 55.

70. Nietzsche, *Gay Science*, 301.

71. Erikson, *Identity*, 17.

72. Medovoi observes that "the very concept of 'identity' as it is commonly understood today was a new one in the 1950s." He argues that Erikson was instrumental in constructing identity as the "normative psychic achievement of selfhood" for the first time in his book *Childhood and Society* and that he was also the first to link identity to race, ethnicity, nationality, and sexuality (*Rebels*, 1, 6).

73. Margaret Talbot, "About a Boy."

74. Ibid.

75. Quoted in Margaret Talbot, "About a Boy."

76. Margaret Talbot, "About a Boy."

77. Gill-Peterson, *Histories of the Transgender Child*, 198.

78. Quoted in Margaret Talbot, "About a Boy."

79. See Halberstam, *In a Queer Time*, 18–21.

80. See Stockton, *Queer Child*; Halberstam, *In a Queer Time*; and Bornstein, *Hello, Cruel World*.

81. Kristeva, *New Maladies of the Soul*, 135.

82. Lowenfeld, "Youth and Health."

83. Ibid.

84. Odlum, *Psychology of Adolescence*, 30.

Chapter 3.
Perverse Reading and the Adolescent Reader

1. Sedgwick, *Tendencies*, 3.

2. Hurley, "Perversions of Children's Literature," 118, 120.

3. Kidd, "Queer Theory's Child," 186.

4. This oppositional relation to adulthood is what leads Stockton to argue that all children are queer. See *Queer Child*.

5. Sedgwick, *Tendencies*, 8.

6. Salinger, *Catcher in the Rye*, 24, 22.

7. Ibid., 25.

8. West, "J. D. Salinger," in Jones, *Censorship*, 2131.

9. Chelton and Clendenning, "Rave Reviews," 224–28.

10. West, "J. D. Salinger," in Jones, *Censorship*, 2131.

11. MacLeod, "Censorship History," 10; Foerstel, *Banned in the USA*, 212.

12. Pavonetti, "Speaking from the NCBLA," 33.

13. This perspective builds on Butler's observation in *Undoing Gender* about the fraught relation between discourse and self: "If I have any agency, it is opened up by the fact that I am constituted by a social world I never chose. That my agency is riven with paradox does not mean that it is impossible. It means that paradox is the condition of its possibility" (*Undoing Gender*, 3).

14. *The Bell Jar* was first published under the pseudonym Victoria Lucas in Britain, presumably because the autobiographical elements were expected to upset the family. The novel was not published in the United States under Plath's name until 1971, nearly a decade after her death.

15. Rose, *Haunting of Sylvia Plath*, 75. I have provided Rose's book for this citation, who attributes this quote to some of Aurelia's notes in the Plath Archive; however, Aurelia Plath can be seen making a similar statement on film in the PBS documentary *Voices and Visions: Sylvia Plath*.

16. Plath, *Bell Jar*, 138–39.

17. Carlsen, *Books and the Teen-Age Reader*, 1. I use Carlsen here as one example of an institutional delineation of adolescence. However, definitions like this one appear frequently in writing about adolescents and reading from the past thirty years. Carlsen implies that this understanding has been around "for centuries," but I would trace it back only to the late nineteenth century and to Hall's emphasis on the "plasticity" of adolescence discussed later in this chapter (1).

18. Kristeva, *Powers of Horror*, 4.

19. Gubar has also linked abjection with adolescence using Kristeva, problematizing the "child empowerment" themes in children's novels with miniature characters who find themselves "in positions of utter abjection" ("Species Trouble," 99).

20. While Kristeva's work might be said to belong to psychoanalysis and feminist theory more significantly than queer theory, her formulation of abjection has been foundational to queer theory's understandings of gay male subjectivity. See, for example, Bersani, *Homos*; and Halperin, *What Do Gay Men Want?*

21. Kristeva, *New Maladies of the Soul*, 135.

22. Rose, *Case of Peter Pan*, 10.

23. Kristeva, *Powers of Horror*, 2.

24. Halperin, *What Do Gay Men Want?*, 70, 69, 70.

25. Kristevea, *New Maladies of the Soul*, 135.

26. Take, for example, Donelson and Nilsen's section, titled "Understanding Young Adults," in *Literature for Today's Young Adults*; Carlsen's chapter "The Teenager's World," in *Books and the Teen-Age Reader*; Cline and McBride's chapter "The Young Adult," in *Guide to Literature*; Probst's section "The Secondary School Literature Student," in *Adolescent Literature*; and Cart's extensive discussion of definitions of "young adult" and "adolescent" in the first chapter of *From Romance to Realism*.

27. Aronson, *Beyond the Pale*, 99.

28. Montgomery, *Anne of Green Gables*, 193.

29. Ibid., 193, 194.

30. Hall, *Adolescence*, 2:476–77, 2:478, 2:477.

31. Ibid., 2:478.

32. Montgomery, *Anne of Green Gables*, 194.

33. Hall, *Adolescence*, 2:478.

34. Trites, *Disturbing the Universe*, x.

35. Montgomery, *Anne of Green Gables*, 81–85, 86–87.

36. Oates, *Big Mouth and Ugly Girl*, 7.

37. Portman, *King Dork*, 98.

38. We need not look very far in popular culture to see this repeating trope of a child who cannot be heard or believed—Spielberg's Elliot in *E.T.* (1982), whose claims about his relationship to his "alien" are ignored, or Bird's Hogarth in *Iron Giant*, who tried to tell his town the Iron Giant is not there to harm them. In both cases and in many others, these plots take for granted that children and adolescents are not listened to, their voices considered irrelevant or silenced because they are deemed irrational, fantastical, or strange.

39. Portman, *King Dork*, 99.

40. Hall, *Adolescence*, 2:454, 1:xv, 1:82, 1:310.

41. I refer to *The Story of a Bad Boy* as a children's novel because a separate category for "adolescent novel" would not have been culturally legible until the early twentieth century. Like *Little Women*, *The Story of a Bad Boy* blurs conceptions of childhood and adolescence, both novels a part of the cultural context that produced Hall's *Adolescence* at the turn of the twentieth century.

42. Aldrich, *Story of a Bad Boy*, 246, 247.

43. Hall, *Adolescence*, 2:478.

44. Aldrich, *Story of a Bad Boy*, 248.

45. Hall, *Adolescence*, 2:478.

46. Foucault, *History of Sexuality*, 139, 136.

47. Hacking reports that "suicide was made the property of medics only at the beginning of the nineteenth century, and a major fight it was. It was generally allowed that there was the noble suicide, the suicide of honor or of the state, but all the rest had to be regarded as part of the new medicine of insanity." And, with this shift of property, suicides and their methods and "causes" were meticulously documented in the nineteenth century in the name of science, the classification of suicide aimed at its prevention and control (*Historical Ontology*, 108). This is a part of the same institutional shift that Foucault describes in *History of Sexuality*.

48. Foucault, *History of Sexuality*, 137.

49. Hall, *Adolescence*, 1:viii.

50. Foucault, *History of Sexuality*, 138.

51. Plath, *Bell Jar*, 94.

52. *Preparing for Adolescence* went through many subsequent editions,

the most recent edition published in 2006 with the claim "over one million copies sold" printed on the cover.

53. Dobson, *Preparing for Adolescence*, 8, 9.

54. Ibid., 14–15.

55. Ibid., 15, 16.

56. Hall, *Adolescence*, 2:478; Edelman, *No Future*.

57. Graduated licensing laws exist in all states, but with different requirements. The most common of them is the requirement of a learner's permit, though some states have subsequent requirements before someone under eighteen can acquire a full driver's license.

58. Allstate Insurance, "Last Year, Nearly 5,000 Teens Died in Car Crashes," advertisement, *Newsweek*, October 12, 2009.

59. Allstate Insurance, "Two Out of Three Teens Admit to Texting While Driving," advertisement, *Newsweek*, December 7, 2009.

60. Allstate Insurance, "Last Year, Nearly 5,000 Teens."

61. Allstate Insurance, "Why Do Most 16-Year-Olds Drive Like They're *Missing a Part of Their Brain?*," advertisement, *New Yorker*, March 2, 2009.

62. For example, this 2016 study demonstrates "that PFC also supports hierarchical rule learning during infancy, challenging the current dogma that PFC is an underdeveloped brain system until adolescence." See Werchan et al., "Role of Prefrontal Cortex," 10314.

63. Allstate Insurance, "Last Year, Nearly 5,000 Teens."

64. Allstate Insurance, "Most 16-Year-Olds."

65. *North Carolina Graduated Driver*, 2–3, 6.

66. Dobson, *Preparing for Adolescence*, 41–42, 46, 61.

67. Hall, *Adolescence*, 2:478.

68. Bornstein, *Hello, Cruel World*, 36–37.

69. Butler, *Undoing Gender*, 29.

70. Rose, *Case of Peter Pan*, 141.

71. Butler, *Undoing Gender*, 19.

72. Frank, *America*, 1.

73. Ibid.

74. Kristeva, *New Maladies of the Soul*, 136, 143, 137.

Chapter 4.
Toward an Ethics of Relationality

1. Duane, "Questioning the Autonomous Subject," in Duane, *Children's Table*, 16.

2. Sánchez-Eppler, *Dependent States*, xxv.

3. Wall, "Childism," in Duane, *Children's Table*, 69.

4. Butler, *Bodies That Matter*, 8.

5. Castañeda, *Figurations*, 1.

6. Abundant comparisons of children to animals in the nineteenth century and in present-day parenting books illustrate this logic.

7. Sheldon, *Child to Come*, 17, 5, 21. See also Morgenstern, *Wild Child*.

8. Barad, *Meeting the Universe Halfway*, 66.

9. Sheldon, *Child to Come*, viii.

10. Castañeda, *Figurations*, 168, 170.

11. See Haraway, *Simians, Cyborgs, and Women*; and Barad, *Meeting the Universe Halfway*.

12. Kohn, *Unconditional Parenting*, 2.

13. Ibid., 6, 8.

14. Alice Miller, *Drama of the Gifted Child*, 5.

15. See Cvetkovich, *Depression*.

16. Kohn, *Unconditional Parenting*, 6.

17. Alice Miller, *Drama of the Gifted Child*, 7.

18. Ibid., 8.

19. Ibid., 8, 14.

20. Gibson, *Adult Children*, 7.

21. Ibid., 6, 27.

22. Martin Miller, *True "Drama,"* 115–19, 19.

23. Ibid., 18.

24. Martin reports that he and his mother were estranged for the last two decades of her life and that their written communications before her suicide (after a terminal cancer diagnosis) in 2010 were strained (Martin Miller, *True "Drama,"* 21–23).

25. Quoted in Martin Miller, *True "Drama,"* 5.

26. Kohn, *Unconditional Parenting*, 16, 223.

27. Quoted in Martin Miller, *True "Drama,"* 8, 6.

28. A. J. Willingham, "Florida Lawmaker Insults Parkland Activists, Saying 'Adults Make the Laws,'" CNN, March 9, 2018, https://www.cnn.com/2018/03/09/politics/elizabeth-porter-parkland-florida-speech-trnd/index.html.

29. Michael Bradley, *Yes, Your Teen Is Crazy!*, xv.

30. See Males, *Framing Youth*, 1–2.

31. David Whitting, "Internet a 'Lord of the Flies': Teen Suicide Rise after Instagram, Snapchat Began," *Orange County Register*, March 21, 2018, https://www.ocregister.com/2018/03/21/teen-suicide-can-be-reduced-if-parents-educators-change-social-media-culture/.

32. Quoted in Whitting, "Internet a 'Lord of the Flies.'"

33. Whitting, "Internet a 'Lord of the Flies.'"

34. Graham, *End of Adolescence*, 75.

35. "Suicide Statistics," American Foundation for Suicide Prevention, accessed July 15, 2019, https://afsp.org/about-suicide/suicide-statistics/.

36. Oren Miron et al., "Suicide Rates among Adolescents and Young Adults in the United States, 2000–2017," *JAMA Network*, June 18, 2019, https://jamanetwork.com/journals/jama/fullarticle/2735809?guestAccess Key=04de2fe2-1b68-4ad8-9afb-e5196b877b2b&utm_source=For_The _Media&utm_medium=referral&utm_campaign=ftm_links&utm_ content=tfl&utm_term=061819.

37. "Suicide Statistics" and Miron et al., "Suicide Rates."

38. These numbers were calculated with a combination of U.S. Census data found at "Explore Data," United States Census Bureau, accessed August 12, 2019, https://www.census.gov/data.html; and the number of suicides by age reported on "Number of Youth Suicides, by Age Group," Kidsdata. org, accessed August 12, 2019, https://www.kidsdata.org/topic/211/suicides-age /trend#fmt=123&loc=2,1&tf=13,84&ch=1309,446,1308&pdist=7.

39. See McKeown, Cuffe, and Schulz, "U.S. Suicide Rates by Age."

40. Miron et al., "Suicide Rates."

41. Males, *Framing Youth*, 224, 228, 229, 231.

42. David Whitting, "New Pressures for Perfection Contribute to Rise in Teen Suicide," *Orange County Register*, March 16, 2018, https://www.ocreg-ister.com/2018/03/16/new-pressures-for-perfection-contribute-to-rise-in-teen-suicide/.

43. Quoted in Whitting, "New Pressures for Perfection."

44. Graham, *End of Adolescence*, 69, 76, 77, 78.

45. See Epstein, *Teen 2.0*.

46. See Musgrove, *Youth and the Social Order*.

47. Twenge, "Have Smartphones Destroyed a Generation?"

48. Twenge's data on the relationship between reports of unhappiness and screen time is compelling, but I am suspicious of the implication that the smartphone or screen time is responsible for the rise in teen suicide rates since 2011. Even Twenge acknowledges that the "teen suicide rate was even higher in the 1990s, before smartphones existed." ("Have Smartphones Destroyed a Generation?")

49. Bornstein, *Hello, Cruel World*, 17.

50. Ibid., 27, 83–87.

51. Nonoptimalrobot, "Refractory Depression in Therapy Part 1," *Word-*

Press (blog), November 14, 2014, https://recklessink.wordpress.com/2014/11/14/treatment-resistant-depression-in-therapy-assignment-1/.

52. Kohn, *Unconditional Parenting*, 40; Gibson, *Adult Children*, 8; Miller, *Drama of the Gifted Child*, 12.

53. Bornstein, *Hello, Cruel World*, 23.

54. Dobson, *Preparing for Adolescence*, 139, 5.

55. Bornstein, *Hello, Cruel World*, 26, 23–24.

56. Quoted in David Whitting, "This 16-Year-Old's Suicide Letters Are a Cry for Help and a National Call for Change," *Orange County Register*, March 19, 2018. https://www.ocregister.com/2018/03/19/this-16-year-olds-suicide-letters-are-a-cry-for-help-and-a-national-call-for-change/.

57. Ibid.

58. A copy of this third letter addressed only to family can be found at Joe Imbriano, "The Tragic Suicide Death of Corona Del Mar High School's Patrick Turner," *Fullerton Informer* (blog), accessed August 12, 2019, https://thefullertoninformer.com/the-tragic-suicide-death-of-corona-del-mar-high-schools-patrick-turner/.

59. Quoted in Whitting, "This 16-Year-Old's Suicide."

60. Ibid.

61. Cvetkovich, *Depression*, 1, 2, 11.

62. Kohn, *Unconditional Parenting*, 17.

63. Giroux, *Youth in a Suspect Society*, 17.

64. Lorde, *Sister Outsider*, 55.

65. Bornstein, *Hello, Cruel World*, 26–27, 17, 100–106.

66. Kohn, *Unconditional Parenting*, 16.

67. Wall, *Ethics in Light of Childhood*, 6.

68. Kincaid, *Child-Loving*, 25, 29.

69. See chapter 3; Montgomery, *Anne of Green Gables*, 193; and Hall, *Adolescence*, 2:478.

70. Joanna Walters, "Teen Prosecuted as Adult for Having Naked Images—of Himself—on Phone," *Guardian U.S.*, September 20, 2015, https://www.theguardian.com/us-news/2015/sep/20/teen-prosecuted-naked-images-himself-phone-selfies.

71. See chapter 1. This example can be found in Bernstein, *Racial Innocence*, 1.

72. Kincaid, *Erotic Innocence*, 18–19; Kincaid, *Child-Loving*, 27.

73. Bornstein, *Hello, Cruel World*, 27–28, 24, 25.

74. Gilbert, "Literature as Sex Education," 234.

75. Silverberg and Smyth, *Sex Is a Funny Word*.

76. Ibid., 4.

77. Cat Fitzpatrick, "Feministing Reads: 'Sex Is a Funny Word' and the Aesthetics of Inclusivity," *Feministing*, August 17, 2015, http://feministing .com/2015/08/17/feministing-reads-sex-is-a-funny-word-and-the-aesthetics -of-inclusivity/.

78. Silverberg and Smyth, *Sex Is a Funny Word*, 20, 21.

79. Gill-Peterson, *Histories of the Transgender Child*, 206–7.

80. Silverberg and Smyth, *Sex Is a Funny Word*, 72, 79, 83, 38.

81. Warner, *Trouble with Normal*, 1, 5.

82. Butler, *Undoing Gender*, 19.

83. Warner, *Trouble with Normal*, 1.

84. Bornstein, *Hello, Cruel World*, 29.

85. Silverberg and Smyth, *Sex Is a Funny Word*, 85.

86. Gilbert, *Sexuality in School*, 28, 29.

87. Bornstein, *Hello, Cruel World*, 29, 32.

88. Butler, *Undoing Gender*, 28, 29.

89. Graham, *End of Adolescence*, 1–2.

90. Gubar, "Hermeneutics of Recuperation," 293, 295, 296, 297, 300.

91. Wall, *Ethics in Light of Childhood*, 5.

92. Castañeda, *Figurations*, 149, 168, 170.

93. Barad, *Meeting the Universe Halfway*, 391, 178.

94. Ibid., 393.

95. Castañeda, *Figurations*, 171.

96. Barad, *Meeting the Universe Halfway*, 393, 158.

97. Butler, *Undoing Gender*, 25.

98. Barad, *Meeting the Universe Halfway*, 160.

99. Butler, *Undoing Gender*, 36.

Epilogue.
Queer Theory in the Age of Alternative Facts

1. *Macon (Ga.) Telegraph*, May 10, 1904.

2. Macaulay, *Told by an Idiot*, 305.

3. F. H. Bradley, "Free Thought," review of *History of Freethought in the Nineteenth Century*, by J. M. Robertson, *London Times Literary Supplement*, December 19, 1929. I encountered this book review in the papers of Dr. Frederick Parkes Weber at the Wellcome Library. Weber was a physician

in London in the early twentieth century, and in his commonplace book he collected "some notes and writings related to the *gradual evolution of the mind and the sense of responsibility in childhood and youth*, especially from the *rational education* point of view," which he connected to Hall's *Adolescence* in his commentary. See "Life, Death, Immortality, Free Will, Etc, 1913," 1903–41, folder PP/FPW/C1, box 168, Archives and Manuscripts, Wellcome Library, London.

4. It is worth remembering here Hall's impassioned and defensive dismissal of the "captivity to epistemology" and the "present lust for theories of the nature of knowledge," which have "become a veritable and multiform psychosis" (Hall, *Adolescence*, 1:v). See chapter 2.

5. Dollimore, *Sexual Dissidence*, 280; Freccero, *Queer/Early/Modern*, 1.

6. McIntyre, *Post-truth*, 6.

7. "Word of the Year 2016," *Oxford Languages*, accessed February 8, 2020, https://languages.oup.com/word-of-the-year/word-of-the-year-2016.

8. McIntyre, *Post-truth*, xiv.

9. See McIntyre, *Post-truth*; Kakutani, *Death of Truth*; D'Ancona, *Post Truth*; Levitin, *Weaponized Lies*; Keyes, *Post-truth Era*; and Ball, *Post-truth*. See also a book from 2004 that predates this trend: Davis, *Post-truth*.

10. "Conway: Press Secretary Gave 'Alternative Facts,'" NBC News, *Meet the Press* video, 3.39, January 22, 2017, https://www.nbcnews.com/meet-the-press/video/conway-press-secretary-gave-alternative-facts-860142147643.

11. Latour, "Why Has Critique Run Out?," 226, 227.

12. Gubar, "Hermeneutics of Recuperation," 293.

13. McIntyre, *Post-truth*, 123.

14. Latour, "Why Has Critique Run Out?," 227.

15. McIntyre, *Post-truth*, 127.

16. For example, according to the *Fuel Project* blog, a platform whose mission is to "spread the gospel," the problem is that "we rejected the Hard Right Conservative virtues, and decided to pursue the Soft Left Liberal virtues instead. This is the simple reason why we now live in a post-truth society. As our culture becomes more Liberal—increasingly driven by the heart than the head—we increasingly are shaped by emotion rather than objective facts. Indeed, we increasingly *hate* the truth for its divisive nature. We call it 'hate speech.' We call people who speak it, 'bigots.'" It will come as no surprise that this article goes on to claim that the "truths" people don't want to hear are that "transgenderism is a psychiatric disorder," homosexuality "is an unnatural and unhealthy perversion," and "Islam is a dangerous ideology."

See "What a 'Post-truth' Society Actually Means: The War on Truth," *Fuel Project* (blog), July 11, 2017, http://thefuelproject.org/blog/2017/7/11/what-a-post-truth-society-actually-means-1. The *Federalist* makes similar moves in a more secular framework, talking about the "postmodern 'cult of nondiscrimination'" and political correctness, suggesting that postmodernism is "nihilism in the presumption that all truth is relative, morality is subjective, and therefore all of our individually preferred 'narratives' that give our lives meaning are equally true and worthy of validation"—the implication being that they definitely are not. A few paragraphs later the blog states that the problem with postmodernism isn't that it *values* everything equally but that it craps on everything equally; it's "an anti-culture that measures success insofar as it deconstructs anything that other people value." And this is what supposedly gave us Trump, who merely exposed the hypocrisy and phoniness of all "Liberals." See David Ernst, "Donald Trump Is the First President to Turn Postmodernism against Itself," *Federalist*, January 23, 2017, https://thefederalist.com/2017/01/23/donald-trump-first-president-turn-postmodernism/.

17. McIntyre, *Post-truth*, 127, 11, 154.

18. See McIntyre, *Post-truth*.

19. "Conway."

20. Adeyemi, "Donald Trump," 59–60.

21. See also Baggini, *Short History of Truth*.

22. Sheldon, *Child to Come*, 133, 118.

23. See also Gill-Peterson, "Value of the Future."

24. Sheldon, *Child to Come*, 20, 118.

25. Ibid., 21, 18, 5, 117, 20.

26. Quoted in Ava Kofman, "Bruno Latour, the Post-Truth Philosopher, Mounts a Defense of Science," *New York Times Magazine*, October 25, 2018, https://www.nytimes.com/2018/10/25/magazine/bruno-latour-post-truth-philosopher-science.html.

27. Giroux, *Youth in a Suspect Society*, 2, 7–8.

28. Ibid., 12; Foucault, *Order of Things*, xxiv.

29. Giroux, *Youth in a Suspect Society*, 24.

30. Sedgwick, *Touching Feeling*, 140, 141, 143; Latour, quoted in Kofman, "Bruno Latour."

31. Latour, "Why Has Critique Run Out?," 232, 246.

32. See Haraway, *Staying with the Trouble*; Sedgwick, *Touching Feeling*; and Barad, *Meeting the Universe Halfway*.

33. Gubar, "Risky Business," 450; Wall, *Ethics in Light of Childhood*; Gill-Peterson, *Histories of the Transgender Child*, 203.

34. Duane, *Children's Table*; Chinn and Duane, "Child"; Gill-Peterson, Sheldon, and Stockton, "Child Now."

35. See Rose, *Case of Peter Pan*; and Lesnik-Oberstein, *Children's Literature*.

bibliography

Adeyemi, Kemi. "Donald Trump Is the Perfect Man for the Job." *QED: A Journal in GLBTQ Worldmaking* 4, no. 2 (2017): 56–62.

Alcott, Louisa May. *Little Women*. Edited by Elaine Showalter. 1868–69. Reprint, New York: Penguin, 1989.

Aldrich, Thomas Bailey. *The Story of a Bad Boy*. 1869. Reprint, Hanover, N.H.: University Press of New England, 1990.

Ariès, Philippe. *Centuries of Childhood: A Social History of Family Life*. Translated by Robert Baldick. New York: Knopf, 1962.

Aronson, Marc. *Beyond the Pale: New Essays for a New Era*. Lanham, Md.: Scarecrow, 2003.

Baggini, Julian. *A Short History of Truth: Consolations for a Post-truth World*. London: Quercus, 2017.

Ball, James. *Post-truth: How Bullshit Conquered the World*. London: Biteback, 2017.

Barad, Karen. *Meeting the Universe Halfway: Quantum Physics and the Entanglement of Matter and Meaning*. Durham, N.C.: Duke University Press, 2007.

Baxter, Kent. *The Modern Age: Turn-of-the-Century American Culture and the Invention of Adolescence*. Tuscaloosa: University of Alabama Press, 2008.

Bernstein, Robin. *Racial Innocence: Performing American Childhood from Slavery to Civil Rights*. New York: New York University Press, 2011.

Bersani, Leo. *Homos*. Cambridge, Mass.: Harvard University Press, 1995.

Bornstein, Kate. *Hello, Cruel World: 101 Alternatives to Suicide for Teens, Freaks and Other Outlaws*. New York: Seven Stories, 2006.

Bradley, Michael J. *Yes, Your Teen Is Crazy! Loving Your Kid without Losing Your Mind*. Gig Harbor, Wash.: Harbor, 2003.

Breslow, Jacob. "Adolescent Citizenship, or Temporality and the Negation of Black Childhood in Two Eras." *American Quarterly* 71, no. 2 (2019): 473–94.

Butler, Judith. *Bodies That Matter: On the Discursive Limits of "Sex."* New York: Routledge, 1993.

———. *Gender Trouble: Feminism and the Subversion of Identity.* New York: Routledge, 1990.

———. *Undoing Gender.* New York: Routledge, 2004.

Carlsen, G. Robert. *Books and the Teen-Age Reader: A Guide for Teachers, Librarians, and Parents.* 2nd ed. New York: Harper and Row, 1980.

Cart, Michael. *From Romance to Realism: 50 Years of Growth and Change in Young Adult Literature.* New York: HarperCollins, 1996.

Castañeda, Claudia. *Figurations: Child, Bodies, World.* Durham, N.C.: Duke University Press, 2002.

Chamberlain, Alexander Francis. *The Child: A Study in the Evolution of Man.* London: Scribner's Sons, 1901.

Chelton, Mary K., and Linda Fuller Clendenning. "Rave Reviews for Popular American Fiction." *Reference and User Services Quarterly* 42, no. 3 (2003): 224–29.

Chinn, Sarah E. *Inventing Modern Adolescence: The Children of Immigrants in Turn-of-the Century America.* New Brunswick: Rutgers University Press, 2009.

———. "'I Was a Lesbian Child': Queer Thoughts about Childhood Studies." In Duane, *Children's Table*, 149–66.

Chinn, Sarah E., and Anna Mae Duane, eds. "Child." Special issue, *WSQ* 43, nos. 1–2 (2015).

Cline, Ruth, and William McBride. *A Guide to Literature for Young Adults: Background, Selection, and Use.* Glenview, Ill.: Scott, Foresman, 1983.

Cohen, Albert K. Foreword to *Youth and the Social Order.* By Frank Musgrove, ix–xix. Bloomington: Indiana University Press, 1964.

Colebrook, Claire. "On Not Becoming Man: The Materialist Politics of Unactualized Potential." In *Material Feminisms*, edited by Stacy Alaimo and Susan Heckman, 52–84. Bloomington: Indiana University Press, 2009.

Cordell, Ryan. "Reprinting, Circulation, and the Network Author in Antebellum Newspapers." *American Literary History* 27, no. 3 (2015): 417–45.

Cordell, Ryan, and David Smith. "The Viral Texts Project: Mapping Networks of Reprinting in 19th-Century Newspapers and Magazines." Viral Texts. 2017. http://viraltexts.org.

Cvetkovich, Ann. *Depression: A Public Feeling.* Durham, N.C.: Duke University Press, 2012.

D'Ancona, Matthew. *Post Truth: The New War on Truth and How to Fight Back*. London: Ebury, 2017.

Darwin, Charles. *On the Origin of the Species by Means of Natural Selection, or The Preservation of Favoured Races in the Struggle for Life*. 1859. In *From So Simple a Beginning: The Four Great Books of Charles Darwin*, edited by Edward O. Wilson, 441–760. New York: Norton, 2006. Originally published London: Murray, 1859.

Davis, Evan. *Post-truth: Why We Have Reached Peak Bullshit and What We Can Do about It*. London: Little, Brown, 2017.

DeLuzio, Crista. *Female Adolescence in American Scientific Thought, 1830–1930*. Baltimore: Johns Hopkins University Press, 2007.

Dinshaw, Carolyn, Lee Edelman, Roderick A. Ferguson, Carla Freccero, Elizabeth Freeman, Jack Halberstam, Annamarie Jagose, Christopher S. Nealon, and Tan Hoang Nguyen, "Theorizing Queer Temporalities: A Roundtable Discussion." *GLQ: A Journal of Lesbian and Gay Studies* 13, nos. 2–3 (2007): 177–95.

Dobson, James. *Preparing for Adolescence: Straight Talk for Parents and Teens*. Ventura, Calif.: Regal Books, 1978.

Dollimore, Jonathan. *Sexual Dissidence: Augustine to Wilde, Freud to Foucault*. Oxford: Clarendon Press, 1991.

Donelson, Kenneth L., and Alleen Pace Nilsen. *Literature for Today's Young Adults*. Glenview, Ill.: Scott, Foresman, 1980.

Duane, Anna Mae, ed. *The Children's Table: Childhood Studies and the Humanities*. Athens: University of Georgia Press, 2013.

———. "Introduction: The Children's Table." In Duane, *Children's Table*, 1–14.

———. "Questioning the Autonomous Subject and Individual Rights." In Duane, *Children's Table*, 15–18.

Edelman, Lee. *No Future: Queer Theory and the Death Drive*. Durham, N.C.: Duke University Press, 2004.

Epstein, Robert. *The Case against Adolescence: Recognizing the Adult in Every Teen*. Sanger, Calif.: Word Dancer, 2007.

———. *Teen 2.0: Saving Our Children and Families from the Torment of Adolescence*. Fresno, Calif.: Quill Driver Books, 2010.

Erikson, Erik. *Childhood and Society*. 1950. Reprint, New York: Norton, 1963.

———. *Identity: Youth and Crisis*. New York: Norton, 1968.

E. T. the Extra-Terrestrial. Directed by Steven Spielberg. Universal City, Calif.: Universal Pictures, 1982.

Fabian, Johannes. *Time and the Other: How Anthropology Makes Its Object*. New York: Columbia University Press, 1983.

Felski, Rita. *The Limits of Critique*. Chicago: University of Chicago Press, 2015.

Foerstel, Herbert N. *Banned in the USA: A Reference Guide to Book Censorship in Schools and Public Libraries*. Westport, Conn.: Greenwood, 2002.

Foucault, Michel. *The History of Sexuality*. Vol. 1. Translated by Robert Hurley. 1976. Reprint, New York: Vintage, 1990.

——. *The Order of Things: An Archeology of the Human Sciences*. 1970. Reprint, New York: Vintage, 1994.

——. *The Use of Pleasure*. Vol. 2 of *The History of Sexuality*. Translated by Robert Hurley. Reprint, New York: Vintage, 1985.

Frank, E. R. *America: A Novel*. New York: Atheneum, 2002.

Freccero, Carla. *Queer/Early/Modern*. Durham, N.C.: Duke University Press, 2006.

Freeman, Elizabeth. "Time Binds, or Erotohistoriography." *Social Text* 23, nos. 3–4 (2005): 57–68.

——. *Time Binds: Queer Temporalities, Queer Histories*. Durham, N.C.: Duke University Press, 2010.

Freud, Sigmund. "A Letter from Freud." 1935. *American Journal of Psychiatry* 107 (1951): 786–87.

——. "The Psychogenesis of a Case of Homosexuality in a Woman." In *The Standard Edition of the Complete Psychological Works of Sigmund Freud*, edited and translated by James Strachey, 18:145–72. London: Hogarth, 1955.

Gibson, Lindsay C. *Adult Children of Emotionally Immature Parents*. Oakland, Calif.: New Harbinger, 2015.

Gibson, Mary, and Nicole Hahn Rafter, eds. Introduction to *Criminal Man*, by Cesare Lombroso, translated by Mary Gibson and Nicole Hahn Rafter, 1–36. Durham, N.C.: Duke University Press, 2006.

Giffney, Noreen. "Queer Apocal(o)ptic/ism: The Death Drive and the Human." In *Queering the Non/Human*, edited by Noreen Giffney and Myra J. Hird, 55–78. Hampshire, UK: Ashgate, 2008.

Gilbert, Jen. "Literature as Sex Education." *Changing English* 11, no. 2 (2004): 233–41.

——. *Sexuality in School: The Limits of Education*. Minneapolis: University of Minnesota Press, 2014.

Gillis, John R. *Youth and History: Tradition and Change in European Age Relations, 1770–Present*. New York: Academic, 1974.

Gill-Peterson, Jules. *Histories of the Transgender Child*. Minneapolis: University of Minnesota Press, 2018.

———. "The Value of the Future: The Child as Human Capital and the Neoliberal Labor of Race." *WSQ: Women's Studies Quarterly* 43, nos. 1–2 (2015): 181–96.

Gill-Peterson, Jules, Rebekah Sheldon, and Kathryn Bond Stockton, eds. "The Child Now." Special issue, *GLQ* 22, no. 4 (2016).

Giroux, Henry. *Youth in a Suspect Society: Democracy or Disposability?* New York: Palgrave Macmillan, 2009.

Goldberg, Jonathan, and Madhavi Menon. "Queering History." *PMLA* 120, no. 5 (2005): 1608–17.

Gordon, Angus. "Turning Back: Adolescence, Narrative, and Queer Theory." *GLQ: A Journal of Lesbian and Gay Studies* 5, no. 1 (1999): 1–24.

Gould, Stephen Jay. *Ontogeny and Phylogeny.* Cambridge, Mass.: Belknap Press of Harvard University Press, 1977.

Graham, Philip. *The End of Adolescence.* Medical Publications. Oxford: Oxford University Press, 2004.

Gubar, Marah. *Artful Dodgers: Reconceiving the Golden Age of Children's Literature.* Oxford: Oxford University Press, 2009.

———. "The Hermeneutics of Recuperation: What a Kinship-Model Approach to Children's Agency Could Do for Children's Literature and Childhood Studies." *Jeunesse: Young People, Texts, Cultures* 8, no. 1 (2016): 291–310.

———. "Risky Business: Talking about Children in Children's Literature Criticism." *Children's Literature Association Quarterly* 38, no. 4 (2013): 450–57.

———. "Species Trouble: The Abjection of Adolescence in E. B. White's *Stuart Little.*" *Lion and the Unicorn* 27 (2003): 98–119.

Hacking, Ian. *Historical Ontology.* Cambridge, Mass.: Harvard University Press, 2002.

Haeckel, Ernst. *Generelle morphologie der organismen [General morphology of organisms].* Berlin: Druck und Verlag von Georg Reimer, 1866.

Halberstam, Jack. *In a Queer Time and Place: Transgender Bodies, Subcultural Lives.* New York: New York University Press, 2005.

Hall, G. Stanley. *Adolescence: Its Psychology and Its Relations to Physiology, Anthropology, Sociology, Sex, Crime, Religion and Education.* 2 vols. New York: Appleton, 1904.

———. *Youth: Its Education, Regimen, and Hygiene.* New York: Appleton, 1907.

Halperin, David M. *What Do Gay Men Want? An Essay on Sex, Risk, and Subjectivity.* Ann Arbor: The University of Michigan Press, 2007.

Haraway, Donna. *Simians, Cyborgs, and Women: The Reinvention of Nature*. New York: Routledge, 1991.

———. *Staying with the Trouble: Making Kin in the Chthulucene*. Durham, N.C.: Duke University Press, 2016.

Huang, Carita Constable. "Making Children Normal: Standardizing Children in the United States (1880–1930)." PhD diss., University of Pennsylvania, 2004.

Hunter, T. A. A., and M. E. M. Herford. *Adolescence: The Years of Indiscretion*. London: Heinemann Medical Books, 1961.

Hurley, Nat. "The Perversions of Children's Literature." *Jeunesse: Young People, Texts, Cultures* 3, no. 2 (2011): 118–32.

The Iron Giant. Directed by Brad Bird. Burbank, Calif.: Warner Bros., 1999.

Kakutani, Michiko. *The Death of Truth: Notes on Falsehood in the Age of Trump*. New York: Duggan, 2018.

Kett, Joseph. *Rites of Passage: Adolescence in America, 1790 to the Present*. New York: Basic Books, 1977.

Keyes, Ralph. *The Post-truth Era: Dishonesty and Deception in Contemporary Life*. New York: St. Martin's Press, 2004.

Kidd, Kenneth. "Queer Theory's Child and Children's Literature Studies." *PMLA* 126. no. 1 (2011): 182–88.

Kincaid, James R. *Child-Loving: The Erotic Child and Victorian Culture*. New York: Routledge, 1992.

———. *Erotic Innocence: The Culture of Child Molesting*. Durham, N.C.: Duke University Press, 1998.

Kohn, Alfie. *Unconditional Parenting: Moving from Rewards and Punishment to Love and Reason*. New York: Atria Paperback, 2005.

Krafft-Ebing, Richard von. *Psychopathia sexualis*. Translated by Charles Gilbert Chaddock. Philadelphia: Davis, 1894.

Kristeva, Julia. *New Maladies of the Soul*. New York: Columbia University Press, 1995.

———. *Powers of Horror: An Essay on Abjection*. Translated by Leon S. Roudiez. New York: Columbia University Press, 1982.

Latour, Bruno. "Why Has Critique Run Out of Steam? From Matters of Fact to Matters of Concern." *Critical Inquiry* 30, no. 2 (2004): 225–48.

Lesko, Nancy. *Act Your Age! A Cultural Construction of Adolescence*. New York: Routledge Falmer, 2001.

Lesnik-Oberstein, Karín. "Childhood, Queer Theory, and Feminism." *Feminist Theory* 11, no. 3 (2010): 309–21.

———. *Children's Literature: Criticism and the Fictional Child*. Oxford: Clarendon, 1994.

Lesnik-Oberstein, Karín, and Stephen Thomson. "What Is Queer Theory Doing with the Child?" *Parallax* 8 (2002): 35–46.

Levitin, Daniel J. *Weaponized Lies: How to Think Critically in the Post-truth Era.* New York: Dutton, 2016.

Lombroso, Cesare. *Criminal Man.* Translated by Mary Gibson and Nicole Hahn Rafter. 1876–97. Reprint, Durham, N.C.: Duke University Press, 2006.

Lorde, Audre. *Sister Outsider: Essays and Speeches.* Berkeley, Calif.: Crossing, 2007.

Lost and Delirious. Directed by Léa Pool. Montreal: Cité-Amérique, 2001.

Macaulay, Rose. *Told by an Idiot.* 1923. Reprint, New York: Doubleday, 1983.

MacLeod, Lanette. "The Censorship History of *The Catcher in the Rye.*" *PNLA Quarterly* 39 (1975): 10–13.

Males, Mike A. *Framing Youth: 10 Myths about the Next Generation.* Monroe, Maine: Common Courage, 1999.

——— . *The Scapegoat Generation: America's War on Adolescents.* Monroe, Maine: Common Courage, 1996.

Mandelbaum, Maurice. *History, Man, and Reason: A Study in Nineteenth-Century Thought.* Baltimore: Johns Hopkins Press, 1971.

McIntyre, Lee. *Post-truth.* Cambridge, Mass.: MIT Press, 2018.

McKeown, Robert E., Steven P. Cuffe, and Richard M. Schulz. "U.S. Suicide Rates by Age Group, 1970–2002: An Examination of Recent Trends." *American Journal of Public Health* 96, no. 10 (2006): 1744–51.

Mead, Margaret. *Coming of Age in Samoa.* New York: Morrow, 1928.

Medovoi, Leerom. *Rebels: Youth and the Cold War Origins of Identity.* Durham, N.C.: Duke University Press, 2005.

Miller, Alice. *The Drama of the Gifted Child: The Search for the True Self.* Rev. ed. New York: Basic Books, 1997.

Miller, Martin. *The True "Drama of the Gifted Child": The Phantom Alice Miller—the Real Person.* Translated by Barbara Rogers and Rebecca Peterson. San Bernardino, Calif.: Privately printed, 2018.

Montgomery, Lucy Maud. *Anne of Green Gables.* Edited by Mary Henley Rubio and Elizabeth Waterston. 1908. Reprint, New York: Norton, 2007.

Moran, Jeffery P. *Teaching Sex: The Shaping of Adolescence in the Twentieth Century.* Cambridge, Mass.: Harvard University Press, 2000.

Moretti, Franco. *The Way of the World: The Bildungsroman in European Culture.* London: Verso, 2000.

Morgenstern, Naomi. *Wild Child: Intensive Parenting and Posthumanist Ethics.* Minneapolis: University of Minnesota Press, 2018.

Muñoz, José Esteban. *Cruising Utopia: The Then and There of Queer Futurity*. New York: New York University Press, 2009.

Musgrove, Frank. *Youth and the Social Order*. Bloomington: Indiana University Press, 1965.

Neubauer, John. *The Fin-de-Siècle Culture of Adolescence*. New Haven, Conn.: Yale University Press, 1992.

Nietzsche, Friedrich. *The Gay Science*. Translated by Walter Kaufmann. New York: Vintage, 1974.

The North Carolina Graduated Driver Licensing System: Urban-Rural Differences. Chapel Hill, N.C.: Highway Safety Research Center, 2001.

Oates, Joyce Carol. *Big Mouth and Ugly Girl*. New York: HarperTempest, 2002.

Pavonetti, Linda M. "Speaking from the NCBLA Committee's Perspective: Where Is the Line between Children's and Young Adult Books? Or, Are Nancy Drew and the Hardy Boys (Not to Mention Holden Caulfield) Getting Younger Day-by-Day?" *Journal of Children's Literature* 30, no. 2 (2004): 33–36.

"Physiology: The Periods of Human Life." In *Classic Cullings and Fugitive Gatherings*, 246. London: Arnold, 1831.

Plath, Sylvia. *The Bell Jar*. 1963. Reprint, New York: Harper and Row, 1971.

Portman, Frank. *King Dork*. New York: Delacorte, 2006.

Probst, Robert E. *Adolescent Literature: Response and Analysis*. Columbus, Ohio: Merrill, 1984.

Prout, Alan. *The Future of Childhood*. London: Routledge Falmer, 2005.

Read, C. Stanford. *The Struggles of Male Adolescence*. London: Allen and Unwin, 1928.

Rebel without a Cause. Directed by Nicholas Ray. Burbank, Calif.: Warner Bros., 1955.

Rollo, Toby. "The Color of Childhood: The Role of the Child/Human Binary in the Production of Anti-black Racism." *Journal of Black Studies* 49, no. 4 (2017): 307–29.

Rose, Jacqueline. *The Case of Peter Pan, or The Impossibility of Children's Fiction*. London: Macmillan, 1984.

———. *The Haunting of Sylvia Plath*. Cambridge, Mass.: Harvard University Press, 1992.

Rudd, David. *Reading the Child in Children's Literature: A Heretical Approach*. London: Palgrave Macmillan, 2013.

Russell, James E. "What Constitutes a Secondary School." *School Review* 4, no. 7 (1896): 529–31.

Salinger, J. D. *The Catcher in the Rye*. New York: Little, Brown, 1951.

Sánchez-Eppler, Karen. *Dependent States: The Child's Part in Nineteenth-Century American Culture*. Chicago: University of Chicago Press, 2005.

Sanger, Margaret. *Woman and the New Race*. New York: Brentano's, 1920.

Sedgwick, Eve Kosofsky. "Paranoid Reading and Reparative Reading, or You're So Paranoid, You Probably Think This Introduction Is about You." In *Novel Gazing: Queer Readings in Fiction*, edited by Eve Kosofsky Sedgwick, 1–37. Durham, N.C.: Duke University Press, 1997.

———. *Tendencies*. Durham, N.C.: Duke University Press, 1995.

———. *Touching Feeling: Affect, Pedagogy, Performativity*. Durham, N.C.: Duke University Press, 2003.

Sheldon, Rebekah. *The Child to Come: Life after the Human Catastrophe*. Minneapolis: University of Minnesota Press, 2016.

Silverberg, Cory, and Fiona Smyth. *Sex Is a Funny Word*. New York: Seven Stories, 2015.

Somerville, Siobhan. *Queering the Color Line: Race and the Invention of Homosexuality in American Culture*. Durham, N.C.: Duke University Press, 2000.

Spacks, Patricia Meyer. *The Adolescent Idea: Myths of Youth and the Adult Imagination*. New York: Basic Books, 1981.

Springhall, John. *Coming of Age: Adolescence in Britain, 1860–1960*. Dublin: Gill and Macmillan, 1986.

Starr, Louis. *The Adolescent Period: Its Features and Management*. London: Lewis, 1915.

Steedman, Carolyn. *Strange Dislocations: Childhood and the Idea of Human Interiority, 1780–1930*. London: Virago, 1995.

Stockton, Kathryn Bond. *The Queer Child, or Growing Sideways in the Twentieth Century*. Durham, N.C.: Duke University Press, 2009.

Stout, L. A. "Words of Welcome." *Journal of Adolescence* 1, no. 1 (1900): 16.

Talbot, Eugene S. *Degeneracy: Its Causes, Signs, and Results*. New York: Scribner's Sons, 1898.

Talbot, Margaret. "About a Boy: Transgender Surgery at Sixteen." *New Yorker*, March 18, 2013. http://www.newyorker.com/magazine/2013/03/18/about-a-boy-2.

Taylor, Charles. *Sources of the Self: The Making of Modern Identity*. Cambridge, Mass.: Harvard University Press, 1989.

Tomboy. Directed by Céline Sciamma. Paris: Hold Up Films, 2011.

Trites, Roberta Seelinger. *Disturbing the Universe: Power and Repression in Adolescent Literature*. Iowa City: University of Iowa Press, 2000.

Twenge, Jean M. "Have Smartphones Destroyed a Generation?" *Atlantic*, September 2017. https://www.theatlantic.com/magazine/archive /2017/09/has-the-smartphone-destroyed-a-generation/534198/.

Upham, A. H., ed. *Transactions and Proceedings of the National Association of State Universities in the United States of America*. Vol. 26. Oxford, Ohio: National Association of State Universities, 1928.

Voices and Visions: Sylvia Plath. Directed by Lawrence Pitkethly. Written by Susan Yankowitz. PBS. 1988. http://www.dailymotion.com/video /x19my4b_voices-visions-sylvia-plath_creation.

Walkerdine, Valerie. "Beyond Developmentalism?" *Theory and Psychology* 3, no. 4 (1993): 451–69.

Wall, John. "Childism: The Challenges of Childhood to Ethics and the Humanities." In Duane, *Children's Table*, 68–84.

——— . *Ethics in Light of Childhood*. Washington, D.C.: Georgetown University Press, 2010.

Warner, Michael. *The Trouble with Normal*. Cambridge, Mass.: Harvard University Press, 1999.

Werchan, Denise M., Anne G. E. Collins, Michael J. Frank, and Dima Amso. "Role of Prefrontal Cortex in Learning and Generalizing Hierarchical Rules in 8-Month-Old Infants." *Journal of Neuroscience* 36, no. 40 (2016): 10314–22.

West, Mark I. "J. D. Salinger." In *Censorship: A World Encyclopedia*, edited by Derek Jones, 2131. Chicago: Dearborn, 2001.

Wheeler, E. G. "Periods of Human Life." *Boston Medical and Surgical Journal* 22, no. 25 (1840): 395–96.

Wheeler, Olive A. *Youth: The Psychology of Adolescence and Its Bearing on the Reorganization of Adolescent Education*. London: University of London Press, 1929.

Winter, Jay M. *The Great War and the British People*. Basingstoke: Palgrave Macmillan, 1986.

Yoder, Albert. [Untitled]. *Journal of Adolescence* 1, no. 1 (1900): 16.

Zelizer, Viviana A. *Pricing the Priceless Child: The Changing Social Value of Children*. New York: Basic Books, 1985.

index

Note: Page numbers in italics indicate illustrations.

Barad, Karen, xvi, 139; on "apparatus," 5, 196n13; on "ethics of
entanglement," 193; on performativity, 19–20, 23; on "relationalities of becoming," 179; on relativity theory, 25; on subjectivity,
177–78, 180
Bardwell, Keith, 58–59
Baxter, Kent, 199n1, 203n58,
206n108
Beatty, Stephen, 93–94
Bell Jar, The (Plath), 106–8, 122–23,
213n15
Bening, Annette, 93
Bernstein, Robin, 58–59, 68; *Racial
Innocence*, 15–16, 204n61
"biogenetic law," 52
biopolitics, 189; Edelman on,
206n99; Foucault on, 6, 57; of
neoliberalism, 190
birth control, 87–88
Bornstein, Kate, 131, 168–69, 178;
Hello, Cruel World, 156–57,
159–61, 163–66, *164*, *165*, 170, 176;
on sexuality, 173–74
Bradley, Francis Herbert, 183
Bradley, Michael J., 150
Breslow, Jacob, 70, 79
Brexit, 185, 188
Burke, Joseph, 39, 202n35
Butler, Judith, 68, 132–33, 137–38;
on autonomy as relationality,
173; on fantasy, 1, 174–75; *Gender
Trouble*, 11, 17–18; on performativity, 19–20, 22; on queer theory,
179–80; *Undoing Gender*, 212n13
Byron, Lord, 120

Cambridge Analytica, 189
Canova, Antonio, 34
Carlsen, G. Robert, 108–11, 213n17

Case of Peter Pan, The (Rose), 9–13
Castañeda, Claudia, 32, 139–40;
on children's status, 138; on
developmentalism, 53, 58, 72;
on intersectionality, 204n61; on
Spencer, 205n84; on subjectivity,
176–77, 178; on Western notions
of adolescence, 207n5
Catcher in the Rye, The (Salinger),
103–6, 108, 112
categories of age, 9, 32–33, 81, 100–
102; functions of, 140; Hall on,
67; Kincaid on, 68, 166–67, 168;
Macaulay on, 183; performative
effects of, 14–22, 55–56, 100, 111,
132; relationality of, 137, 148–49;
Rose on, 2–3, 68; Sánchez-
Eppler on, 196n21; Sheldon
on, 138; Springhall on, 199n1,
207n108; Steedman on, 32–33;
Twenge on, 156; Wheeler on,
36–38, 37. *See also* adolescence
Cheney, Lynne, 187
child abuse, 141, 143, 145, 167–68;
Kincaid on, 12, 197n32; Stockton
on, 208n21
"child trouble," 8–14
childhood, 32–33; "difference
model" of, 176; "plasticity" of,
73–74; racial notions about, 15–
16, 68, 204n61, 208n21; Sánchez-
Eppler on, 196n21; Steedman on,
32; theories of, 14–15, 72. *See also*
categories of age
"childism," 137
children, 144; adolescents versus,
8–9, 39, 81, 113, 166; agency of,
175–76, 177; gifted, 13, 142–49, 158;
"good," 141–49, 160; Lombroso
on, 77–78; as "priceless," 68,
208n18; suicide among, 151

children's literature, 102, 112, 193; Gubar on, 3, 9–10; queer theory and, 100; Rose on, 2, 9–10, 109
Chinn, Sarah, 27, 80–82, 204n61
climatic theories of development, 75–76
Cohen, Albert K., xii–xiii
Colebrook, Claire, 57
colonialism, 31, 40–44, 54–55
Columbine (Colo.) shootings, 79, 118
conformity, 6, 72, 75–77, 80; Dobson on, 130, 133–34, 159–60; Erikson on, 91; Talbot on, 94
Conway, Kellyanne, 185, 188
Cordell, Ryan, 200n4
critical race studies, 138, 193
Cvetkovich, Ann, 162–63

Darwin, Charles, 49, 52–53, 113, 205n83. *See also* evolution
Dean, James, 101, 101–2
DeLuzio, Crista, 204n61
depression, 150, 158; Cvetkovich on, 162; Miller on, 142, 143; rates of, 154–56; Talbot on, 93
Derrida, Jacques, 17, 186, 187
developmentalism, 26–27, 53–54, 95; of Castañeda, 53, 58, 72; climatic theories of, 75–76; definitions of, xiv, 32; deviance and, 74–75; of Hall, 5, 46–47, 116–17; heterosexuality and, 76; logic of, xv, 32–33, 46, 49, 72; race and, xv, 54–55, 78–81; representationalism versus, 38–41; of Spencer, 52, 53, 205nn83–84
deviance, 70, 74–75; delinquency and, 67, 78, 82, 88, 91, 138; Sanger on, 88; Stout on, 81–82; Talbot on, 77

Dinesen, Isak, 103–4, 108
"disability," 71–72, 179
Dobson, James, 124–26, 129–31, 153, 159–60
Dollimore, John, 183–84
Duane, Anna Mae, 16, 137, 193
Dunn, Robert, 72

Edelman, Lee, 13; on biopolitics, 206n99; *No Future*, 11–14, 60; on "reproductive futurism," 57–58, 74, 90, 113–14, 122
Einstein, Albert, 25
endocrinology, 73, 74, 78, 78
entanglement, 23, 68, 169, 205n76; autonomy and, 140, 148, 149; dependency and, 136–37, 143; ethics of, 140, 144–45, 166, 175–81, 193
Epstein, Robert, x, 155
Erikson, Erik, 64, 91–92, 204n72, 211n72
Ernst, David, 221n16
ethics: of entanglement, 140, 144–45, 166, 175–81, 193; of futurity, 55–62; of relationality, 20, 136–40, 144, 169, 173, 181; sexual, 172–73
eugenics, 73–74, 87–88, 90; biopolitics and, 189; sex education and, 84, 95
evolution, 78; Darwin on, 49, 52–53, 205n83; Hall on, 49–53; Spencer on, 52, 53, 205nn83–84

Fabian, Johannes, 53, 67, 205n83
Felski, Rita, 3–4, 186
feminism, 77, 138, 193; "childism" and, 137; queer theory and, 132, 213n20; Sanger and, 87–88
feminist science studies, xvi, 140, 186
Finnegans Wake (Joyce), 106–8

Fitzpatrick, Cat, 170–71

Focus on the Family (organization), 124–25

Foucault, Michel, 38, 87, 186, 187; on biopolitics, 6, 57; on historicity, 32, 48; *The History of Sexuality*, 16–17, 179, 196n17, 214n47; on homosexuality, 45; *The Order of Things*, 24, 47; on representationalism, 38; on suicide, 121, 122

fracking, 139–40

Frank, E. R., 133–34

Freccero, Carla, 25–26, 184

Freeman, Elizabeth, 47–48, 54

Freud, Sigmund, 6, 54, 76, 77

Fuel Project blog, 220n16

"futurism, reproductive," 57–58, 74, 90, 113–14, 122

futurity, 14, 70, 113, 142–43; ethics of, 55–62; normative, 74. *See also* temporality

gangs, 150. *See also* juvenile delinquency

gender, 67–70; performativity of, 179–80; "plasticity" of, 73–75, 119–20, 213n17; sexuality and, 27, 173–74. *See also* transgender

gender roles, 93, 159–60

gender studies, 9, 132–33

Gender Trouble (Butler), 11, 17–18

Gibson, Lindsay C., 143–44, 159

Giffney, Noreen, 58

Gilbert, Jen, 170, 174

Gillis, John R., 206n108

Gill-Peterson, Jules, 73, 90, 93, 171, 193, 205n76

Giroux, Henry, 163, 191

Goethe, Johann Wolfgang von, 121

Goldberg, Jonathan, 25

Gould, Stephen Jay, 51

graduated driver licensing (GDL) laws, 129, 215n57

Graham, Philip, x, 151, 154–55, 175

Gubar, Marah, 3–4, 15–16, 175–76, 186; on abjection, 213n19; on agency, 175–76, 177; on children's literature, 3, 9–10; on Golden Age histories, 15; "kinship model" of, 176, 193; on theorizing childhood, 14–15

Hacking, Ian, 45; on deviance, 198n65; on suicide, 214n47

Haeckel, Ernst, 50–52

Halberstam, Jack, 60

Hall, G. Stanley, xiii–xiv, 30–31, 41, 46–55; *Adolescence*, 5, 30, 44–46, 57, 64–67, 82; on adolescent readers, xv, 115–17, 121, 167; career of, 24–25; as "creator" of adolescence, 30, 199n1; developmentalism of, 5, 46–47, 116–17; on epistemology, 220n4; on evolution, 49–53; historicism of, 67; on humanism, 71; Mead and, 21, 203n58; Montgomery and, 113; Portman and, 119–20; racial notions of, 50, 71–73; on scientific epistemology, 66–67; on "superfetation," 116–17, 126

Halperin, David, 110–11

Haraway, Donna, 192–93

Harris, Eric, 79

hate speech, 220n16

Hello, Cruel World (Bornstein), 156–57, 159–61, 163–66, *164*, *165*, 170, 176

Herford, M. E. M., 82

"hermeneutic of the self," 7, 196n17

"hermeneutics of suspicion," 3

historicism, 26; of Hall, 67; of

index

Moran, Jeffery P., 199n1
Mothers' Union, 89
Muñoz, José Esteban, 60–61
Musgrove, Frank, xi–xiii, 155

Napoleon Bonaparte, 41, 202n43
nationalism, 31, 40–43, 54–55
nature/nurture debates, 22, 139–40
neoliberalism, 162–63, 189, 191; bio-politics of, 190; Bornstein on, 169
Neubauer, John, 199n1
Newman, Lawrence, 74
Nietzsche, Friedrich, 91
No Future (Edelman), 11–14, 60

Oates, Joyce Carol, 118–19
obedience, 141
Odlum, Doris M., 75–76, 86–87, 97–98, 209n34
Order of Things, The (Foucault), 24, 47

"paranoid reading," 3–4
parenting, 80–91, 141–50
Parkland (Fla.) shootings, 149
Pasteur, Louis, 96
Pavonetti, Linda M., 104
pedophilia, 12, 167–68, 197n32
performativity, 4, 13, 22–24, 27, 31; Barad on, 19–20, 23; Butler on, 19–20, 22, 179–80; categories of age and, 14–22, 55–56, 100, 111, 132; definitions of, 19; Kincaid on, 12; Sedgwick on, 17–19, 21
"Periods of Human Life, The," 36–38, 37
"perverse reading," 2, 100, 115
phrenology, 72
Plath, Aurelia, 106, 213n15
Plath, Sylvia, 121; *The Bell Jar*, 106–8, 122–23, 212n14

Porter, Elizabeth, 149
Portman, Frank, 119
"post-truth," 184–85
Pout, Muriel, 85–86
Preparing for Adolescence (Dobson), 124–26, 129–31, 153, 159–60
Pricing the Priceless Child (Zelizer), 208n18
prostitution, 76, 88, 89, 138
Prout, Alan, 13
Psychology of Adolescence, The (Odlum), 75–76, 86–87, 97–98, 209n34
puberty, 74–75; Dobson on, 125; onset of, xi, 195n6, 209n36; Springhall on, 35

queer possibility, 131–35
queer theory, 60, 102, 138; in age of alternative facts, 182–94; Butler on, 179–80; children's literature and, 100; Kristeva and, 213n20; methods of, 1–4, 22–29, 194; of self-hood, 94. *See also* homosexuality
"queer time," 60–61

race, 67–70, 192, 209n36; childhood and, 15–16, 68, 204n61, 208n21; climatic theories of, 75–76; critical studies of, 138, 193; develop-mentalism and, xv, 54–55, 78–81; eugenics and, 87–88; Hall's notions of, 50, 71–73
Racial Innocence (Bernstein), 15–16, 204n61
Radcliffe, Ann, 121
Read, C. Stanford, 82
reading: "illiterate," 99, 103, 108; "paranoid," 3–4; "perverse," 2, 100, 115. *See also* adolescent readers

CPSIA information can be obtained
at www.ICGtesting.com
Printed in the USA
LVHW041629211120
672336LV00002B/215